COMMENTARY ON THE EPISTLE
TO THE EPHESIANS

Commentary
on the
Epistle
to the
Ephesians

CHARLES HODGE

WILLIAM B. EERDMANS PUBLISHING COMPANY
GRAND RAPIDS, MICHIGAN

Published by Wm. B. Eerdmans Publishing Co.
255 Jefferson Ave. S.E., Grand Rapids, Michigan 49503

Paperback edition published 1994

Printed in the United States of America

ISBN 0-8028-8024-X

INTRODUCTION

§ I. *The City of Ephesus.*

THE city of Ephesus, under the Romans, the capital of Proconsular Asia, was situated on a plain near the mouth of the river Cayster. It was originally a Greek colony, but became in no small degree orientalized by the influences which surrounded it. Being a free city, it enjoyed under the Romans to a great extent the right of self-government. Its constitution was essentially democratic. The municipal authority was vested in a Senate, and in the Assembly of the people. The γραμματεύς, "Town Clerk," or, Recorder, was an officer in charge of the archives of the city, the promulgator of the laws, and was clothed with great authority. It was by his remonstrance the tumultuous assembly of which mention is made in Acts 19, 24–40, was induced to disperse.

The city was principally celebrated for its temple of Diana. From the earliest period of its history, Ephesus was regarded as sacred to that goddess. The attributes belonging to the Grecian Diana, however, seem to have been combined with those which belonged to the Phœnician Astarte. Her image, as revered in Ephesus, was not a product of Grecian Art, but a many-breasted, mummy-like figure of oriental symbolism. Her famous Temple was, however, a Greek building of the Ionic order. It had become so celebrated, that its destruction three hundred and fifty-six years before the birth of Christ has conferred immortality on the author of the deed. All Greece and Western Asia contributed to its restoration, which was a work of centuries. Its vast dimensions, its costly materials, its extended colonnades, the numerous statues and paintings with which it was adorned, its long accumulated wealth, the sacred effigies of the goddess, made it one of the wonders of the world. It was this temple which gave unity to the city, and to the character of its inhabitants. Oxford in England is not more Oxford on account of its University, than Ephesus was Ephesus on account of the Temple of Diana. The highest title the city could have assumed, and that which was impressed on its coins, was Νεωκόρος, *Temple-sweeper*,—servant of the great goddess. One of the most lucrative occupations of the people was the manufacture of miniature representations of the temple, wrought in silver, which being carried about by travellers, or reverenced at home, found an extensive sale, both foreign and domestic.

With the worship of Diana the practice of sorcery was from the earliest times connected. The " Ephesian letters," mystical monograms, used as charms or amulets, are spoken of frequently by heathen writers. Ephesus was, therefore, the chief seat of necromancy, exorcism, and all forms of magic arts for all Asia. The site of this once famous city is now occupied by an inconsiderable village called Ajaloluk, supposed by some to be a corruption of ἅγιος θεόλογος, (pronounced Seologos by the Greeks), the title of the apostle John, as the great teacher of the divinity of Christ. If this is so, it is a singular confirmation of the tradition which makes Ephesus the seat of St. John's labours. Others explain the name from the Turkish, in which language the word is said to mean, *City of the Moon;* and then the connection is with Ephesus as the worshipper of Diana.

§ II. *Paul's labours in Ephesus.*

In this city, the capital of Asia, renowned through the world for the temple of Diana, and for skill in sorcery and magic, the place of concourse for people from all the surrounding countries, Paul laboured for nearly three years.

After remaining eighteen months in Corinth, at the conclusion of his second missionary tour, he sailed thence to Ephesus in company with Priscilla and Aquila. He left his companions there, but he himself entered into the synagogue, and reasoned with the Jews. When they desired him to tarry longer with them he consented not: but bade them farewell, saying, I must by all means keep this feast that cometh in Jerusalem; but I will return again unto you, if God will. And he sailed from Ephesus. After his departure, Apollos, "an eloquent man, and mighty in the Scriptures, came to Ephesus. This man was instructed in the way of the Lord; and being fervent in the Spirit, he spake and taught diligently the things of the Lord, knowing only the baptism of John. And he began to speak boldly in the synagogue; whom, when Aquila and Priscilla had heard, they took him unto them, and expounded unto him the way of God more perfectly." Acts 18, 18–26.

Paul, agreeably to his promise, returned to Ephesus, probably in the fall of the year 54. Here he found certain disciples who had received only John's baptism, to whom Paul said: " John verily baptized with the baptism of repentance, saying unto the people, that they should believe on him which should come after him, that is, on Christ Jesus. When they heard this they were baptized in the name of the Lord Jesus. And when Paul had laid his hands upon them, the Holy Ghost came upon them, and they spake with tongues and prophesied." Acts 19, 3–6.

It seems from the narrative that there was in the apostolic period a class of persons who had renounced Judaism, and professed their faith in the person and doctrines of Christ, (for Apollos, it is said, was instructed in the way of the Lord,) and yet passed for John's disciples, in distinction from the other followers of Christ. They were Christians, for they are called " disciples," and yet had not received Christian Baptism. That is, they had been baptized with water, but not with the Holy

Ghost. They may have received the inward saving influences of the Spirit, but they had not been made partakers of those extraordinary gifts, the power of speaking with tongues and of prophesying, which those converted and baptized by the apostles had received. They were Christians through the instructions and testimony of John the Baptist, as distinguished from those made Christians by the preaching of the apostles. Their knowledge of the Gospel was, therefore, necessarily imperfect. This, at least, is one answer to the question concerning the disciples of John spoken of in Acts.

After this the apostle continued for three months to attend the synagogue, " disputing and persuading the things concerning the kingdom of God." Meeting with opposition from the Jews, he withdrew " and separated the disciples, disputing daily in the school of one Tyrannus. And this continued by the space of two years, so that all they that dwelt in Asia heard the word of the Lord Jesus, both Jews and Greeks. And God wrought special miracles by the hands of Paul. So that from his body were brought unto the sick handkerchiefs, or aprons, and the diseases departed from them, and the evil spirits went out of them." Acts 19, 8–12.

It appears from this, and from the subsequent account given by the sacred historian, that the effects of Paul's preaching in Ephesus, were: 1. The conversion of a great number of the Jews and Greeks. 2. The diffusion of the knowledge of the Gospel throughout proconsular Asia. 3. Such an influence on the popular mind, that certain exorcists attempted to work miracles in the name of that Jesus, whom Paul's preaching had proved to be so powerful; and that other magicians, convinced of the folly and wickedness of their arts, made public confession, and burnt their books of divination and mystic charms. 4. Such a marked diminution of the zeal and numbers of the worshippers of Diana, as to excite general alarm that her temple would be despised. 5. A large and flourishing church was there established. This is proved from the facts recorded in the twentieth chapter of the Acts of the Apostles. Having spent a few months in visiting the churches in Macedonia and Greece, Paul, when he arrived at Miletus on his way to Jerusalem, sent for the elders of Ephesus, and addressed them in terms which show that they had an important church committed to their care. In this address the apostle predicted that false teachers would soon rise up among them, not sparing the flock. From the epistle to this church, in the Book of Revelation, it appears that this prediction was soon fulfilled. The church is there commended for its faith and patience, and especially for its resistance to the inroads of heresy.

§ III. *The date of this Epistle and the place whence it was sent.*

As the apostle speaks of himself in this epistle as being in bonds, it is plain it was written either during his imprisonment at Rome or at Cæsarea. Every thing conspires to favour the assumption that it was written at Rome, which until a recent period has been the universally received opinion. In the first place, it is clear that the Epistles to the Ephesians, to the Colossians, to Philemon, and to the Philippians, all belong to the same period. As to the first three, it is expressly stated that they were sent together by Tychicus and Onesimus. Comp. Eph. 6, 21. Col. 4, 7–9. Philem. v. 12. And that the fourth belongs to the same period is plain, 1. Because Timothy is mentioned as being with Paul when he wrote to the Philippians, and he was with him when he wrote to the Colossians and to Philemon. 2. Because he enjoyed great liberty of preaching at the time when the Epistle to the Philippians was written, Phil. 1, 13; and so he did when that to the Ephesians was written. Eph. 6, 20. 3. Because he expresses both to the Philippians and to Philemon the expectation of being soon set at liberty. Phil. 2, 11. Philem. v. 22. If, therefore, one of these letters was written from Rome, they all were. But it is almost certain that the Epistle to the Philippians at least, was written during his imprisonment at Rome. In ch. 1, 12, 13, he says, " The things which happened unto me have fallen out rather unto the furtherance of the gospel; so that my bonds are manifest in all the palace and in all other places." Even admitting that the word πραιτώριον here used, does not necessarily refer either to the well known pretorian camp at Rome, or to the imperial palace, yet, when taken in connection with what is said in ch. 4, 22, there is little doubt that the reference is to the place of abode of the pretorian guard in immediate attendance on the Emperor. The phrase οἱ ἐκ τῆς Καίσαρος οἰκίας, can only mean, *those of Cæsar's household;* and as they sent their salutations to the Philippians, there is no reasonable doubt that the Epistle to the church in Philippi was written at Rome. If, therefore, it was during the same imprisonment that he wrote the four epistles above mentioned, then it follows that the Epistle to the Ephesians was written from Rome.

In the second place, every thing contained in the Epistles to the Ephesians, Colossians, and to Philemon, which are admitted to belong to the same period, agrees with this assumption. 1. The persons mentioned in these epistles are known to have been with the apostle at Rome, but are not known to have been with him at Cæsarea. 2. Paul, according to Acts 28, 30, 31, enjoyed liberty to preach the gospel at Rome, but it is not known that he had that liberty in Cæsarea. 3. He had at Rome the prospect of being soon set at liberty, which he did not enjoy during his imprisonment under Felix and Festus. 4. The reasons assigned by the few modern critics who refer these epistles to the time of his confinement at Cæsarea, have very little weight. It is said that Onesimus, a fugitive slave, would more probably seek refuge in Cæsarea than in a place so distant as Rome; that it is to be inferred from Eph. 6, 21, that Paul expected the Epistle to the Colossians to reach its destination before the letter to the Ephesians came into their hands. This would be the case if Tychicus travelled from Cæsarea, not if Rome was his point of departure. Besides, it is said, that Paul cherished the purpose to visit Spain as soon as he obtained his liberty at Rome; whereas he wrote to Philemon that he hoped to see him soon at Colosse; whence it is inferred that he could not have been in Rome when he wrote that letter. The two former of these reasons have no force. If the third proves any thing with regard to the date of the Epistle to Philemon, it proves the same respecting that to the Philippians, because in that also he expresses the hope of being soon at Philippi. These expressions only prove that the apostle had been led to postpone the execution of the purpose which he had formed long before of visiting Spain. There seems, therefore, to be no reason to depart from the commonly received opinion that the Epistle to the Ephesians was written from Rome.

§ IV. *The persons to whom this Epistle was addressed.*

As to this point there are three opinions. 1. That it was addressed to the Ephesians. 2. That it was addressed to the Laodiceans. 3. That it was a circular letter designed for all the churches in that part of Asia Minor.

In favour of the first of these opinions it is urged, 1. That the epistle is directed τοῖς οὖσιν ἐν Εφέσῳ *to those who are in Ephesus.* If this is the true reading, it settles the question, at least so far as this, that whatever may have been its further destination, it was primarily designed for the church in Ephesus. That the reading above given is the true one, is proved because it is found in all extant MSS., in all the ancient versions, and in all the Fathers. This array of external evidence is decisive. No critic would venture to alter the text against these authorities. The only opposing evidence of a critical nature is, that it appears from the comment of Basil that the words ἐν Εφέσῳ were not in the copy which he used, and that in the MS. B. they stand in the margin and not in the text, and in MS. 67, they are inserted as a correction. This is altogether insufficient to outweigh the concurrent testimony above mentioned. On all critical principles, therefore, the reading ἐν Εφέσῳ must be pronounced genuine.

2. That this epistle was addressed to the Ephesians is proved by the concurrent testimony of the ancient church. This Basil does not question; he only explains τοῖς οὖσιν in such a way as to show that they were not followed in his copy by the words ἐν Εφέσῳ. These two considerations would seem to

be decisive. How came the epistle to be addressed to the Ephesians, if not designed for them? How came the whole ancient church to regard it as addressed to the church in Ephesus, if such were not the fact? It is a fundamental principle in historical criticism to allow greater weight to historical testimony than to conjectures drawn from circumstantial evidence.

The objections to this view are: 1. That there is evidence that in some of the ancient MSS. no longer extant, the words ἐν Ἐφέσῳ were not in the text. 2. That although Paul was personally so well acquainted with the Ephesian Christians, he speaks as though he were a stranger to them and they to him. The passages, however, cited in proof of this point, admit of an interpretation perfectly consistent with the common hypothesis. When Paul speaks in ch. 1, 15, of having *heard* of their faith and love, he may refer to the intelligence which had reached him at Rome. And the expression in ch. 3, 2, εἴγε ἀκούσατε does not necessarily express doubt of their knowledge of him or of his being an apostle. 3. It is objected that the epistle contains no reference to the peculiar circumstances of the Ephesians. It is so general, that it might as well be addressed to one church as another. 4. It contains no salutations from Paul or from his companions to any one in Ephesus. 5. It contemplates exclusively heathen Christians, whereas the church in Ephesus was composed of both Jewish and Gentile converts. The facts on which these last three arguments are founded are undoubtedly true and very remarkable, and certainly distinguish this epistle from all others addressed by Paul to particular churches. They prove, however, nothing more than that the apostle's object in writing this epistle was peculiar. They cannot be allowed to outweigh the direct critical and historical testimony in support of the fact that it was addressed to the Ephesians.

In favour of the hypothesis that this epistle was written to the church in Laodicea, it is urged: 1. That Marcion so entitled it. But Marcion was a notorious falsifier of Scripture. 2. That in Col. 4, 16, it is said, "When this epistle is read among you, cause that it be read also in the church of the

Laodiceans, and that ye also read *the epistle* from Laodicea."
It cannot, however, be inferred that "the epistle *from* Laodicea" was an epistle which Paul wrote *to* Laodicea; much less that the epistle intended was the one addressed to the Ephesians.   Paul may have written to the Laodiceans a letter which is no longer extant.   3. It is urged that on this hypothesis all the peculiarities of the epistle can be readily explained.   But those peculiarities can be explained without resorting to a hypothesis destitute of all historical foundation.

The assumption that this epistle was not designed specially for any one church, but intended equally for all the churches in that part of Asia Minor, has met with more favour.   This view, first suggested by Archbishop Usher, has been adopted, variously modified, by Bengel, Benson, Michælis, Eichhorn, Koppe, Hug, Flatt, Guericke, Neander, Olshausen and many others.   The great objection to it is the overwhelming authority in favour of the reading ἐν Ἐφέσῳ in the salutation, and the unanimous testimony of the early church.   Perhaps the most probable solution of the problem is, that the epistle was written to the Ephesians and addressed to them, but being intended specially for the Gentile Christians as a class, rather than for the Ephesians as a church, it was designedly thrown into such a form as to suit it to all such Christians in the neighbouring churches, to whom no doubt the apostle wished it to be communicated.   This would account for the absence of any reference to the peculiar circumstances of the saints in Ephesus.   This seems to have been substantially the opinion of Beza, who says : Suspicor non tam ad Ephesios ipsos proprie missam epistolam, quam ad Ephesum, ut ad cæteras Asiaticas ecclesias transmitteretur.

§ V. *The relation between this Epistle and that to the Colossians.*

This relation is, in the first place, one of remarkable similarity.   This similarity is observable, 1. In the occurrence in both epistles of the same words and forms of expressions.   2. In passages which are identical in thought and language.   3.

In passages in which the thought is the same and the expression is varied. 4. In others where the same topic is more fully handled in the one epistle than in the other. 5. In passages in which different topics follow each other in the same order.

In the second place, although there are these striking points of resemblance between the two epistles, there are no less striking points of difference. 1. While the Epistle to the Colossians has every indication of having been written to a particular congregation and in reference to their peculiar circumstances, the absence of these features is the most marked characteristic of the Epistle to the Ephesians. 2. In the Epistle to the Ephesians the doctrinal element prevails over the practical; in the Epistle to the Colossians it is just the reverse. 3. The main object of the Epistle to the Colossians is to warn the church against "philosophy falsely so called." Of this there is no indication in the Epistle to the Ephesians; the great design of which is to unfold the glories of the plan of redemption as embracing both Jews and Gentiles, and designed to be the great medium for the manifestation of the grace and wisdom of God to all intelligent creatures. 4. There are, therefore, topics discussed in the one epistle, to which there is nothing to correspond in the other. 5. The order of sequence, or the concatenation of subjects, except in the case of some particular exhortations, is entirely different in the two epistles. 6. The Epistle to the Ephesians has much greater unity than that to the Colossians. This evidently arose from the different purposes with which they are written.

In the third place, the two epistles are evidently independent the one of the other. Each is a complete whole. In each one topic flows naturally from another, the association of ideas in every case being clearly indicated. Neither is a patchwork, but both are a closely woven web.

All these characteristics of similarity, dissimilarity, and mutual independence, are naturally accounted for on the assumption that the two epistles were written at the same time, the one for a particular congregation, the other for a particular class of readers.

§ VI. *The Genuineness of the Epistle.*

1. The epistle announces itself as written by Paul the Apostle. 2. There is nothing in its contents inconsistent with the assumption of his being its author. 3. All the incidental references which it contains to the office, character and circumstances of the writer, agree with what is known to be true concerning Paul. The writer was an apostle, an apostle of the Gentiles, a prisoner, one to whom Tychicus stood in the relation of a companion and fellow-labourer. 4. The style, the doctrines, the sentiments, the spirit, the character revealed, are those of Paul. 5. The whole ancient church received it as genuine. As to this point the judgment of the early ages is unanimous. Even Marcion, though he dissented from the common opinion as to its destination, admitted its Pauline origin. 6. Finally and mainly, the epistle reveals itself as the work of the Holy Ghost, as clearly as the stars declare their maker to be God. In no portion of the Sacred Scriptures are the self-evidencing light and power of divine truth more concentrated than they are here. Had it been first discovered in the nineteenth century, in a forsaken monastery, it would command the faith of the whole church.

The genuineness of this epistle, therefore, has never been doubted, except by a few modern critics to whom nothing is sacred. These critics object: 1. That Paul was familiarly acquainted with the Ephesians, whereas the writer of this epistle had only heard of their conversion and of their faith and love. This objection is fully met by showing that the expressions referred to, may be understood of information received by Paul, during his long imprisonment, first at Cæsarea, and afterwards at Rome; or, on the assumption that the epistle, though addressed to the Ephesians, was designed for a large class of readers, with many of whom Paul had no personal acquaintance. 2. They object that this epistle is merely a verbose imitation of the Epistle to the Colossians. Nothing can be more inconsistent with the fact. The relation between the two epistles, instead of being a ground of objection

against either, is a strong proof of the genuineness of both.
Of this any reader may satisfy himself by a careful comparison of the two. 3. It is objected that the epistle contains no
reference to the peculiar circumstances of the Ephesians, so
that the address and contents are irreconcilable. This absence of specific reference, as before remarked, is accounted for
from the design of the epistle as addressed to Gentile believers,
as Christians, not as Ephesians. REUSS remarks in reference
to such objections, " If Paul wrote friendly letters, these critics
say they are spurious, because they are not doctrinal; and if he
wrote doctrinal epistles, they say they are spurious, because
not friendly." 4. It is objected that the style is not that of
Paul. The very reverse, in the judgment of the vast majority
of competent readers, is the fact. There is the same fervour
and force of expression, the same length and complication in
his sentences, clause linked with clause, till he is forced to stop,
and begin the sentence anew. *Idem in epistola,* says Erasmus,
*Pauli fervor, eadem profunditas, idem omnino spiritus ac
pectus.* DE WETTE, the originator of these and similar objections, admits that they do not justify the rejection of the
epistle, which, he says, contains much that is worthy of the
apostle, and which all antiquity acknowledged as genuine.
Unfortunately, however, he afterwards retracted this admission.
It is to the honour of the German critics, for whom in general,
novelty is every thing, the last opinion always being the best, that
with the exception of the destructive school of Tubingen, few,
if any, of their number attach any weight to the arguments
against the apostolic origin of this epistle. 5. The principal
objection urged by Baur of Tubingen, in addition to those suggested by De Wette, is that the Epistle to the Ephesians contains allusions to Gnostic opinions, which did not prevail until
after the apostolic age. But, in the first place, the great majority of scholars deny that this epistle contains any reference
to Gnostic sentiments; and, in the second place, even if it did,
the Epistle to the Colossians affords abundant evidence that
principles afterwards developed into Gnosticism, had manifested themselves in the age of the apostles. If it be said that the

allusions in the Epistle to the Colossians to those principles proved that it also is spurious ; that would be only a *dictum* in the face of all evidence, and utterly subversive of all history. There is no portion of the New Testament the genuineness of which the church has from the beginning, with more cordial unanimity, acknowledged, than that of this epistle.

§ VII. *Contents of the Epistle.*

The apostle addresses himself principally to Gentile Christians. His object was, 1. To bring them to a just appreciation of the plan of redemption, as a scheme devised from eternity by God, for the manifestation of the glory of his grace. 2. To make them sensible of the greatness of the blessing which they enjoyed in being partakers of its benefits. 3. To lead them to enter into the spirit of the gospel as a system which ignored the distinction between Jews and Gentiles, and united all the members of the church in one living body destined to be brought into full conformity to the image of Christ. 4. To induce them to live as it became a religion which had delivered them from the degradation of their condition as heathen, and exalted them to the dignity of the sons of God.

He begins, therefore, with the primal fountain of all spiritual blessings. He refers them to their predestination to sonship, and their consequent election to holiness, before the foundation of the world. From this flowed their actual redemption by the blood of Christ; and the revelation of the divine purpose to unite all the subjects of redemption in one body in Christ; in whom first the Jews, and then the Gentiles, had been made the heirs of eternal life. Ch. 1, 1–14.

He next earnestly prays that God would enable them to appreciate the hope which they were thus entitled to cherish ; the glory of the inheritance in reserve for them; and the exceeding greatness of that power which had already wrought in them a change analogous to that effected in the resurrection and exaltation of Christ. For as Christ was dead and deposited in the tomb, so they were spiritually dead; and as Christ was raised and exalted above all creatures, so they also were quickened and exalted to a heavenly state in Him.   Ch. 1, 15. 2, 10.

He therefore calls upon them to contrast their former condition as heathen, with their present state.   Formerly they were without Christ, aliens from the commonwealth of Israel, without God, and without hope.   But by the blood of Christ a two-fold reconciliation had been effected.   The Jews and Gentiles are united as one body, and both are reconciled to God, and have equally free access to his presence.   The Gentiles, therefore, are now fellow-citizens of the saints, members of the family of God, and living stones in that temple in which God dwells by his Spirit.   Ch. 2, 11–22.

This great mystery of the union of Jews and Gentiles, had been partially revealed under the Old Dispensation, but it was not then made known so clearly as it had since been revealed to the apostles and prophets of the New Dispensation; whose great vocation it was to preach the unsearchable riches of Christ, and to make all men understand the plan of redemption, hid for ages in God, but now revealed, that through the church might be made known to principalities and powers the manifold wisdom of God.   Ch. 3, 1–13.

The apostle, therefore, bows his knees before the common Father of the redeemed, and prays that Christ may dwell in their hearts by faith ; that they being rooted and grounded in love, might be able to apprehend the infinite love of Christ, and be filled with the fulness of God, who is able to do for us far more than we are able either to ask or to think.   Ch. 3, 14–21.

The Gentiles, therefore, are bound to enter into the spirit of this great scheme—to remember that the church, composed of Jews and Gentiles, bond and free, wise and unwise, is one body, filled by one Spirit, subject to the same Lord, having one faith, one hope, one baptism, and one God and Father, who is in, through, and over all.   They should also bear in mind that diversity in gifts and office was not inconsistent with this unity of the church, but essential to its edification.   For the ascended Saviour had constituted some apostles, some prophets, some evangelists, some pastors and teachers, for the very purpose of building up the church, and through them as the channels of the truth and grace of Christ, the church was to be brought to the end of its high calling. Ch. 4, 1–16.

They should not, therefore, live as did the other Gentiles, who, being in a state of darkness and alienation from God, gave themselves up to uncleanness and avarice. On the contrary, having been taught by Christ, they should put off the old man, and be renewed after the image of God. Avoiding all falsehood, all undue anger, all dishonesty, all improper language, all malice, all impurity and covetousness, they should walk as children of the light, reproving evil, striving to do good, and expressing their joy by singing hymns to Christ, and giving thanks to God. Ch. 4, 17. 5, 20.

He impresses upon his readers reverence for the Lord Jesus Christ as the great principle of Christian obedience. He applies this principle especially to the domestic obligations of men. The marriage relation is illustrated by a reference to the union between Christ and the church. The former is an obscure adumbration of the latter. Marriage is shown to be not merely a civil contract, not simply a voluntary compact between the parties, but a vital union producing a sacred identity. The violation of the marriage relation is, therefore, presented as one of the greatest of crimes and one of the greatest of evils. Parents and children are bound together not only by natural ties, but also by spiritual bands ; and, therefore, the obedience on the part of the child, and nurture on the part of the parent, should be religious. Masters and slaves, however different their condition before men, stand on the same level before God ; a consideration which exalts the slave, and humbles and restrains the master. Finally, the apostle teaches his readers the nature of that great spiritual conflict on which they have entered ; a conflict, not with men but with the powers of darkness. He tells them what armour they need, how it is to be used, and whence strength is to be obtained to bring them off victorious. Ch. 5, 21. 6, 1–20.

§ VIII. *Commentaries.*

The most important modern commentaries on this epistle are the following: *Koppe*, in the sixth vol. of his Annotations on the epistles of the N. T. *Flatt*, in a distinct volume. *J. A. Holzhausen*, 1833, pp. 195. *L. J. Ruckert*, 1833, pp. 306. This is a valuable work, though the author prides himself on his independence not only of theological system, but also of the Scriptures, and writes with a certain air of superiority over the apostle. *F. H. Meier*, 1834, pp. 231, less important. *G. C. A. Harless*, 1834, pp. 574. This is the most elaborate commentary on this epistle which has yet been published. It is orthodox and devout, but is wearisome from its diffuseness and lack of force. *De Wette*, in the second volume of his Exegetisches Handbuch—very condensed, but evinces little regard to the authority of the sacred writers. *Olshausen*, in the fourth volume of his Commentar über das N. T., devout, able, and mystical. *H. A. W. Meyer*, Achte Abtheilung of his Kritisch Exegetischer Commentar über das N. T. Meyer is, perhaps, the ablest commentator on the New Testament of modern times. His theological stand-point is that of high Arianism. He evinces deference to authority of Scripture, but does not hesitate to impute error or false reasoning to the apostles. *John Eadie, D.D.*, Professor of Bib. Literature to the United Presbyterian Church, 1854, pp. 466. This is a work of great research, and contains a full exhibition of the views of all preceding commentators. It is an important and valuable addition to our exegetical literature.

EPISTLE TO THE EPHESIANS

---•◆•---

CHAPTER I

THE SALUTATION.

1.   Paul, an apostle of Jesus Christ by the will of God, to the
saints which are at Ephesus, and to the faithful in Christ Jesus:

2. grace *be* to you, and peace from God our Father, and *from*
the Lord Jesus Christ.

COMMENTARY.

V. 1. *An apostle of Jesus Christ.*—The word *apostle*
is used in three senses in the New Testament. 1. In
its primary sense of messenger, John 13, 16 (the messenger), he that is sent is not greater than he that sent
him.   Phil. 2, 25, your messenger. 2 Cor. 8, 23, messengers of the churches. Ἀπόστολοι ἐκκλησιῶν ; του-
τέστιν, says Chrysostom, ὑπὸ ἐκκλησιῶν πεμφθέντες.
Theophylact adds καὶ χειροτονηθέντες. 2. In the sense

of missionaries, men sent by the church to preach the Gospel.—In this sense Paul and Barnabas are called apostles, Acts 14, 4. 14; and probably Andronicus and Junias, Rom. 16, 7. 3. In the sense of plenipotentiaries of Christ; men whom he personally selected and sent forth invested with full authority to teach and rule in his name. In this sense it is always used when "the apostles," "the twelve," or "the apostles of the Lord," are spoken of as a well-known, definite class. They were appointed as witnesses of Christ's miracles, doctrines, resurrection; and therefore it was necessary that they should not only have seen him after his resurrection, but that their knowledge of the Gospel should be immediately from Christ, John 15, 26. Acts 1, 22. 2, 32. 3, 15. 13, 31. 26, 16. 1 Cor. 9, 1. Gal. 1, 12. They were not confined to any one field but had a general jurisdiction over the churches, as is manifest from their epistles.—To qualify them for this office of authoritatively teaching, organizing, and governing the church, they were rendered infallible by the inspiration of the Holy Ghost, and their divine mission was confirmed by miraculous powers.—Their authority therefore rested first on their commission, and secondly on their inspiration. Hence it is evident that none can have the authority of an apostle who has not apostolic gifts. In this respect Romanists are consistent, for they claim infallibility for those whom they regard as the official successors of the apostles. They are, however, inconsistent with their own theory, and at variance with the Scripture, in making this infallibility the prerogative of the prelates in their collective capacity, instead of claiming it for each individual bishop.

$\Delta\iota\grave{a}$ $\Theta\epsilon\lambda\acute{\eta}\mu\alpha\tau\sigma$ $\Theta\epsilon\sigma\hat{v}$, *by the will of God.* There are two ideas included in this phrase. 1. That the apostleship was a gift, or grace from God, Rom. 1, 5. Eph. 3, 7. 8. 2. That the commission or authority of the apostles was immediately from God. Paul in Gal. 1, 1, as well as in other passages, asserts that apostleship was neither derived from men nor conveyed through the instrumentality of men, but conferred directly by God through Christ.

To the saints which are at Ephesus. The Israelites, under the old dispensation, were called saints, because separated from other nations and consecrated to God. In the New Testament the word is applied to believers, not merely as externally consecrated, but as reconciled to God and inwardly purified. The word $\dot{a}\gamma\iota\acute{a}\zeta\epsilon\iota\nu$ signifies *to cleanse,* either from guilt by a propitiatory sacrifice, as in Heb. 2, 11. 10, 10. 14, or from inward pollution, and also to consecrate. Hence the $\ddot{a}\gamma\iota\sigma\iota$, *saints,* are those who are cleansed by the blood of Christ, and by the renewing of the Holy Ghost, and thus separated from the world and consecrated to God. On the words, *which are at Ephesus,* see the Introduction.

And to the faithful in Christ Jesus. The word $\pi\iota\sigma\tau\acute{o}\varsigma$, *faithful,* may mean preserving faith, worthy of faith, or exercising faith. In the last sense, which is its meaning here, it is equivalent to believing. The faithful, therefore, are believers. *In Christ,* belongs

equally to the two preceding clauses : τοῖς ἁγίοις—καὶ
πιστοῖς ἐν Χριστῷ, 'To the saints and faithful who
are in Christ Jesus.' Those whom he calls *saints* he
also calls *faithful;* Ergo, says Calvin, nemo fidelis,
nisi qui etiam sanctus : et nemo rursum sanctus, nisi
qui fidelis. *No one is a believer who is not holy ; and
no one is holy who is not a believer.*

V. 2. Contains the usual apostolic benediction.
Paul prays that grace and peace may be granted to his
readers. Grace is unmerited favour ; and the grace or
favour of God is the source of all good. Peace, according to the usage of the corresponding Hebrew word,
means well-being in general. It comprehends all blessings flowing from the goodness of God. The apostle
prays to Christ, and seeks from him blessings which
God only can bestow. Christ therefore was to him the
object of habitual worship. He lived in communion
with Christ as a divine person, the ground of his confidence and the source of all good.

God is our Father : 1. As He is the author of our
being ; 2. As we were formed in his likeness. He as
a spirit is the Father of spirits. 3. As we are born
again by his Spirit and adopted into his family. It is
in reference to the last-mentioned relationship that the
expression is almost always used in the New Testament.
Those who are the children of God are such by regeneration and adoption.

Jesus Christ is our supreme and absolute Lord and
proprietor. The word κύριος is indeed used in Scripture in the sense of master, and as a mere honorary title

as in English Master or Sir. But, on the other hand, it is the translation of Adonai, supreme Lord, an incommunicable name of God, and the substitute for Jehovah, a name the Jews would not pronounce. It is in this sense that Christ is, The Lord, The Lord of Lords, The Lord God; Lord in that sense in which God alone can be Lord—having a dominion of which divine perfection is the only adequate or possible foundation. This is the reason why no one can call him Lord, but by the Holy Ghost, 1 Cor. 12, 3. It is a confession which implies the apprehension of the glory of God as it shines in Him. It is an acknowledgment that he is God manifested in the flesh. Blessed are all they who make this acknowledgment with sincerity; for flesh and blood cannot reveal the truth therein confessed, but the Father who is in heaven.

SECTION II.—Vs. 3–14.

3. Blessed *be* the God and Father of our Lord Jesus Christ, who hath blessed us with all spiritual blessings in heavenly

4. *places* in Christ: according as he hath chosen us in him before the foundation of the world, that we should be holy and

5. without blame before him in love: having predestinated us unto the adoption of children by Jesus Christ to himself, ac-

6. cording to the good pleasure of his will, to the praise of the glory of his grace, wherein he hath made us accepted in the

7. beloved. In whom we have redemption through his blood, the forgiveness of sins, according to the riches of his grace;

8. wherein he hath abounded towards us in all wisdom and pru-

9. dence; having made known unto us the mystery of his will,

according to his good pleasure which he hath purposed in
10. himself; that in the dispensation of the fulness of times he might
gather together in one all things in Christ, both which are in
11. heaven, and which are on earth; *even* in him: in whom also
we have obtained an inheritance, being predestinated according to the purpose of him who worketh all things after the
12. counsel of his own will; that we should be to the praise of his
13. glory, who first trusted in Christ. In whom ye also *trusted*
after that ye heard the word of truth, the gospel of your salvation : in whom also after that ye believed ye were sealed with
14. that holy Spirit of promise, which is the earnest of our inheritance until the redemption of the purchased possession, unto
the praise of his glory.

ANALYSIS.

The apostle blesses God for the spiritual gifts bestowed upon his people, v. 3. Of these the first in
order and the source of all the others, is election, v. 4.
This election is, 1st. Of individuals. 2d. In Christ;
3d. It is from eternity. 4th. It is to holiness, and to
the dignity of sons of God. 5th. It is founded on the
sovereign pleasure of God, vs. 4. 5. 6th. Its final
object is the glory of God, or the manifestation of his
grace, v. 6.

The second blessing here mentioned is actual redemption through the blood of Christ; the free remission of sins according to the riches of his grace, vs. 7. 8.

The third blessing is the revelation of the divine
purpose in relation to the economy of redemption;
which has for its object the reduction of all things to a
harmonious whole under Jesus Christ, vs. 9. 10.

Through this Redeemer, the Jewish Christians who had long looked for the Messiah are, agreeably to the divine purpose, made the heirs of God, vs. 11. 12.

The Gentile converts are partakers of the same inheritance; because, having believed in Christ, they are assured of their redemption by the possession of the Holy Spirit, the pledge of the inheritance until its actual and complete enjoyment, vs. 13. 14.

COMMENTARY.

V. 3. Εὐλογητὸς ὁ Θεός, *Blessed be God.* The word εὐλογεῖν, like its English equivalent, *to bless,* signifies to praise, as when we bless God; to pray for blessings, as when we bless others; and to bestow blessings, as when God blesses us. Blessed be God who hath blessed us, is then the expression of thanksgiving and praise to God on account of those peculiar benefits which we receive from him through Christ.

God is here designated as the God and Father of our Lord Jesus Christ. That is, he is at once God and Father, sustaining both these relations to Christ. Our Saviour used a similar form of expression, when he said, ' I ascend unto my Father and your Father ; and to my God and your God.' John 20, 17. The God in whom the Israelites trusted was the God of Abraham, Isaac, and Jacob ; their covenant God. This designation served to remind the ancient people of God of his promise to their fathers, and of their peculiar consequent relationship to him. The God in whom we are called upon to trust, and to whom we are to look as the source of all good, is not the absolute Jehovah, nor the God who stood in a special relation to the Israelites; but the God of redemption; the God whom the Lord Jesus revealed, whose will he came to accomplish, and who was his Father. It is this relationship which is the ground of our confidence. It is because God has sent the Lord Jesus into the world, because He spared not his own Son, that he is our God and Father, or that we have access to him as such.

It is this reconciled God, the God of the covenant of grace, ὁ εὐλογήσας ἡμᾶς ἐν πάσῃ εὐλογίᾳ πνευματικῇ, *who hath blessed us with all spiritual blessings.* The past tense, *hath blessed,* is used because the apostle contemplates his readers as actually redeemed, and in present possession of the unspeakable blessings which Christ has procured. These blessings are *spiritual* not merely because they pertain to the soul, but because derived from the Holy Spirit, whose presence and influence are the great blessing purchased by Christ.

" In heavenly *places.*" The words ἐν τοῖς ἐπουρανίοις may be rendered either *in* or *with* *heavenly things*, or *in* *heavenly* *places*, i. e. in heaven. If the former method be adopted the sense is, ' Hath blessed us with all spiritual blessings, i. e. with heavenly things.' The words however occur five times in this epistle and always elsewhere in a local sense. See v. 20. 2, 6. 3, 10. 6, 12, which therefore should be preferred here. They are to be connected with the immediately preceding word, ' Blessings in heaven.'

The meaning is that these blessings pertain to that heavenly state into which the believer is introduced. Here on earth he is, as the apostle says, in ch. 2, 6, ' in heavenly places.' He is a citizen of heaven, Phil. 3, 10. The word heaven, in Scripture, is not confined in its application to the place or state of future blessedness, but sometimes is nearly equivalent to ' kingdom of heaven.' The old writers, therefore, were accustomed to distinguish between the *coelum gloriae*, the heaven of glory ; *coelum naturae*, the visible heavens, and *coelum gratiae*, the heaven of grace here on earth. These blessings connected with this heavenly state, are conferred upon believers *in Christ*. It is as they are in him, and in virtue of that union that they are partakers of these benefits.

V. 4. All these blessings have their source in the electing love of God. $E\nu\lambda o\gamma\eta\sigma a\varsigma - \kappa a\theta\dot{\omega}\varsigma\ \dot{\epsilon}\xi\epsilon\lambda\dot{\epsilon}\xi a\tau o$ $\dot{\eta}\mu\hat{a}\varsigma$, *he blessed us—because he chose us.* $Ka\theta\dot{\omega}\varsigma$, *according as*, or, *inasmuch as*, *because*, see John 17, 2. Rom. 1, 28. 1 Cor. 1, 6. Election is the cause or source of all subsequent benefits.

He hath chosen *us*. By *us* is not meant the apostle alone, because there is nothing in the context to indicate or justify this restriction. The blessings consequent on the election here spoken of, are in no sense peculiar to the apostle. Neither does the word refer to any external community or society as such. It is not us Ephesians, as Ephesians, nor us Corinthians, nor us Romans, as formerly the Jews were chosen by a national election. But it is us believers, scattered here and there. It is those who are the actual recipients of the blessings spoken of, viz. holiness, sonship, remission of sins, and eternal life.

We are said to be chosen *in Him ;* an expression which is variously explained. Some refer the pronoun to God, ' chosen us in himself;' which is contrary not only to the context but to the signification of the words ἐν αὐτῷ, which is the received text. Others say the meaning is, ' He hath chosen us because we are in him.' The foresight of our faith or union with Christ, being the ground of this election. This however cannot be admitted. 1. Because faith, or a living union with Christ, is the very blessing to which we are chosen. 2. Because it introduces into the passage more than the words express. 3. Because in this immediate connection, as well as elsewhere, the ground of this election is declared to be the good pleasure of God.—A third interpretation also supposes an ellipsis. The full expression would be : εἰς τὸ εἶναι ἡμᾶς ἐν αὐτῷ, Chosen us *to be* in Him; *in ipso, videlicet adoptandos*, as Beza explains it. The objection to this is that it introduces more than the words contain, and that the end to which we are chosen is expressed in the following clause, εἶναι ἡμᾶς ἁγίους. It is best therefore to take the words as they stand, and to inquire in what sense our election is in Christ. The purpose of election is very comprehensive. It is the purpose of God to bring his people to holiness, sonship, and eternal glory. He never intended to do this irrespective of Christ. On the contrary it was his purpose, as revealed in Scripture, to bring his people to these exalted privileges through a Redeemer. It was in Christ as their head and representative they were chosen to holiness and eternal life, and therefore in virtue of what he was to do in their behalf. There is a federal union with Christ which is antecedent to all actual union, and is the source of it. God gave a people to his Son in the covenant of redemption. Those included in that covenant, and because they are included in it—in other words, because they are in Christ as their head and representative—receive in time the gift of the Holy Spirit and all other benefits of redemption. Their voluntary union with Christ by faith, is not the ground of their federal union, but, on the contrary, their federal union is the ground of their voluntary union. It is, therefore, in Christ, i. e. as united to him in the covenant of redemption, that the people of God are elected to eternal life and to all the blessings therewith connected. Much in the same sense the Israelites are said to have been chosen in Abraham. Their relation to Abraham and God's covenant with him, were the ground and reason of all the peculiar blessings they enjoyed. So our covenant union with Christ is the ground of all the benefits which we as the people of God possess or hope for. We were chosen in Christ, as the Jews were chosen in Abraham. The same truth is expressed in 3, 11, where it is said that the carrying out or application of the plan of redemption is "according to the eternal purpose which He purposed in Christ Jesus our Lord."

God purposed to save men in Christ, He elected them in him to salvation.

Again, this election is from eternity. He chose us πρὸ καταβολῆς κόσμου, *before the foundation of the world.* Comp. 2 Thess. 2, 13. Matt. 25, 34. As our idea of time arises from the perception of motion or consciousness of succession, the natural expression for eternity is ' before time,' before the existence of creatures who exist in time. Hence what has been from eternity is said in Scriptures to have been before the world was, John 17, 24. 1 Pet. 1, 20 ; or before the ages, 1 Cor. 2, 7. 2 Tim. 1, 9. " The grace given us in Christ Jesus πρὸ χρόνων αἰωνίων, before the world began."—There seem to be two things intended by this reference to the eternity of the divine purpose. The one is, to represent God as doing every thing in time according to a preconceived plan ; or as working all things after the counsel of his own will. From eternity the whole scheme of redemption with all its details and in all its results lay matured in the divine mind. Hence every thing is certain. There is no possibility either of failure or of any change of purpose. The eternity of God's purpose is, therefore, a strong ground of confidence and comfort. The other is, to express the sovereignty of the divine purpose. The grace was given to us before we existed, before the world began, and of course before we had done any good or evil. It was, therefore, not for works of righteousness which we have done, but according to his mercy he saved us. If the one aspect of the truth that God chose us before the foundation of the world, is adapted to produce confidence; the other aspect is no less adapted to produce humility.

This election is to holiness. We are chosen εἶναι ἁγίους καὶ ἀμώμους κατενώπιον αὐτοῦ, *to be holy and without blame before him.* These words admit of two interpretations. They may be understood to refer to our justification, or to our sanctification. They express either that freedom from guilt and blame in the sight of God, which is the proximate effect of the death of Christ; or that subjective purification of the soul which is its indirect, but certain effect produced by the Holy Spirit which his death secures for his people. The words admit of either interpretation; because ἁγιάζειν, as remarked above on v. 1, often means to cleanse from guilt, to atone for; and ἅγιος means *clean from guilt, atoned for;* and ἄμωμος may mean *free from any ground of blame; unsträflich* (not deserving of punishment), as Luther renders it. In favour of this interpretation it is urged, first, that it is unscriptural as well as contrary to experience, to make perfect purity and freedom from all blemish, the end of election. There is little force in this argument, because the end of election is not fully attained in this life. It might as well be said that the υἱοθεσία (*the adoption of sons*), to which in v. 5 we are said to be predestinated, includes nothing more than what is experienced in this world. Besides, in 5, 27, it is said, Christ gave himself for the church, "That he might present it to himself a glorious church, not having spot or wrinkle, or any such thing;

but (ἵνα ᾖ ἁγία καὶ ἄμωμος) that it should be holy and
without blemish." This certainly is descriptive of a
degree of inward purity not attained by the church
militant. Comp. Col. 1, 22. Secondly, it is urged that
the whole context treats of the effect of the ἱλαστήριον
or propitiatory sacrifice of Christ, and therefore these
words must be understood of justification, because sanctification is not the effect of a sacrifice. But the Scriptures often speak of the remote, as well as of the immediate end of Christ's death. We are reconciled to God
by the death of his Son in order that we should be
holy. Propitiation is in order to holiness. Therefore, it
is said, " He gave himself for us that he might redeem
us from all iniquity, and purify us unto himself a people
zealous of good works." Titus 2, 14. In many other
passages sanctification is said to be the end for which
Christ died. There is nothing in the context, therefore,
which requires us to depart from the ordinary interpretation of this passage. If the words ἐν ἀγάπῃ (in
love) are to be connected with the preceding clause,
it is decisive as to its meaning ' We are chosen to be
holy and without blame in love.' It is a state of moral
excellence which consists in love. That is, it is no
mere external consecration to God, as was the case
with the Jews, nor any mere ceremonial freedom
from blemish, to which we are elected. This is altogether the most natural connection of the words, from
which no one would have thought of departing, had it
not been assumed that the words " holy and without
blame" refer to sacrificial purification. To connect

ἐν ἀγαπῃ with *ἐξελέξατο,* would give the sense, ' Hath chosen us in love ;' but this the position of the words forbids. To connect them with *προορίσας,* which follows, would give the sense, ' In love having predestinated us.' But this also is unnatural ; and besides, the word *predestinated* has its limitation or explanation in the following clause, " according to the good pleasure of his will.' It would be tautological to say : ' He hath predestinated us in love according to the good pleasure of his will." The majority of commentators, therefore, adopt the construction followed by our translators.

If election is to holiness as the apostle here teaches, it follows, first, that individuals, and not communities or nations, are the objects of election ; secondly, that holiness in no form can be the ground of election If men are chosen to be holy, they cannot be chosen because they are holy. And, thirdly, it follows that holiness is the only evidence of election. For one who lives in sin to claim to be elected unto holiness, is a contradiction.

V. 5. The apostle says, God hath chosen us to holiness, having predestinated us to sonship ; that is, because he has thus predestinated us. Holiness, therefore, must be a necessary condition or prerequisite for the sonship here spoken of. Sonship in reference to God includes—1. Participation of his nature, or conformity to his image. 2. The enjoyment of his favour, or being the special objects of his love. 3. Heirship, or a participation of the glory and blessedness of God.

Sometimes one and sometimes another of these ideas is the most prominent. In the present case it is the second and third. God having predestinated his people to the high dignity and glory of sons of God, elected them to holiness, without which that dignity could neither be possessed nor enjoyed. It is *through Jesus Christ*, that we are made the sons of God. As many as received him, to them gave he the power to become the sons of God. John 1, 12. For we are all the children of God by faith of Jesus Christ. Gal. 3, 26. Christ has purchased this dignity for his people. He died for them on condition that they should be the sons of God, restored to their Father's family and reinstated in all the privileges of this divine relationship.

The words εἰς αὐτόν, *to himself*, in the clause, 'Predestinated us to sonship by Jesus Christ to himself,' are somewhat difficult. The text, in the first place, is uncertain. Some editors read εἰς αὐτόν, *unto himself*, and others εἰς αὐτόν, *unto him*. In either case, however, the reference is to God. They admit of three explanations. 1. They may limit or explain the word *sonship*. 'Sonship unto himself,' i. e. sons in relation to God. 2. They may express the design of this adoption. 'Sonship for himself,' i. e. for his benefit or glory. This assumes that εἰς is here equivalent to the dative. 3. They may be connected immediately with the words Jesus Christ. 'Through Jesus Christ to himself,' i. e. to be brought to him by Jesus Christ. The first is generally preferred, because it gives a good sense, and is consistent with the force of the preposition.

The ground of this predestination and of the election founded upon it, is expressed by the clause, κατὰ τὴν εὐδοκίαν τοῦ θελήματος αὐτοῦ, *according to the good pleasure of his will.* The word εὐδοκία means either *benevolence, favour,* as in Luke 2, 14; or *good pleasure, free* or *sovereign purpose,* as in Matt. 11, 26; and Luke 10, 21. Phil. 2, 13. The meaning therefore may be either: ' according to his benevolent will,' or ' according to his sovereign will,' i. e. his good pleasure. The latter is to be preferred. 1. Because it agrees better with the usage of the word in the N. T. In Matt. 11, 26, ὅτι οὕτως ἐγένετο εὐδοκία ἔμπροσθέν σου means, ' Because thus it seemed good in thy sight.' In Luke 10, 21, the same words occur in the same sense. In Phil. 2, 13, ὑπὲρ τῆς εὐδοκίας means, ' Of good pleasure.' 2. The words εὐδοκία τοῦ θελή-ματος naturally mean *voluntas liberrima, beneplacitum, sovereign purpose;* to make them mean *benevolent will,* is contrary to scriptural usage. 3. In this connection it is not the predestinated that are the objects of εὐδοκία, but the act of predestination itself. God chose to have that purpose. It seemed good to him. 4. The expressions, " purpose of his will," " counsel of his will," v. 11, are used interchangeably with that in the text, and determine its meaning. 5. The analogy of Scripture is in favour of this interpretation, because the ground of election is always said to be the good pleasure of God.

V. 6. The final end of election is the glory of God. He has predestinated us to sonship, εἰς ἔπαινον δόξης τῆς χάριτος αὐτοῦ, *to the praise of the glory of his grace.* That is, in order that in the exaltation and blessedness of his people, matter for celebrating his grace might be abundantly afforded. It is worthy of remark that here, as in 2, 7. 1 Cor. 1, 27–29, and elsewhere, the specific design of redemption and of the mode in which its blessings are dispensed, is declared to be the manifestation of *the grace* or unmerited favour of God. Nothing therefore can be more foreign to the nature of the Gospel than the doctrine of merit in any form. It is uncongenial with that great scheme of mercy whose principal design is to exhibit the grace of God.

It is to weaken the language of the apostle to make δόξης a mere qualification either of ἔπαινον (praise), or of χάριτος (grace). It is neither glorious praise, nor glorious grace, but *to the praise of the glory of his grace. The glory of grace,* is the divine excellence of that attribute manifested as an object of admiration. The glory of God is the manifested excellence of God, and the glory of any one of his attributes, is the manifestation of that attribute as an object of praise. The design of redemption, therefore, is to exhibit the grace of God in such a conspicuous manner as to fill all hearts with wonder and all lips with praise.

Wherein he hath made us accepted. The Text in this clause is uncertain. Some MSS. have ἐν ᾗ which is the common text; and others ἧς. Mill, Griesbach,

Lachmann, Rückert adopt the latter; Knapp, Scholz, Harless, De Wette the former. If the genitive be preferred, ἧς is for ἥν, and the phrase χάριν χαριτοῦν would be analogous to others of frequent occurrence, as κλῆσιν καλεῖν, ἀγάπην ἀγαπᾶν. This clause admits of two interpretations. The word χαριτόω, agreeably to the analogy of words of the same formation, signifies to impart χάρις grace. The literal rendering therefore of the words ἐν ᾗ (χάριτι) ἐχαρίτωσεν ἡμᾶς would be, *with which grace he has graced us*, or conferred grace upon us. But as grace sometimes means a disposition and sometimes a gift, the sense may be either, 'Wherein (i. e. in the exercise of which) he has been gracious towards us;' or, 'With which he has made us gracious or well pleasing.' In the former case, grace refers to the goodness or unmerited favour of God exercised towards us; in the latter, to the sanctifying effect produced on us. It is the grace by which he has sanctified or rendered us gracious (in the subjective sense of that word) in his sight. The Greek and Romish interpreters prefer the latter interpretation; the great body of Protestant commentators the former. The reasons in favour of the former are, 1. The word grace in the context is used in the sense of *kind disposition* on the part of God, and not in the sense of a gift. 2. The verb in the only other case where it occurs in the New Testament, is used in the sense of *showing favour*. Luke 1, 28: "Hail, thou favoured one!" 3. The parallel passage and analogous expression 2, 4 is in favour of this interpretation. There it is said, "His great love wherewith he hath loved

us," and here the same idea is expressed by saying,
‘His grace wherein he favoured us, or which he has
exercised towards us.’   4. The whole context demands
this interpretation.   The apostle is speaking of the
love or grace of God as manifested in our redemption.
He has predestinated us to the adoption of sons to the
praise of the glory of his grace ; which grace he has
exercised towards us, in the remission of sins.   The
same idea is expressed 2, 7, where it is said, God hath
quickened us, that in the ages to come he might show
the exceeding riches of his grace in his kindness
towards us, through Jesus Christ.   “ To make accepted,” therefore, here means, to accept, to treat with
favour ; or rather, such is the meaning of the apostle's
language ; *gratia amplexus est*, as the word is rendered
by Bengel.   To which agrees the explanation of Beza :
gratis nos sibi acceptos effecit.

This grace is exercised towards us *in the Beloved.*
In ourselves we are unworthy.   All kindness towards
us is of the nature of grace.   Christ is the beloved for
his own sake ; and it is to us only as in him and for
his sake that the grace of God is manifested.   This is
a truth which the apostle keeps constantly in view,
2, 5. 6. 7.

V. 7. *In whom we have redemption.*   In whom,
i. e. not in ourselves.   We are not self-redeemed.
Christ is our Redeemer.   The word *redemption*, ἀπο-
λύτρωσις, sometimes means deliverance in the general,
without reference to the mode in which it is accomplished.   When used of the work of Christ it is always

to be understood in its strict sense, viz. deliverance by ransom ; because this particular mode of redemption is always either expressed or implied. We are redeemed neither by power, nor truth, but by blood ; that is, by the sacrificial death of the Lord Jesus. A sacrifice is a ransom, as to its effect. It delivers those for whom it is offered and accepted. The words διὰ τοῦ αἵματος αὐτοῦ, *by his blood*, are explanatory of the words *in whom*. In whom, i. e. by means of his blood. They serve to explain the method in which Christ redeems.

The redemption of which the apostle here speaks is not the inward deliverance from sin, but it is an outward work, viz. *the forgiveness of sins*, as the words τὴν ἄφεσιν τῶν παραπτωμάτων necessarily mean. It is true this is not the whole of redemption, but it is all the sacred writer here brings into view, because forgiveness is the immediate end of expiation. Though this clause is in apposition with the preceding, it is by no means coextensive with it. So in Rom. 8, 23, where believers are said to be waiting for the adoption, *to wit*, the redemption of the body, the two clauses are not coextensive in meaning. The redemption of the body does not exhaust the idea of adoption. Neither in this passage does the forgiveness of sin exhaust the idea of redemption. This passage is often quoted in controversy to prove that justification is merely pardon.

This redemption is not only gratuitous, but it is, in all its circumstances, an exhibition and therefore a proof of *the riches of his grace.* The word πλοῦτος *riches* in such connections is a favorite one with the apostle, who speaks of the riches of glory, the riches of wisdom, and the exceeding riches of grace It is the overflowing abundance of unmerited love, inexhaustible in God and freely accessible through Christ. There is, therefore, nothing incompatible between redemption, i. e. deliverance on the ground of a ransom (or a complete satisfaction to justice), and grace The grace consists—1. In providing this satisfaction and in accepting it in behalf of sinners. 2. In accept ing those who are entirely destitute of merit. 3. In bestowing this redemption and all its benefits without regard to the comparative goodness of men. It is not because one is wiser, better, or more noble than others, that he is made a partaker of this grace; but God chooses the foolish, the ignorant, and those who are of no account, that they who glory may glory only in the Lord.

V. 8. *Wherein he hath abounded towards us,* ἧς ἐπερίσσευσεν εἰς ἡμᾶς. As the word περισσεύω is both transitive and intransitive, the clause may be rendered as above, ἧς being for ῇ ; or, *which he has caused to abound towards us,* ἧς being for ἥν. The sense is the same ; but as the attraction of the dative is very rare, the latter explanation is to be preferred. We are redeemed according to the riches of that grace, which God has so freely exercised towards us.

In all wisdom and prudence, ἐν πάσῃ σοφίᾳ καὶ φρονήσει. These words admit of a threefold connection

and explanation.   1. They may be connected with the
preceding verb ·and qualify the action of God therein
expressed.   God, in the exercise of wisdom and prudence, has abounded in grace towards us.   2. They
may be connected with the following clause : ' In all
wisdom and prudence making known, &c.'   3. They
may be connected with the preceding relative pronoun.
' Which (grace) in connection with, or together with,
all wisdom and prudence he has caused to abound.'
That is, the grace manifested by God and received by
us, is received in connection with the divine wisdom or
knowledge of which the subsequent clause goes on to
speak.   This last explanation seems decidedly preferable because the terms here used, particularly the word
φρόνησις *prudence,* is not in its ordinary sense properly
referable to God.   Cicero de Off. 1. 43. Prudentia enim,
quam Graeci φρόνησιν dicunt, est rerum expetendarum
fugiendarumque scientia.   And because the sense afforded by the third mentioned interpretation is so appropriate to the context and so agreeable to other passages
of Scripture.   The apostle often celebrates the goodness of God in communicating to men the true wisdom ;
not the wisdom of this world, nor of the princes of this
world, but the wisdom of God in a mystery, even the
hidden wisdom, which God ordained before the world
to our glory. See 1 Cor. 1, 17 to the end, and the whole
second chapter of that epistle.—Similar modes of expression are common with the apostle.   As here he
speaks of grace being given (ἐν) *in connection with
wisdom,* so in v. 17 he prays that the Ephesians may

receive wisdom (ἐν) *in connection with* the knowledge of himself.

The wisdom then which the apostle says God has communicated to us, is the divine wisdom in the Gospel, the mystery of redemption, which had been hid for ages in God, but which he has now revealed to his holy apostles and prophets by the Spirit. See the glorious doxology for this revelation contained in Rom. 16, 25–27. Indeed this whole Epistle to the Ephesians is a thanksgiving to God for the communication of this mysterious wisdom. Mysterious, not so much in the sense of incomprehensible, as in that of undiscoverable by human reason, and a matter of divine revelation. With wisdom the apostle connects φρόνησις, which is here used much in the same sense as σύνεσις in Col. 1, 9, ' That ye may be filled with the knowledge of his will in all wisdom and *spiritual understanding.*' The verb φρονέω is used for any mental exercise or state whether of the understanding or of the feelings. In the New Testament it is commonly employed to express a state of the affections, or rather, of the whole soul, as in Mark 8, 33, " Thou savourest not the things which be of God." Rom. 8, 5, " To mind the things of the flesh." Col. 3, 2, " Set your affections on things above," &c. &c. Hence its derivative φρόνημα is used not only for thought, but more generally for a state of mind, what is in the mind or soul, including the affections as well as the understanding. Hence we have such expressions as φρόνημα τῆς σαρκός *a carnal state of mind;* and φρόνημα τοῦ πνεύματος *a state of mind produced*

by the Spirit. The word φρόνησις is equally compre
hensive. It is not confined to strictly intellectual
exercises, but expresses also those of the affections.
In other words, when used in reference to spiritual
things, it includes all that is meant by spiritual discernment. It is the apprehension of the spiritual
excellence of the things of God, and the answering
affection towards them. It is not therefore a mere
outward revelation of which the apostle here speaks.
The wisdom and understanding which God has so
abundantly communicated, includes both the objective
revelation and the subjective apprehension of it. This
is the third great blessing of which the context treats.
The first is election; the second redemption; the third
is this revelation both outward and inward. The first
is the work of God, the everlasting Father; the second
the work of the Son; and the third the work of the
Holy Spirit, who thus applies to believers the redemption purchased by Christ.

V. 9. God has caused this wisdom to abound, or
has communicated it, *having made known unto us the
mystery of his will,* γνωρίσας ἡμῖν τὸ μυστήριον τοῦ
θελήματος αὐτοῦ. In other words, by the revelation
of the Gospel. The word μυστήριον, *mystery,* means a
secret, something into which we must be initiated;
something, which being undiscoverable by us, can be
known only as it is revealed. In this sense the Gospel
is a mystery; and any fact or truth, however simple in
itself, in the New Testament sense of the word, is a mystery, if it lies beyond the reach of our powers. Comp.

Rom. 16, 25.   1 Cor. 2, 7–10.   Eph. 3, 9.   Co⁙. 1, 26.
For the same reason any doctrine imperfectly revealed
is a mystery.   It remains in a measure secret.   Thus
in the fifth chapter of this epistle Paul calls the union
of Christ and believers a great mystery ; and in 1 Tim.
3, 16 he calls the manifestation of God in the flesn, the
great mystery of godliness.

In the present case *the mystery of his will* means
his secret purpose ; that purpose of redemption, which
having been hid for ages, he has now graciously revealed.

According to his good pleasure, κατὰ τὴν εὐδοκίαν
αὐτοῦ, ἣν προέθετο ἐν αὐτῷ.   There are three interpretations of this clause.   The first is to make it qualify
the word *will.*   ' His will which was according to his
good pleasure ;' i. e. his kind and sovereign will.   But
this is forbidden by the absence of the connecting article in the Greek, and also by the following clause.
The second interpretation connects this clause with the
beginning of the verse, ' Having, according to his good
pleasure, made known the mystery of his will.'   The
sense in this case is good, but this interpretation supposes the relative *which,* in the following clause, to
refer to the mystery of his will, which its grammatical
form in the Greek forbids.   *Which* (ἣν) must refer to
good pleasure (εὐδοκία).   The third explanation, which
alone seems consistent with the context, supposes εὐδοκία to mean here not *benevolence,* but *kind intention,*
or, *sovereign purpose.*   The sense then is : ' Having
made known the mystery of his will, according to his

CHAP. I. VER. 10.

kind intention or purpose (viz. of redemption) which
he had purposed in himself.' Instead of *in himself*,
many commentators read *in him*, referring to Christ.
But this would introduce tautology into the passage.
The apostle would then say: ' Which he purposed in
Christ, to bring together in Christ.'

V. 10. This verse is beset with difficulties. The
general sense seems to be this : The purpose spoken
of in the preceding verse had reference to the scheme
of redemption ; the design of which is to unite all the
subjects of redemption, as one harmonious body, under
Jesus Christ.

*Εἰς οἰκονομίαν τοῦ πληρώματος τῶν καιρῶν, ἀνα-
κεφαλαιώσασθαι, κτλ.* The first question relates to the
connection with what precedes. This is indicated by
the preposition *εἰς*, which does not here mean *in*, as
though the sense were, He purposed in, or during, the
dispensation, &c.; much less *until ;* but *as to, in reference to.* The purpose which God has revealed relates
to the economy here spoken of. The second question
is, what is here the meaning of the word *οἰκονομία* ?
The word has two general senses in the New Testament.
When used in reference to one in authority, it means
plan, scheme, or economy. When spoken of one under authority, it means an office, stewardship, or administration of such office. In this latter sense Paul
speaks of an *οἰκονομία* as having been committed unto
him. As the business of a steward is to administer, or
dispense, so the apostle was a steward of the mysteries
of God. It was his office to dispense to others the

truths which God had revealed to him. Many take
the word in the latter sense here. The meaning would
then be : 'In reference to the administration of the
fulness of times, i. e. the last times, or Messianic period;
the times which yet remain.' The former sense of the
word however is much better suited to the context.
The apostle is speaking of God's purpose, of what He
intended to do. It was a purpose having reference to
a plan or economy of his own ; an economy here designated as that of the *fulness of times*. This phrase does
not indicate a protracted period—*the times which remain*—but the termination of the times; the end of the
preceding and commencement of the new dispensation.
The prophets being ignorant of the time of the Messiah's advent, predicted his coming when the time
determined by God should be accomplished. Hence
the expressions, " end of the ages," 1 Cor. 10, 11 ;
" end of days," Heb. 1, 1 ; " fulness of the time," Gal.
4, 4 ; and here, " the fulness of times," are all used to
designate the time of Christ's advent. By the *economy
of the fulness of times* is therefore to be understood,
that economy which was to be clearly revealed and
carried out when the fulness of time had come.

The infinitive ἀνακεφαλαιώσασθαι, *to bring together
in one*, may be referred either to the immediately preceding clause : 'The plan of the fulness of times to
bring together in one ;' or to the preceding verse :
'The purpose which he purposed (in reference to the
economy of the fulness of times), to gather together in
one.' The sense is substantially the same. The verb

κεφαλαιόω means *summatim colligere*, ἀνακεφαλαιόω, *summatim recolligere*. In the New Testament it means either: 1. To reduce to one sum, i. e. to sum up, to recapitulate. Rom. 13, 9: 'All the commands are summed up in, or under, one precept.' 2. To unite under one head; or, 3. To renew. Many of the Fathers adopt the last signification in this place, and consider this passage as parallel with Rom. 8, 19–22. Through Christ God purposes to restore or renovate all things; to effect a παλιγγενεσία or regeneration of the universe, i. e. of the whole creation which now groans under the burden of corruption. This sense of the word however is remote. The first and second meanings just mentioned differ but little. They both include the idea expressed in our version, that of regathering together in one, the force of ἀνά, *iterum*, being retained. Beza explains the word: *partes disjectas et divulsas in unum corpus conjungere.*—The purpose of God, which he has been pleased to reveal, and which was hidden for ages, is his intention to reunite all things as one harmonious whole under Jesus Christ.

The words τὰ πάντα, *all things*, are explained by the following clause: τὰ ἐν τοῖς οὐρανοῖς καὶ τὰ ἐπὶ τῆς γῆς, *both which are in heaven and which are on earth*. The totality here referred to includes every thing in heaven and on earth, which the nature of the subject spoken of admits of being comprehended. There is nothing to limit these comprehensive terms, but the nature of the union to which the apostle refers. As, therefore, the Scriptures speak of the whole uni-

verse, material and rational, as being placed under
Jesus Christ; as they speak especially of all orders
of intelligent creatures being subject to him; as they
teach the union of the long disjected members of the
human family, the Jews and Gentiles, in one body in
Christ, of which union this epistle says so much and in
such exalted strains; and as finally they speak of the
union of the saints of all ages and nations, of those now
in heaven and of those now on earth, in one great
family above; the words, ALL THINGS, are very variously explained.   1. Some understand them to include the
whole creation, material and spiritual, and apply the
passage to the final restoration of all things; or to that
redemption of the creature from the bondage of corruption of which the apostle speaks in Rom. 8, 19–22.
2. Others restrict the "all things" to all intelligent
creatures—good and bad, angels and men—fallen spirits
and the finally impenitent.   In this view the reduction
to unity, here spoken of, is understood by the advocates
of the restoration of all things to the favour of God, to
refer to the destruction of all sin and the banishment
of all misery from the universe.   But those who believe
that the Scriptures teach that the fallen angels and the
finally impenitent among men, are not to be restored
to holiness and happiness, and who give the phrase "all
things" the wide sense just mentioned, understand the
apostle to refer to the final triumph of Christ over all
his enemies, of which he speaks in 1 Cor. 15, 23–28.
All things in heaven above, in the earth beneath, and
in the waters under the earth, are to be made subject

to Christ; but this subjection will be either voluntary or coerced. The good will joyfully acknowledge his supremacy; the evil he will restrain and confine, that they no longer trouble or pervert his people. 3. Others again understand the words under consideration, of all good angels and men. The inhabitants of heaven, or the angels, and the inhabitants of the earth, or the saints, are to be united as a harmonious whole under Jesus Christ. 4. The words are restricted to the members of the human family; and the distinction between those in heaven and those on earth, is supposed to refer to the Jews and Gentiles, who, having been so long separated, are under the Gospel and by the redemption of Christ, united in one body in him. The Jews are said to be in heaven because in the kingdom of heaven, or the theocracy; and the Gentiles are said to be on earth, or in the world as distinguished from the church. 5. The words may be confined to the people of God, the redeemed from among men, some of whom are now in heaven and others are still on earth. The whole body of the redeemed are to be gathered together in one, so that there shall be one fold and one shepherd. The form of expression is analogous to Eph. 3, 15, where the apostle speaks of the whole family in heaven and earth.

The decision which of these several interpretations is to be adopted, depends mainly on the nature of the union here spoken of, and on the means by which it is accomplished. If the union is merely a union under a triumphant king, effected by his power converting

some and coercing others, then of course we must understand the passage as referring to all intelligent
creatures. But if the union spoken of be a union with
God, involving conformity to his image and the enjoyment of his favour, and effected by the redemption of
Christ, then the terms here employed must be restricted
to the subjects of redemption. And then if the Scriptures teach that all men and even fallen angels are
redeemed by Christ, and restored to the favour of God,
they must be included in the all things in heaven and
earth here spoken of. If the Scriptures teach that good
angels are the subjects of redemption, then they must
be comprehended in the scope of this passage.* But if
the doctrine of the Bible be, that only a certain portion
of the human family are redeemed and saved by the
blood of Christ, then to them alone can the passage be
understood to refer. In order therefore to establish the
correctness of the fifth interpretation mentioned above,
all that is necessary is to prove, first, that the passage

---

* CALVIN thinks there is a sense in which good angels may be said to
be redeemed by Christ. On this passage, he says: Nihil tamen impedit,
quominus angelos quoque dicamus recollectos fuisse, non ex dissipatione,
sed primum ut perfecte et solide adhereant Deo ; deinde ut perpetuum
statum retineant . . . . Quis neget, tam angelos quam homines, in firmum
ordinem Christo gratia fuisse redactos ? homines enim perditi erant, an
geli vero non erant extra periculum. Again, on the parallel passage in
Colossians, he says : Duabus de causis angelos quoque oportuit cum Deo
pacificari, nam quum creaturae sint extra lapsus periculum non erant, non
nisi Christi gratia fuissent confirmati . . . . Deinde in hac ipsa obedientia,
quam præstant Deo, non est tam exquisita perfectio, ut Deo omni ex
parte et extra veniam satisfaciat.

speaks of that union which is effected by the redemption of Christ; and secondly, that the church alone is the subject of redemption.

That the passage does speak of that union which is effected by redemption, may be argued—1. From the context. Paul, as we have seen, gives thanks first for the election of God's people; secondly, for their actual redemption; thirdly, for the revelation of the gracious purpose of God relative to their redemption. It is of the redemption of the elect, therefore, that the whole context treats. 2. Secondly, the union here spoken of is an union in Christ. God has purposed " to gather together all things in Christ." The things in heaven and the things on earth are to be united in Him. But believers alone, the members of his body, are ever said to be in Christ. It is not true that angels good or bad, or the whole mass of mankind are in Him in any scriptural sense of that expression. 3. The word here used expresses directly or indirectly the idea of the union of all things under Christ as their head. Christ is not the head of angels, nor of the material universe in the sense in which the context here demands. He is the head of his body, i. e. his church. It is therefore only of the redemption of the church of which this passage can be understood. 4. The obviously parallel passage in Colossians 1, 20 seems decisive on this point. It is there said: " It pleased *the Father* .... having made peace through the blood of his cross, by him to reconcile all things unto himself; by him, *I say*, whether they be things in earth, or things in heaven." From this passage it is plain that the union to be effected is a reconciliation, which implies previous alienation, and a reconciliation effected by the blood of the cross. It is, therefore, not a union of subjection merely to the same Lord, but it is one effected by the blood of Christ, and consequently the passage can be understood only of the subjects of redemption.

That the church or people of God, excluding angels good or bad, and the finally impenitent among men, are alone the subjects of redemption, is proved, as to evil angels and impenitent men, by the numerous passages of Scripture which speak of their final destruction ; and as to good angels, by the entire silence of Scripture as to their being redeemed by Christ, and by the nature of the work itself. Redemption, in the scriptural sense, is deliverance from sin and misery, and therefore cannot be predicated of those angels who kept their first estate.

These considerations exclude all the interpretations above enumerated except the fourth and fifth. The fourth, which supposes the passage to refer to the union of the Jews and Gentiles, is excluded by its opposition to the uniform language of Scripture. The Jews are never designated as 'inhabitants of heaven.' It is in violation of all usage, therefore, to suppose they are here indicated by that phrase. Nothing therefore remains but the assumption that the apostle refers to the union of all the people of God, i. e. of all the redeemed, in one body under Jesus Christ their head.

They are to be constituted an everlasting kingdom; or, according to another symbol—a living temple, of which Jesus Christ is the chief corner stone.

V. 11. God having formed and revealed the purpose of gathering the redeemed as one body in Christ, it is in the execution of this purpose, the apostle says: ἐν ᾧ καὶ ἐκληρώθημεν, *in whom we also have obtained an inheritance.* By *we,* in this clause, is to be understood neither the apostle individually, nor believers indiscriminately, but *we,* who first hoped in Christ; *we* as contrasted with *you also* in v. 13 ; *you* who were formerly Gentiles in the flesh, 2, 11. It is, therefore, the Jewish Christians to whom this clause refers.

Have obtained an inheritance. The word κληρόω, means *to cast lots, to distribute by lot, to choose by lot,* and in the middle voice, *to obtain by lot* or *inheritance,* or simply, *to obtain.* There are three interpretations of the word ἐκληρώθημεν in this passage, all consistent with its signification and usage. 1. Some prefer the sense *to choose:* ' *In whom we also were chosen,* as it were, by lot, i. e. freely.' The Vulgate translates the passage : Sorte vocati sumus ; and Erasmus : Sorte electi sumus. 2. As in the Old Testament the people of God are called his inheritance, many suppose the apostle has reference to that usage and meant to say : ' In whom we have become the inheritance of God.' 3. The majority of commentators prefer the interpretation adopted in our version : ' In whom we have obtained an inheritance.' This view is sustained by the following considerations. 1. Though the verb is in the passive, the above rendering may be justified either by the remark of Grotius : as the active form signifies to give a possession, the passive may signify to accept it ;* or by a reference to that usage of the passive voice illustrated in such passages as Rom. 3, 2. Gal. 2, 7. With verbs, which in the active have the accusative and dative, in the passive construction what was in the dative, becomes the nominative. Hence ἐκληρώθημεν is the same as ἐκλήρωσε ἡμῖν κληρονομίαν ; just as πεπίστευμαι τὸ εὐαγγέλιον is equivalent to ἐπίστευσέ μοι τὸ εὐαγγέλιον. 2. The inheritance of which the apostle speaks in the context, as in vs. 14 and 18, is that which believers enjoy. They are not themselves the inheritance, they are the heirs. Therefore in this place it is more natural to understand him as referring to what believers attain in Christ, than to their becoming the inheritance of God. As the Israelites of old obtained an inheritance in the promised land, so those in Christ become partakers of that heavenly inheritance which he has secured for them. To this analogy such frequent reference is made in Scripture as to leave little doubt as to the meaning of this passage. 3. The parallel passage in Col. 1, 12, also serves to determine the sense of the clause under consideration. What is there expressed by saying : ' Hath made us partakers of the inheritance of the saints in light ; ' is here expressed by saying : ' We have obtained an inheritance.' *Kaì*,

---

* His words are : κληροῦν dicitur, qui alteri dat possessionem, κληροῦσθαι, qui eam accipit.

also, belongs to the verb and not to tne pronoun implied in the form of the verb. The sense is not *we also*, i. e. we as well as other; but, 'we have also obtained an inheritance.' We have not only been made partakers of the knowledge of redemption, but are actually heirs of its blessings.

There are two sentiments with which the mind of the apostle was thoroughly imbued. The one is, a sense of the absolute supremacy of God, and the other a corresponding sense of the dependence of man and the consequent conviction of the entirely gratuitous nature of all the benefits of redemption. To these sentiments he seldom fails to give expression on any fit occasion. In the present instance having said we have in Christ obtained a glorious inheritance, the question suggests itself, Why? His answer is: *Having been predestinated according to the purpose of Him who worketh all things after the counsel of his own will.* It is neither by chance nor by our own desert or efforts, that we, and not others, have been thus highly favoured. It has been brought about according to the purpose and by the efficiency of God. What has happened He predetermined should occur; and to his "working" the event is to be exclusively referred. We are said to be predestinated, κατὰ πρόθεσιν, *according to the purpose* of God. In v. 5 the same thing is expressed by saying: 'We were predestinated according to the good pleasure of his will;' and in Rom. 8, 28, by saying: 'We are called according to his purpose.' Two things are included in these forms of expression.

1st. That what occurs was foreseen and foreordained. The plan of God embraced and ordered the events here referred to. 2d. That the ground or reason of these occurrences is to be sought in God, in the determination of his will. This however is not a singular case. The bringing certain persons to the enjoyment of the inheritance purchased by Christ, is not the only thing foreordained by God and brought about by his efficiency, and, therefore, the apostle generalizes the truth here expressed, by saying: 'We are predestinated according to the purpose of Him who worketh *all things* after the counsel of his own will.' Every thing is comprehended in his purpose, and every thing is ordered by his efficient control. That control, however, is exercised in accordance with the nature of his creatures, so that no violence is done to the constitution which he has given them. He is glorified, and his purposes are accomplished without any injustice or violence.

The counsel of his will, κατὰ τὴν βουλὴν τοῦ θελήματος αὐτοῦ, means the counsel which has its origin in his will; neither suggested by others, nor determined by any thing out of himself. It is therefore equivalent to his sovereign will.

V. 12. *That we should be to the praise of his glory,* εἰς τὸ εἶναι ἡμᾶς, εἰς ἔπαινον τῆς δόξης αὐτοῦ, that is, that we should be the means of causing his divine majesty or excellence to be praised. Here, as in v. 6, the glory of God is declared to be the design of the plan of redemption and of every thing connected with its administration. The persons here spoken of are described as τοὺς προηλπικότας ἐν τῷ Χριστῷ, *those who first hoped in Christ.* That is, who hoped in him of old, or before his advent; or, who hoped in him before others, mentioned in v. 13, had heard of him. In either case it designates not the first converts to Christianity, but the Jews who, before the Gentiles, had the Messiah as the object of their hopes. The form of expression here used (ἐλπίζειν ἐν), does not mean simply *to expect,* but to place one's hope or confidence in any one. Comp. 1 Cor. 15, 19. It is not, therefore, the Jews as such, but the believing Jews, who are here spoken of as in Christ the partakers of the inheritance which he has purchased.

The construction of these several clauses adopted in the foregoing exposition is that which takes them in their natural order, and gives a sense consistent with the usage of the words and agreeable to the analogy of Scripture. The first clause of this verse is made to depend upon the last clause of v. 11 : ' Having predestinated us to be the praise of his glory ;' and the last clause, ' Who first hoped in Christ,' is merely explanatory of the class of persons spoken of. The whole then hangs naturally together : ' We have obtained an inheritance, having been predestinated to be the praise of his glory, we, who first hoped in Christ.' There are, however, two other modes of construction possible. The one connects the beginning of v. 12 with the first clause of v. 11, and renders ἐκληρώθημεν, *we have attained.* The sense would then be, ' We have attained, or, it has happened unto us to be to the praise of his glory.' This however not only unnaturally dissevers contiguous clauses, but assigns to ἐκληρώθημεν a weakened sense inconsistent with the Scripture usage of that and its cognate words. A second method connects the last clause of the 12th verse with the second clause of the 11th.—'Having predestinated us to be the first who hȯped in Christ.' But this also rends the clauses apart, and does not express a sense so suitable to the context. It is saying much more, and much more in the way of an explanation of the fact affirmed in the first clause of v. 11, to say, 'We were predestinated to be the praise of God's glory;' than to say, 'We were predestinated to be the first who hoped in Christ.' The majority of commentators therefore take the clauses as they stand, and as they are concatenated in our version.

V. 13. The apostle having in v. 10 declared that the purpose of God is to bring all the subjects of redemption into one harmonious body, says in v. 11 that this purpose is realized in the conversion of the Jewish Christians, and he here adds that another class, viz. the Gentile Christians, to whom his epistle is specially addressed, are comprehended in the same purpose. The first clause, ἐν ᾧ καὶ ὑμεῖς, κτλ., is elliptical. *In whom ye also, after that ye heard*, &c. There are therefore several modes of construction possible. 1. Our translators borrow the verb ἠλπίκατε from the immediately preceding clause.—'We, who first *trusted* in Christ, in whom ye also *trusted*.' But the preceding clause is merely subordinate and explanatory, and does not express the main idea of the context. This construction also overlooks the obvious antithesis between the *we* of the 11th verse and the *you* of this clause. 2. Others supply simply the verb *are*. ' In whom you also *are*.' This is better, but it is liable to the latter objection just mentioned. 3. Others make *you* the nominative to the verb *were sealed* in the following clause.—' In whom you also (having heard, &c.) were sealed.' But this requires the clauses to be broken by a parenthesis. It supposes also the construction to be irregular, for the words *in whom also* are repeated before the verb *ye were sealed*. The passage according to this construction would read, ' In whom ye also—, in whom also ye were sealed.' Besides, the sealing is not the first benefit the Gentile Christians received. They were first brought into union with Christ and made partakers of his inheritance and then sealed. 4. It is therefore more consistent not only with the drift of the whole passage, and with the relation between this verse and verse 11, but also with the construction of this and the following verse to supply the word ἐκληρώθητε, *have obtained an inheritance*. Every thing is thus natural. In v. 11, the apostle says, ' In whom we have obtained an inheritance ;' and here, ' In whom ye also have obtained an inheritance.' Both Jews and Gentiles are by the mediation of Christ, and in union with him, brought to be partakers of the benefits of that plan of mercy which God had purposed in himself, and which he has now revealed for the salvation of men.

The clause that follows expresses the means by which the Gentile Christians were brought to be partakers of this inheritance.—'In whom ye also have obtained an inheritance, ἀκούσαντες τὸν λόγον τῆς ἀληθείας,· τὸ εὐαγγ. τῆς σωτηρίας ὑμῶν, *having heard the word of truth, the gospel of your salvation.*' The latter of these expressions is explanatory of the former. By the word of truth, is to be understood, the Gospel. *The word of truth* does not mean simply true doctrine; but that word which is truth, or in which divine or saving truth is. Col. 1, 5. 2 Cor. 6, 7. *The gospel of your salvation*, is the gospel concerning your salvation; or rather, the gospel which saves you. It is that gospel which is, as is said Rom. 1, 16, the power of God unto salvation. As it was by hearing this gospel the Gentiles in the days of the apostle were brought to be partakers of the inheritance of God, so it is by the same means men are to be saved now and in all coming ages until the consummation. It is by the word of truth, and not truth in general, but by that truth which constitutes the glad news of salvation.

In whom also, after that ye believed, ye were sealed. This is more than a translation, it is an exposition of the original, ἐν ᾧ καὶ πιστεύσαντες ἐσφραγίσθητε. There are three interpretations of this clause possible, of which our translators have chosen the best. The relative (ἐν ᾧ) may be referred to the word gospel. '*In which* having believed;' or it may be referred to Christ and connected with the following participle, '*In whom* having believed;' or it may be taken as in our version, by itself, ' In whom, i. e. united to whom, after that ye believed, ye were sealed.' This is to be preferred not only because the other construction is unusual (i. e. it is rare that πιστεύειν is followed by ἐν), but because the words, *in whom*, occur so frequently in the context in the same sense with that here given to them. In Christ, the Gentile Christians had obtained an inheritance, and in him also, they were sealed—after having believed. Whatever is meant by sealing, it is something which follows faith.

There are several purposes for which a seal is used. 1. To authenticate or confirm as genuine and true. 2. To mark as one's property. 3. To render secure. In all these senses believers are sealed. They are authenticated as the true children of God; they have the witness within themselves, 1 John 5, 10. Rom. 8, 16. 5, 5. They are thus assured of their reconciliation and acceptance. They are moreover marked as belonging to God, Rev. 7, 3 ; that is, they are indicated to others, by the seal impressed upon them, as his chosen ones. And thirdly, they are sealed unto salvation; i. e. they are rendered certain of being saved. The sealing of God secures their safety. Thus believers are said Eph. 4, 30, " to be sealed unto the day of redemption ;" and in 2 Cor. 1, 21, the apostle says : " Now he which establisheth us with you in Christ, and hath anointed us, is God; who also hath sealed us, and given us the earnest of the Spirit in our hearts. " The sealing then of which this passage speaks answers all these ends. It assures of the favour of God; it indicates those who belong to him; and it renders their salvation certain.

This sealing is *by the Holy Spirit of promise.* That is, by the Spirit who was promised; or who comes in virtue of the promise. This promise was given frequently through the ancient prophets, who predicted that when the Messiah came and in virtue of his mediation, God would pour his Spirit on all flesh. Christ when on earth frequently repeated this promise; assuring his disciples that when he had gone to the Father, he would send them the Comforter, even the Spirit of truth, to abide with them for ever. After his resurrection he commanded the apostles to abide in Jerusalem until they had received "the promise of the Father," Acts 1, 4; meaning thereby the gift of the Holy Ghost. In Gal. 3, 14, it is said to be the end for which Christ redeemed us from the curse of the law, that we should receive the promise of the Spirit. This then is the great gift which Christ secures for his people; the indwelling of the Holy Spirit, as the source of truth, holiness, consolation, and eternal life.

V. 14. This Spirit is ὁ ἀῤῥαβὼν τῆς κληρονομίας ἡμῶν, *the earnest of our inheritance.* It is at once the foretaste and the pledge of all that is laid up for the believer in heaven. The word ἀῤῥαβὼν is a Hebrew term which passed first into the Greek and then into the Latin vocabulary, retaining its original sense. It means first, a part of the price of any thing purchased, paid, as a security for the full payment, and then more generally a pledge. It occurs three times in reference

to the Holy Spirit in the New Testament, 2 Cor. 1, 22.
5, 5 ; and in the passage before us. In the same sense
the Scriptures speak of " the first fruits of the Spirit,"
Rom. 8, 23. Those influences of the Spirit which believers now enjoy are at once a prelibation or antepast
of future blessedness, the same in kind though immea-
surably less in degree ; and a pledge of the certain
enjoyment of that blessedness. Just as the first fruits
were a part of the harvest, and an earnest of its in-
gathering. It is because the Spirit is an earnest of our
inheritance, that his indwelling is a seal. It assures
those in whom he dwells of their salvation, and renders
that salvation certain. Hence it is a most precious
gift to be most religiously cherished.

Until the redemption of the purchased possession,
εἰς ἀπολύτρωσιν τῆς περιποιήσεως. It is doubtful whether these words should be connected with the preceding clause or with the words *were sealed* in the 13th
verse. Our translators have adopted the former method. ' The Spirit is an earnest until the redemption,'
&c. The latter, however, is perhaps on the whole
preferable. ' Ye were sealed until, or in reference to,
the redemption,' &c. This view is sustained by a comparison with 4, 30, where it is said : ' Ye were sealed
unto the day of redemption.'

The word redemption, in its Christian sense, sometimes means that deliverance from the curse of the
law and restoration to the favour of God, of which
believers are in this life the subjects. Sometimes it
refers to that final deliverance from all evil, which is

to take a place at the second advent of Christ. Thus in Luke 21, 28, "They shall see the Son of man coming in a cloud with power and great glory ; . . . . then lift up your heads; for your redemption draweth nigh." Rom. 8, 23. Eph. 4, 30. There can be no doubt that it here refers to this final deliverance.

The word rendered *purchased possession*, is περιποίησις; which means either the *act of acquiring*, or, *the thing acquired*. If the former signification be adopted here, the word can only be taken as a participial qualification of the preceding word. 'The redemption of acquisition,' for 'acquired or purchased redemption.' But this is unnatural. Redemption in itself includes the idea of purchased deliverance. 'Purchased redemption' is therefore tautological. If the word be taken for 'the thing acquired,' then it may refer to heaven, or the inheritance here spoken of. But heaven is never said to be redeemed. It is therefore most naturally understood of God's people. They are his possession, his peculium. They are in 1 Pet. 2, 9 called λαὸς εἰς περιποίησιν, *a peculiar people*. And in Mal. 3, 17 it is said, They shall be to me for a possession, ἔσονταί μοι εἰς περιποίησιν. Comp. Acts 20, 28, ἐκκλησία ἣν περιεποιήσατο. This interpretation is, therefore, peculiarly suited to the scriptural usage, and the sense is perfectly appropriate. Ye are sealed, says the apostle, until the redemption of God's peculiar people ; i. e. unto the great day of redemption spoken of in 4, 30.

Unto the praise of his glory, i. e. that his glory or

excellence should be praised. Comp. vs. 6 and 12. This is the end both of the final redemption and of the present acceptance of believers. This clause, therefore, is to be referred to the whole of the preceding passage. Ye have received an inheritance, have been sealed, and have received the Holy Spirit as an earnest, in order that God may be glorified. This is the last and highest end of redemption.

SECTION III.—Vs. 15–23.

15. Wherefore I also, after I heard of your faith in the Lord
16. Jesus, and love unto all the saints, cease not to give thanks for
17. you, making mention of you in my prayers; that the God of our Lord Jesus Christ, the Father of glory, may give unto you the spirit of wisdom and revelation in the knowledge of him:
18. the eyes of your understanding being enlightened; that ye may know what is the hope of his calling, and what the riches
19. of the glory of his inheritance in the saints, and what *is* the exceeding greatness of his power to us-ward who believe, ac-
20. cording to the working of his mighty power, which he wrought in Christ, when he raised him from the dead, and set *him* at
21. his own right hand in the heavenly *places*, far above all principality, and power, and might, and dominion, and every name that is named, not only in this world, but also in that which
22. is to come: and hath put all *things* under his feet, and gave
23. him *to be* the head over all *things* to his church: which is his body, the fulness of him that filleth all in all..

ANALYSIS.

Having in the preceding Section unfolded the nature of those blessings of which the Ephesians had

become partakers, the apostle gives thanks to God for
their conversion, and assures them of their interest in
his prayers, vs. 15. 16.   He prays that God would give
them that wisdom and knowledge of himself of which
the Spirit is the author, v. 17; that their eyes might
be enlightened properly to apprehend the nature and
value of that hope which is founded in the call of God;
and the glory of the inheritance to be enjoyed among
the saints, v. 18; and the greatness of that power which
had been already exercised in their conversion, v. 19.
The power which effected their spiritual resurrection,
was the same as that which raised Christ from the
dead, and exalted him above all created beings and
associated him in the glory and dominion of God, vs.
20. 21.   To him all things are made subject, and he is
constituted the supreme head of the church, which is his
body, the fulness or complement of the mystical person
of him who fills the universe with his presence and
power, vs. 22. 23.

COMMENTARY.

V. 15. *Wherefore.* This word is to be referred
either to the whole preceding paragraph, or specially
to v. 13. ' Because you Ephesians, you Gentile Christians, have obtained a portion in this inheritance, and,
after having believed, have been sealed with the Holy
Spirit of promise, &c.'—' *I also,* i. e. as well as others,
and especially yourselves.' The Ephesians might well
be expected to be filled with gratitude for their con-

version. The apostle assures them he joins them in their perpetual thanksgiving over this glorious event.

Having heard of your faith in the Lord Jesus As Paul was the founder of the church in Ephesus and had laboured long in that city, it has always excited remark that he should speak of having heard of their faith, as though he had no personal acquaintance with them. This form of expression is one of the reasons why many have adopted the opinion, as mentioned in the Introduction, that this epistle was addressed not to the Ephesians alone or principally, but to all the churches in the western part of Asia Minor. It is, however, not unnatural that the apostle should speak thus of so large and constantly changing a congregation, after having been for a time absent from them. Besides, the expression need mean nothing more than that he continued to hear of their good estate. The two leading graces of the Christian character are faith and love—faith in Christ and love to the brethren. Of these, therefore, the apostle here speaks. *Your faith;* τὴν καθ' ὑμᾶς πίστιν, which either means *the faith which is with you;* or as our version renders the words, *your faith.* Comp. in the Greek Acts 17, 28. 18, 15. *Faith in the Lord Jesus,* i. e. faith or trust which has its ground in him. For examples of the construction of πίστις with ἐν, see Gal. 3, 26. Col. 1, 4. 1 Tim. 1, 14. 3, 13. 2 Tim. 1, 13. 3, 15. Comp. Mark 1, 15, and in the Septuagint Jer. 12, 6. Ps. 78, 22. This construction, though comparatively rare, is not to be denied, nor are forced interpretations of pas sages where it occurs to be justified, in order to get rid of it.

In the Old Testament the phrases, the Lord said, the Lord did, our Lord, and the like, are of constant occurrence; and are used only, in this general way, of the Supreme God. We never hear of the Lord, nor our Lord, when reference is had to Moses or any other of the prophets. In the New Testament, however, what is so common in the Old Testament in reference to God, is no less common in reference to Christ. He is the Lord; the Lord Jesus; our Lord, &c. &c. It is this constant mode of speaking, together with the exhibition of his divine excellence, and holding him up as the object of faith and love, even more than any particular declaration, which conveys to the Christian reader the conviction of his true divinity. His being the object of faith and the ground of trust to immortal beings, is irreconcilable with any other assumption than that he is the true God and eternal life.

And love towards all the saints, i. e. towards those who are saints; those who have been cleansed, separated from the world, and consecrated to God. This love is founded upon the character and relations of its objects as the people of God, and therefore it embraces *all* the saints.

V. 16. *I cease not giving thanks for you, making mention of you,* &c. This does not mean, 'praying I give thanks;' but two things are mentioned—constant thanksgiving on their account, and intercession.

V. 17. The burden of his prayer is contained in this

and the verses following. The object of his prayer, or the person to whom it is addressed, is designated, first, *as the God of our Lord Jesus Christ*, i. e. the God whose work Christ came to do, by whom he was sent, of whom he testified and to whom he has gone;—and secondly, ὁ πατὴρ τῆς δόξης, *the Father of glory*. This designation is variously explained. By *glory* many of the Fathers understood the divine nature of Christ, and remarked that Paul here calls God, the God of Christ as a man, but his Father as God.* This interpretation of the phrase ' Father of glory,' is without the least support from the analogy of Scripture. It means either, the source or author of glory; or the possessor of glory, i. e. who is glorious. Comp. Acts 7, 1. 1 Cor. 2, 8, "Lord of glory." James 2, 1, and in Ps. 24, 7, "the king of glory."

There are three leading petitions expressed in the prayer here recorded. First, for adequate knowledge of divine truth. Second, for due appreciation of the future blessedness of the saints. Third, for a proper understanding of what they themselves had already experienced in their conversion.

His first prayer is thus expressed: *That he may give unto you the Spirit of wisdom and revelation, in the knowledge of him.* By πνεῦμα σοφίας, the *Spirit of wisdom*, is to be understood the Holy Spirit, the author of wisdom, and not merely a state of mind,

---

* So BENGEL, who explains the expression thus : Pater gloriae, infinitae illius, quae refulget in facie Christi ; immo gloriae quae est ipse filius Dei.

which consists in wisdom. It is true the word spirit is sometimes used in periphrases expressive of mental acts or states. As in 1 Cor. 4, 21, "spirit of meekness;" and 2 Cor. 4, 13, "The same spirit of faith," i. e. the same confidence. But in the present case the former interpretation is to be preferred. 1. Because the Holy Spirit is so constantly recognized as the source of all right knowledge; and 2. Because the analogy of Scripture is in favour of this view of the passage. In such passages as the following the word spirit evidently is to be understood of the Holy Spirit. John 15, 26, "Spirit of truth;" Rom. 8, 15, "Spirit of adoption;" comp. Gal. 4, 6, "God sent forth the Spirit of his Son into your hearts, crying, Abba, Father." 1 Thess. 1, 6, "Joy of the Holy Spirit." Rom. 15, 30, "Love of the Spirit." Gal. 5, 5, "We by the Spirit wait," &c. The Holy Spirit is the author of that wisdom of which the apostle speaks so fully in 1 Cor. 2, 6–10; and which he describes, first negatively as not of this world, and then affirmatively, as the hidden wisdom of God, which he had revealed, by the Spirit, for our glory. It is the whole system of divine truth, which constitutes the Gospel. Those who have this wisdom are the wise. There is a twofold revelation of this wisdom, the one outward, by inspiration, or through inspired men; the other inward, by spiritual illumination. Of both these the apostle speaks in 1 Cor. 2, 10–16, and both are here brought into view. Comp. Phil. 3, 15. By ἀποκάλυψις, *revelation*, therefore, in this passage is not to be understood, the knowledge of future events, nor the prophetic gift, nor inspiration. It is something which all believers need and for which they should pray. It is that manifestation of the nature or excellence of the things of God, which the Spirit makes to all who are spiritually enlightened, and of which our Saviour spoke, when he said in reference to believers, They shall all be taught of God.

In the knowledge of him. The pronoun *him* refers not to Christ, but to God the immediate subject in this context. The word ἐπίγνωσις here rendered *knowledge* means accurate and certain, and especially, experimental knowledge; as in Rom. 3, 20, "By the law is the knowledge (the conviction) of sin." Eph. 4, 13. Phil. 1, 9. 1 Tim. 2, 4. The word expresses adequate and proper knowledge, the precise nature of which depends on the object known. The phrase is ἐν ἐπιγνώσει, which some render as though εἰς with the accusative were used—unto knowledge, i. e. so as to know. Others connect these words with those which precede, and translate, ' wisdom in knowledge,' i. e. wisdom consisting in knowledge. Others again connect them with the following clause, ' Through knowledge your eyes being enlightened.' The simplest method is to refer them to what precedes. ' May give you wisdom together with the knowledge of himself.' Comp. v. 8, and Phil. 1, 9, "That your love may abound in, i. e. together with, knowledge." The apostle's prayer is for the Holy Spirit to dwell in them, as the author of divine wisdom, and as the revealer of the

things of God, which insight into the things of the
Spirit, is connected with that knowledge of God in
which eternal life essentially consists.

V. 18. *The eyes of your understanding being enlightened.* Instead of διανοίας *understanding*, the great
majority of ancient manuscripts and versions read καρδίας *heart*, which is no doubt the true reading. The
word *heart* in Scripture is often used as we use the
word *soul*, to designate the whole spiritual nature in
man. Rom. 1, 21. 2 Cor. 4, 6.

This clause πεφωτισμένους τοὺς ὀφθαλμοὺς τῆς καρδίας ὑμῶν, may either be taken absolutely as our translators have understood it—or considered as in apposition and explanatory of what precedes. 'That he may
give you the spirit of wisdom, &c., eyes enlightened,
&c.' This latter mode of explanation is the one commonly adopted. The effect of the gift of the spirit of
wisdom is this illumination, not of the speculative understanding merely, but of the whole soul. For light
and knowledge in Scripture often include the ideas of
holiness and happiness, as well as that of intellectual
apprehension. Comp. such passages as John 8, 12,
"Light of life." Acts 26, 18, "To turn from darkness
to light." Eph. 5, 8, "Ye were sometime darkness,
but now are ye light in the Lord." Believers, therefore, are called "children of the light." Luke 16, 8.
1 Thess. 5, 5.

The residue of this verse εἰς τὸ εἰδέναι ὑμᾶς, κτλ.
contains a second petition. Having prayed that the
Ephesians might be enlightened in the knowledge of

God and of divine things, the apostle here prays, as
the effect of that illumination, that they may have a
proper appreciation of the inheritance to which they
have attained.

That ye may know what is the hope of his calling,
i. e. the hope of which his calling is the source; or to
which he has called you. The vocation here spoken
of is not merely the external call of the Gospel, but
the effectual call of God by the Spirit, to which the
word κλῆσις in the epistles of Paul always refers. The
word *hope* is by many here understood objectively for
the things hoped for; as in Rom. 8, 24, and Col. 1, 5,
"The hope laid up for you in heaven." It is then
identical with the inheritance mentioned in the latter
part of the verse. This, however, is a reason against
that interpretation. There are two things which the
apostle mentions and which he desires they may
know. First, the nature and value of the hope which
they are now, on the call of God, authorized to indulge;
and secondly, the glory of the inheritance in reserve
for them. It is better, therefore, to take the word in
its ordinary subjective sense. It is a great thing to
know, or estimate aright the value of a well founded
hope of salvation.

And what the riches of the glory of his inheritance,
καὶ τίς ὁ πλοῦτος τῆς δόξης τῆς κληρονομίας αὐτοῦ, i. e.
what is the abundance and greatness of the excellence
of that inheritance of which God is the author. The
apostle labours here, and still more in the following
verses, for language to express the greatness of his con-

ceptions. This inheritance is not only divine as having God for its author; but it is a glorious inheritance; and not simply glorious, but the glory of it is inconceivably great.

In the saints, ἐν τοῖς ἁγίοις. These words admit of different constructions, but the most natural is to refer them to the immediately preceding clause, *His inheritance in the saints;* i. e. which is to be enjoyed among them. Comp. Acts 20, 32, and 26, 18, "An inheritance among them that are sanctified." Col. 1, 12, "Partakers of the inheritance of the saints in l ght." It was one part of the peculiar blessedness of the Gentile Christians, who had been strangers and foreigners, that they were become fellow-citizens of the saints. It was therefore an exaltation of the inheritance, now set before them, to call it the inheritance prepared for the saints, or peculiar people of God.

V. 19. *And what is the exceeding greatness of his power to us-ward who believe.* This is the third petition in the apostle's prayer. He prays that his readers may have right apprehensions of the greatness of the change which they had experienced. It was no mere moral reformation effected by rational considerations; nor was it a self-wrought change, but one due to the almighty power of God. Grotius indeed, and commentators of that class, understand the passage to refer to the exertion of the power of God in the future resurrection and salvation of believers. But 1. It evidently refers to the past and not to the future. It is something which believers, as believers, had already expe-

rienced that he wished them to understand. 2. The
apostle never compares the salvation of believers with
the resurrection of Christ, whereas the analogy between
his natural resurrection and the spiritual resurrection
of his people, is one to which he often refers. 3. This
is the analogy which he insists upon in this immediate
connection. As God raised Christ from the dead and
set him at his own right hand in heavenly places; so
you, that were dead in sins, hath he quickened and
raised you up together in him. This analogy is the
very thing he would have them understand. They had
undergone a great change; they had been brought to
life; they had been raised from the dead by the same
almighty power which wrought in Christ. There was
as great a difference between their present and their
former condition, as between Christ in the tomb and
Christ at the right hand of God. This was something
which they ought to know. 4. The parallel passage
in Col. 2, 12, seems decisive of this interpretation.
"Buried with him in baptism, wherein also ye are
risen with him through faith of the operation of God,
who raised him from the dead. And you, being dead
in your sins and the uncircumcision of your flesh, hath
he quickened together with him, having forgiven you
all trespasses." In this passage it cannot be doubted
that the apostle compares the spiritual resurrection of
believers with the resurrection of Christ, and refers
both events to the operation of God, or to the divine
power. Such also is doubtless the meaning of the passage before us; and in this interpretation there has

been a remarkable coincidence of judgment among commentators. Chrysostom says: "The conversion of souls is more wonderful than the resurrection of the dead." Oecumenius remarks on this passage: "To raise us from spiritual death is an exercise of the same power that raised Christ from natural death." Calvin says, "Some (i. e. Stulti homines) regard the language of the apostle in this passage as frigid hyperbole, but those who are properly exercised find nothing here beyond the truth." He adds: "Lest believers should be cast down under a sense of their unworthiness, the apostle recalls them to a consideration of the power of God; as though he had said, their regeneration is a work of God, and no common work, but one in which his almighty power is wonderfully displayed." Luther, in reference to the parallel passage in Colossians, uses the following language: "Faith is no such easy matter as our opposers imagine, when they say, 'Believe, Believe, how easy is it to believe.' Neither is it a mere human work, which I can perform for myself, but it is a divine power in the heart, by which we are new born, and whereby we are able to overcome the mighty power of the Devil and of death; as Paul says to the Colossians, 'In whom ye are raised up again through the faith which God works.'"

It is then a great truth which the apostle here teaches. He prays that his readers may properly understand τί τὸ ὑπερβάλλον μέγεθος τῆς δυνάμεως αὐτοῦ. The conversion of the soul is not a small matter; nor is it a work effected by any human power. It is a re-

surrection due to the exceeding greatness of the power
of God.

According to the working of his mighty power,
κατὰ τὴν ἐνέργειαν τοῦ κράτους τῆς ἰσχύος αὐτοῦ. The
original here offers a remarkable accumulation of
words.—'According to the energy of the might of his
power.' Ἰσχύς, κράτος, ἐνέργεια ; *Robur, Potentia,
Efficacia.* The first is inherent strength ; the second
power ; the third the exercise or efficiency of that
strength. Or, as Calvin says, The first is the root, the
second the tree, the third the fruit. Whatever be the
precise distinction in the signification of the words,
their accumulation expresses the highest form of power.
It was nothing short of the omnipotence of God to which
the effect here spoken of is due. No created power
can raise the dead, or quicken those dead in trespasses
and sins.

The connection of this clause is somewhat doubtful.
It may be referred to the words *exceeding greatness of
his power,* i. e. κατὰ ἐνέργειαν may be referred to τὸ ὑπερβάλλον μέγεθος, κτλ. The sense would then be—'That
ye may know the exceeding greatness of his power, to
us-ward that believe, *which was,* according to, or like,
the working of his mighty power which wrought in
Christ.' Or, πιστεύοντας κατὰ ἐνέργειαν may be connected, 'Who believe in virtue of the working of his
mighty power.' In the one case this clause is a mere
illustration or amplification of the idea of the divine
power of which believers are the subject. In the other,
it expresses more definitely the reason why the power

which they had experienced was to be considered so great, viz., because their faith was due to the same energy that raised Christ from the dead. In either case the doctrinal import of the passage is the same. The considerations in favour of the latter mode of construction are: 1. The position of the clauses. According to this interpretation they are taken just as they stand. 'Us who believe in virtue of (κατά) the working, &c.' 2. The frequency with which the apostle uses the preposition κατά in the sense thus given to it. In ch. 3, 7, he says, 'his conversion and vocation were (κατά) *in virtue* of the working of God's power.' See also 3, 20. 1 Cor. 12, 8. Phil. 3, 21. Christ will fashion our bodies (κατά) 'in virtue of the energy whereby he is able to subdue all things unto himself.' Col. 1, 29. 2 Thess. 2, 9. To say, therefore, 'we believe in virtue of, &c.,' is in accordance with a usage familiar to this apostle. 3. The parallel passage in Col. 2, 12, expresses the same idea. There the phrase is πίστις τῆς ἐνεργείας, *faith of the operation* of God, i. e. which he operates; here it is πίστις κατὰ τὴν ἐνέργειαν, *faith in virtue of the operation.* The analogy between the expressions is so striking, that the one explains and authenticates the other.

The prayer recorded in these verses is a very comprehensive one. In praying that the Ephesians might be enlightened with spiritual apprehensions of the truth, the apostle prays for their sanctification. In praying that they might have just conceptions of the inheritance to which they were called, he prayed that they might be elevated above the world. And in praying that they might know the exceeding greatness of the power exercised in their conversion, he prayed that they might be at once humble and confident; humble, in view of the death of sin from which they had been raised; and confident, in view of the omnipotence of that God who had begun their salvation.

V. 20. *Which he wrought in Christ when he raised him from the dead,* ἣν ἐνήργησεν, κτλ. There are two things evidently intended in these words. First, that the power which raises the believer from spiritual death, is the same as that which raised Christ from the grave. And secondly, that there is a striking analogy between these events and an intimate connection between them. The one was not only the symbol, but the pledge and procuring cause of the other. The resurrection of Christ is both the type and the cause of the spiritual resurrection of his people, as well of their future rising from the grave in his glorious likeness. On this analogy and connection the apostle speaks at large in Rom. 6, 1–10, and also in the following chapters of this epistle. As often therefore as the believer contemplates Christ as risen and seated at the right hand of God, he has at once an illustration of the change which has been effected in his own spiritual state, and a pledge that the work commenced in regeneration shall be consummated in glory.

And caused him to sit at his own right hand in the heavenly places. Kings place at their right hand those whom they design to honour, or whom they associate with themselves in dominion. No creature can be thus associated in honour and authority with God, and therefore to none of the angels hath he ever said: Sit thou at my right hand. Heb. 1, 13. That divine honour and authority are expressed by sitting at the right hand of God, is further evident from those passages which speak of the extent of that dominion and of the nature of that honour to which the exalted Redeemer is entitled. It is an universal dominion. Matt. 28, 18. Phil. 2, 9. 1 Pet. 3, 22; and it is such honour as is due to God alone. John 5, 23.

V. 21. The immediate subject of discourse in this chapter is the blessings of redemption conferred on believers. The resurrection and exaltation of Christ are introduced incidentally by way of illustration. The apostle dwells for a moment on the nature of this exaltation, and on the relation of Christ, at the right hand of God, to his church, and then, at the beginning of the following chapter, reverts to his main topic.

The subject of the exaltation here spoken of is not the Logos, but Christ; the Theanthropos, or God-man. The possession of divine perfections was the necessary condition of this exaltation because, as just remarked, the nature and extent of the dominion granted to him, demand such perfections. It is a dominion not only absolutely universal, but it extends over the heart and conscience, and requires the obedience not only of the outward conduct but of the inward life, which is due to God alone. We therefore find the divine nature of Christ presented in the Scriptures as the reason of his being invested with this peculiar dominion. Thus in the second Psalm, it is said, "Thou art my Son; ask of me, I will give thee the heathen for thine inheritance, &c." That is, because thou art my son, ask and I will give thee this dominion. And in the first chapter of the epistle to the Hebrews, it is said, The Son, being the brightness of the Father's glory, and the express image of his person, and upholding a.. things by the word of his power, is set down at the right hand of the majesty on high. That is, because he is of the same nature with the Father and possesses the same almighty power, he is associated with him in his dominion. While the divine nature of Christ is the necessary condition of his exaltation, his mediatorial work is the immediate ground of the Theanthropos, God manifested in the flesh, being invested with this universal dominion. This is expressly asserted, as in Phil. 2, 9. Though equal with God, he humbled himself to become obedient unto death, wherefore also God hath highly exalted him.

In illustration of the exaltation of Christ mentioned in v. 20, the apostle here says, He is seated ὑπὲρ ἄνω, *up above, high above all principality, and power, and might, and dominion.* That these terms refer to angels is plain from the context, and from such passages as Rom. 8, 38. Col. 1, 16. Eph. 3, 10. 6, 12. Where angels are either expressly named, or the powers spoken of are said to be in heaven, or they are opposed to "flesh and blood," i. e. man, as a different order of beings. The origin of the application of these terms to angels cannot be historically traced. The names themselves suggest the reason of their use. Angels are called principalities, powers and dominions, either because of their exalted nature; or because through them God exercises his power and dominion; or because of their relation to each other. It is possible indeed that Paul had a polemic object in the use of these terms. This epistle and especially that to the Colossians, contain many intimations that the emanation theory, which afterwards assumed the form of Gnosticism, had already made its appearance in Asia Minor. And as the advocates of that theory used these terms to designate the different effluxes from the central Being, Paul may have borrowed their phraseology in order to refute their doctrine. Be this as it may, the obvious meaning of the passage is that Christ is exalted above all created beings.

And every name, i. e., as the connection shows, *every* name of excellence or honour, *that is named*. That is, above every creature bearing such name as prince, potentate, ruler, or whatever other title there may be.

Not only in this world, but also in that which is to come, ἐν τῷ αἰῶνι τούτῳ, ἀλλὰ καὶ ἐν τῷ μέλλοντι. That is, not only in this age, but in the age to come. The words may have the general sense of, *here or hereafter;* as in Matt. 12, 32. According to Jewish usage, they designate the period before and the period after the advent of the Messiah. To this, however, there is no reference in the context. As in Matthew these words are used to express in the strongest terms that the sin against the Holy Ghost can never be forgiven; so here they are intended to add universality to the preceding negation. There is no name here or hereafter, in this world or in the next, over which Christ is not highly exalted.

V. 22. *And hath put all things under his feet.* Christ is not only exalted above all creatures, but he has dominion over them; all are placed in absolute subjection to him. They are under his feet. This passage is a quotation from Ps. 8, 7. It is applied to Christ by this same apostle in 1 Cor. 15, 27, and Heb. 2, 8. In both of these passages the word *all* is pressed to the full extent of its meaning. It is made to include all creatures, all capable of subjection; all beings save God alone, are made subject to man in the person of Jesus Christ, the Lord of lords, and King of kings.

There are two principles on which the application of this passage of Ps. 8 to Christ may be explained. The one is that the Psalm is a prophetic exhibition of the goodness of God to Christ, and of the dominion to be given to him. There is nothing, however, in the contents of the Psalm to favour the assumption of its having special reference to the Messiah. The other principle admits the reference of the Psalm to men generally, but assumes its full meaning to be what the apostle here declares it to be, viz., that the dominion which belongs to man is nothing less than universal. But this dominion is realized only in the Man Christ Jesus, and in those who are associated with him in his kingdom. This latter mode of explanation satisfies all the exigencies both of the original Psalm and of the passages where it is quoted in the New Testament.

And gave him to be head over all things to the church, καὶ αὐτὸν ἔδωκε κεφαλὴν ὑπὲρ πάντα τῇ ἐκκλησίᾳ. This may mean either, he gave him *to* the church as her head; or, he constituted him head *for* the church. The former is more consistent with the meaning of the verb δίδωμι. It may, however, also signify to constitute; see 4, 11, and compare 1 Cor. 12, 28. In either case, Christ is declared to be head not of the universe, but of the church. This being admitted, ὑπὲρ πάντα may be taken in immediate connection with κεφαλήν, *head over all,* i. e. supreme head. This does not mean head over all the members of the church, as the Vulgate translates : *caput super omnem ecclesiam;* for πάντα and ἐκκλησίᾳ are not grammatically connected ; but simply supreme head. Or we may adopt the interpretation of Chrysostom : τὸν ὄντα ὑπὲρ πάντα τὰ ὁρώμενα καὶ τὰ νοούμενα Χριστόν, " Him, who is over all things visible and invisible, he gave to the church as her head." This gives a good sense, but supposes an unnatural trajection of the words. Luther also transposes the words : Und hat ihn gesetzt zum Haupt der Gemeinde über alles. So does De Wette : Und ihn gesetzet über alles zum Haupte der Gemeinde, *And placed him over all as head of the church.* In all these interpretations the main idea is retained ; viz. that Christ is the head of the church. As in Col. 2, 10, it is said Christ is ἡ κεφαλὴ πάσης ἀρχῆς καὶ ἐξουσίας,

the head of all principality and power, in the sense of
supreme ruler; and as here in the immediately preceding context he is said to be exalted over all principality and power, and in the following context he is
said to be the head of the church, which is his body,
the two ideas may be here combined. 'Him he gave
as head over all things, as head to his church.'—This is
Meyer's interpretation. He, the exalted Saviour, the
incarnate Son of God, seated as head of the universe,
is made head of his church. This view of the passage
has the advantage of giving πάντα the same reference
here that it has in the preceding verse. *All things*
are placed under his feet, and he head over all things,
is head of the church.

The sense in which Christ is the head of the church,
is that he is the source of its life, its supreme ruler,
ever present with it, sympathizing with it, and loving
it as a man loves his own flesh. See 4, 15. 16. 5, 23. 29.
Rom. 12, 5. 1 Cor. 12, 27. Intimate union, dependence, and community of life, are the main ideas expressed by this figure.

V. 23. *Which is his body.* This is the radical, or
formative idea of the church. From this idea are to
be developed its nature, its attributes, and its prerogatives. It is the indwelling of the Spirit of Christ, that
constitutes the church his body. And, therefore, those
only in whom the Spirit dwells are constituent members of the true church. But the Spirit does not dwell
in church officers, nor especially in prelates, as such;
nor in the baptized, as such; nor in the mere external

professors of the true religion ; but in true believers,
who therefore constitute that church which is the body
of Christ, and to which its attributes and prerogatives
belong.

The main question which this verse presents for
consideration is : In what sense is the church the fulness of Christ ?　There are, however, two other points
which must be previously determined.　In the first
place, it is the church, and not Christ to whom the
word *fulness* here refers.　Some commentators adopt
the following interpretation of the passage : ' Christ,
the supreme head to the church (which is his body),
the fulness, i. e. Christ is the fulness, of him that filleth
all in all.'　But 1. This interpretation violates the
grammatical construction of the passage.　2. It rends
the clauses very unnaturally asunder.　3. It assumes
that the last clause of the verse, viz. ' who fills all in
all,' refers to God, whereas it refers to Christ.　4. The
sense thus obtained is unscriptural.　The fulness of the
Godhead is said to be in Christ ; but Christ is never
said to be the fulness of God.

In the second place, the church is here declared to
be the fulness of Christ, and not the fulness of God.—
Some commentators understand the passage thus :
' The church, which is the body of Christ, is the fulness
of him who fills all in all, i. e. of God.'　But to this it
is objected, 1. That the construction of the passage
requires that the last clause in the verse be referred to
Christ ; and 2. This interpretation supposes the word
πλήρωμα *fulness*, to mean *multitude*.　' The multitude

belonging to him who fills all in all.' But this is a signification which the word never has in itself, but only in virtue of the word with which it is at times connected. The expression πλήρωμα τῆς πόλεως may be freely rendered, *the multitude of the city*, because that which fills a city is a multitude. But this does not prove that the word πλήρωμα itself signifies a multitude. There is no good reason then for departing from the ordinary interpretation, according to which, the church is declared to be the fulness of Christ.

There are two opinions as to the meaning of this phrase, between which commentators are principally divided. First, the church may be called the fulness of Christ, because it is filled by him. As the body is filled, or pervaded by the soul, so the church is filled by the Spirit of Christ. Or, as God of old dwelt in the temple, and filled it with his glory, so Christ now dwells in his church and fills it with his presence. The sense is then good and scriptural. ' The church is filled by him, who fills all in all.' Or secondly, the church is the fulness of Christ, because it fills him, i. e. completes his mystical person. He is the head, the church is the body. It is the complement, or that which completes, or renders whole. As both these interpretations give a sense that is scriptural and consistent with the context, the choice between them must be decided principally by the New Testament usage of the word πλήρωμα. The former interpretation supposes the word to have a passive signification—*that which is filled*. But in every other case in which it occurs in the New

Testament, it is used actively—*that which does fill.*
Matt. 9, 16, The piece put into an old garment is
called its fulness, i. e. 'that which is put in to fill it
up.' Mark 6, 43, The fragments which filled the bas-
kets, are called their fulness. John 1, 16, ' Of his fulness,' means the plenitude of grace and truth that is
in him. Gal. 4, 4, The fulness of the time, is that
which renders full the specified time. Col. 2, 9, The
fulness of the Godhead, is all that is in the Godhead.
Eph. 3, 19, The fulness of God, is that of which God is
full—the plenitude of divine perfections. 1 Cor. 10, 26,
The fulness of the earth, is that which fills the earth.
The common usage of the word in the New Testament
is therefore clearly in favour of its being taken in an active sense here. The church is the fulness of Christ—
in that it is the complement of his mystic person. He
is the head, the church is his body.

In favour of the other interpretation it may be
urged,—1. That πλήρωμα has in the Classics, in Philo,
in the writings of the Gnostics, at times, a passive
sense. 2. The meaning thus afforded is preferable.
It is a more scriptural and more intelligible statement,
to say that Christ fills his church, as the soul pervades
the body—or as the glory of the Lord filled the temple, than to say that the church in any sense fills Christ.
3. Πλήρωμα must be taken in a sense which suits the
participle πληρουμένου ; ' the church is filled by him
who fills all things.' The second and third of these
reasons are so strong as to give this interpretation the
preference in the minds of those to whom the *usus*

loquendi of the New Testament is not an insuperable objection.

That filleth all in all, τοῦ τὰ πάντα ἐν πᾶσι πληρουμένου. This clause, as before remarked, refers to Christ, as the construction obviously demands. The participle πληρουμένου is by almost all commentators assumed to have in this case an active signification. This assumption is justified by the exigency of the place, and by the fact that in common Greek the passive forms of this verb are at times used in an active sense. That there is no such case in the New Testament, is not therefore a sufficient reason for departing from the ordinary interpretation.

The expression, τὰ πάντα ἐν πᾶσι, *all in all*, or, *all with all*, does not mean all the church in all its members, or with all grace, but the universe in all its parts. There is nothing in the context to restrict or limit τὰ πάντα. The words must have the latitude here which belongs to them in the preceding verses. The analogy of Scripture is in favour of this interpretation. God's relation to the world, or totality of things external to himself, is elsewhere expressed in the same terms. Jer. 23, 24, "Do not I fill heaven and earth? saith the Lord." Comp. 1 Kings 8, 27. Ps. 139, 7. In the New Testament Christ is set forth as creating, sustaining, and pervading the universe. Col. 1, 16. 17. Heb. 1, 3. Eph. 4, 10. This, therefore, determines the sense in which he is here said to fill all things. It is not that he replenishes all his people with his grace; but that he fills heaven and earth with his presence.

There is no place where he is not. There is no creature from which he is absent. By him all things consist; they are upheld by his presence in them and
with them. The union, therefore, which the church
sustains, and which is the source of its life and blessedness, is not with a mere creature, but with Christ,
God manifested in the flesh, who pervades and governs
all things by his omnipresent power. The source of
life, therefore, to the church is inexhaustible and immortal.

CHAPTER II

THE APOSTLE CONTRASTS THE SPIRITUAL STATE OF THE EPHESIANS BEFORE
THEIR CONVERSION, WITH THAT INTO WHICH THEY HAD BEEN INTRO-
DUCED BY THE GRACE OF GOD, VS. 1–10.—HE CONTRASTS THEIR PRE-
VIOUS CONDITION AS ALIENS, WITH THAT OF FELLOW-CITIZENS OF THE
SAINTS AND MEMBERS OF THE FAMILY OF GOD, VS. 11–22.

SECTION I.—Vs. 1–10.

And you *hath he quickened*, who were dead in trespasses
2. and sins; wherein in time past ye walked according to the
course of this world, according to the prince of the power
of the air, the spirit that now worketh in the children of dis-
3. obedience : among whom also we all had our conversation in
times past in the lusts of our flesh, fulfilling the desires of the
flesh and of the mind ; and were by nature the children of
4. wrath, even as others. But God, who is rich in mercy, for
5. his great love wherewith he loved us, even when we were
dead in sins, hath quickened us together with Christ, (by grace
6. ye are saved ;) and hath raised *us* up together, and made *us*
7. sit together in heavenly *places* in Christ Jesus : that in the
ages to come he might show the exceeding riches of his grace
8. in *his* kindness towards us, through Christ Jesus. For by
grace are ye saved through faith ; and that not of yourselves :
9. *it is* the gift of God : not of works, lest any man should boast.

10. For we are his workmanship, created in Christ Jesus unto
good works, which God hath before ordained that we should
walk in them.

ANALYSIS.

There are three principal topics treated of in this
Section. First, the spiritual state of the Ephesians
before their conversion. Second, the change which
God had wrought in them. Third, the design for
which that change had been effected.

I. The state of the Ephesians before their conversion, and the natural state of men universally, is one
of spiritual death, which includes—1. A state of sin.
2. A state of subjection to Satan and to our own corrupt affections. 3. A state of condemnation, vs. 1–3.

II. The change which they had experienced was a
spiritual resurrection ; concerning which the apostle
teaches—1. That God is its author. 2. That it is a work
of love and grace. 3. That it was through Christ, or
in virtue of union with him. 4. That it involves great
exaltation, even an association with Christ in his glory,
vs. 4–6.

III. The design of this dispensation is the manifestation through all coming ages of the grace of God. It
is a manifestation of grace—1. Because salvation in
general is of grace. 2. Because the fact that the Ephesian Christians believed or accepted of this salvation
was due not to themselves but to God. Faith is his
gift. 3. Because good works are the fruits not of
nature, but of grace. We are created unto good works.

COMMENTARY.

V. 1. *And you* hath he quickened, *who were dead in trespasses and sins.* There is an intimate connection between this clause and the preceding paragraph. In v. 19 of the first chapter the apostle prays that the Ephesians might duly appreciate the greatness of that power which had been exercised in their conversion. It was to be known from its effects. It was that power which was exercised in the resurrection and exaltation of Christ, and which had wrought an analogous change in them. The same power which quickened Christ has quickened you. The conjunction καί therefore is not to be rendered *also*, " you also," you as well as others. It serves to connect this clause with what precedes. ' God raised Christ from the dead, and he has given life to you dead in trespasses and sins.'

The grammatical construction of these words is doubtful. Some connect them immediately with the last clause of the first chapter.—' Who fills all in all and you also,' i. e. ὑμᾶς is made to depend on πληρουμένου. This, however, to make any tolerable sense, supposes the preceding clause to have a meaning which the words will not bear. Others refer the beginning of this verse to the 20th ver. of the preceding chapter— or at least borrow from that verse the verb required to complete the sense in this. ' God raised Christ, and he *has raised* you,' ἐγείρας τὸν Χριστὸν, καὶ ὑμᾶς ἤγειρε. There is indeed this association of ideas, but the two passages are not grammatically thus related. The first seven verses of this chapter form one sentence, which is so long and complicated that the apostle is forced, before getting to the end of it, slightly to vary the construction; a thing of very frequent occurrence in his writings. He dwells so long in vs. 2, 3, 4, on the natural state of the Ephesians, that he is obliged in v. 5, to repeat substantially the beginning of v. 1, in order to complete the sentence there commenced. 'You dead on account of sin,—wherein ye walked according to the course of the world, subject to Satan, associated with the children of disobedience, among whom we also had our conversation, and were the children of wrath even as others—us, dead on account of trespasses hath God quickened.' This is the way the passage stands. It is plain, therefore, that the sentence begun in the first verse, is resumed with slight variation in the fifth. This is the view taken by our translators, who borrow from the fifth verse the verb ἐζωοποίησε necessary to complete the sense of the first.

Paul describes his readers before their conversion as dead. In Scripture the word life is the term commonly used to express a state of union with God, and death a state of alienation from him. Life, therefore, includes holiness, happiness and activity; and death, corruption, misery and helplessness. All the higher forms of life are wanting in those spiritually dead; they are secluded from all the sources of true blessedness, and they are beyond the reach of any help from creatures. They are dead.

The English version renders the clause, τοῖς παραπτώμασι καὶ ταῖς ἁμαρτίαις, 'dead *in* trespasses and sins.' But there is no preposition in the original text, and therefore, the great majority of commentators consider the apostle as assigning the cause, and not describing the nature of this death, 'Dead on account of trespasses and sins.' * The former of these words is generally considered as referring to outward transgressions, the latter is more indefinite, and includes all sinful manifestations of ἁμαρτία, i. e. of sin considered as an inherent principle.†

V. 2. *Wherein in time past ye walked.* Their former condition, briefly described in the first verse, as a state of spiritual death, is in this and the verses following more particularly characterized. They walked in sin. They were daily conversant with it, and devoted to it. They were surrounded by it, and clothed with it. They lived *according to the course of this world.* In this clause we have not only the character of their life stated, but the governing principle which controlled their conduct. They lived according to, and under the control of, the spirit of the world. The expression τὸν αἰῶνα τοῦ κόσμου does not elsewhere occur, and is variously ex-

---

* Dicit *mortuos fuisse:* et simul exprimit mortis causam ; nempe peccata.—CALVIN.

† "The word ἁμαρτίαι," says HARLESS, "has, according to the metonymical use of the plurals of abstract nouns, a different sense from the singular ; viz. manifestations of sin, undetermined however, whether by word or deed or some other way. The assertion of David Schulz that ἁμαρτία never expresses a *condition,* but always an act, deserves no refutation, as such refutation may be found in any grammar."

plained. The most common interpretation assumes
that the word αἰών is here used in its classical, rather
than its Jewish sense. It is referred to the old verb ἄω,
to breathe, and hence means, *breath, vital principle, life,
life-time*, and then *duration* indefinitely. *According
to the life of this world*, therefore, means 'according to
the ruling principle, or spirit of the world.' This is
substantially the sense expressed in our version, and is
much to be preferred to any other interpretation. In
all such forms of speech the depravity of men is taken
for granted. To live after the manner of men, or according to the spirit of the world, is to live wickedly,
which of course implies that men are wicked; that
such is the character of the race in the sight of God.

Others, adhering to the New Testament sense of the
αἰών, translate this clause thus: *according to the age of
this world*, i. e. in a way suited to the present age of the
world, as it is now, compared to what it is to be when
Christ comes. Others again give αἰών a Gnostic sense—
according to the Eon of this world, i. e. the devil. To
this Meyer objects: 1. That it is more than doubtful
whether any distinct reference to nascent Gnosticism
is to be found in this epistle; and 2. That such a designation of Satan would have been unintelligible to all
classes of readers.

This subjection to sin is, at the same time, a subjection to Satan, and therefore the apostle adds, κατὰ τὸν
ἄρχοντα τῆς ἐξουσίας τοῦ ἀέρος, *according to the prince
of the power of the air*. In 2 Cor. 4, 4, Satan is called
the god, and in John 12, 31, the prince, of this world.

He is said to be the prince of the demons. Matt. 9, 34.
A kingdom is ascribed to him, which is called the
kingdom of darkness. All wicked men and evil spirits
are his subjects, and are led captive by him at his will.
It is according to this ruler of the darkness of this
world, agreeably to his will and under his control, that
the Ephesians lived before their conversion. Though
there is perfect unanimity among commentators, that
the phrase τὸν ἄρχοντα τῆς ἐξουσίας is a designation of
Satan, there is much difference of opinion as to the
precise import of the terms. First, the genitive, ἐξουσίας, may be taken as qualifying the preceding noun—
'Prince of the power,' for 'powerful prince,' or, 'prince
to whom power belongs.' Or, secondly, ἐξουσία may be
taken metonymically for those over whom power is exercised, i. e. *kingdom*, as it is used in Col. 1, 13. Or,
thirdly, it may designate those to whom power belongs,
as in the preceding ch. v. 21. 'All principality and
power' there means, all those who have dominion and
power. This last mentioned explanation is the one
generally preferred, because most in accordance with
Paul's use of the word, and because the sense thus obtained is so suited to the context and the analogy of
Scripture. Satan is the prince of the powers of the
air, i. e. of those evil spirits, who are elsewhere spoken
of as subject to his dominion.

Of the air. The word ἀήρ signifies either the atmosphere, or darkness. The whole phrase, therefore,
may mean either, the powers who dwell in the air, or
the powers of darkness. In favour of the former ex-

planation is the common meaning of the word, and the undoubted fact that both among the Greeks and Jews it was the current opinion of that age that our atmosphere was the special abode of spirits. In favour of the latter, it may be urged that the Scriptures nowhere else recognize or sanction the doctrine that the air is the dwelling place of spirits. That opinion, therefore, in the negative sense at least, is unscriptural, i. e. has no scriptural basis, unless in this place. And secondly, the word σκότος, *darkness*, is so often used just as ἀήρ is here employed, as to create a strong presumption that the latter was meant to convey the same meaning as the former. Thus, "the power of darkness," Luke 22, 53; "the rulers of darkness," Eph. 6, 12; "the kingdom of darkness," Col. 1, 13, are all scriptural expressions, and are all used to designate the kingdom of Satan. Thirdly, this signification of the word is not without the authority of usage. The word properly, especially in the earlier writers, means the lower, obscure, misty atmosphere, as opposed to αἰθήρ, the pure air. Hence it means obscurity, darkness, whatever hides from sight.

There is a third interpretation of this phrase, which retains the common meaning of the word, but makes it express the nature and not the abode of the powers spoken of. 'Of the earth' may mean *earthy;* so 'of the air' may mean aerial. These demons do not belong to our earth, they have not a corporeal nature; they belong to a different and higher order of beings. They are aerial or spiritual. This passage is thus brought into accordance with what is said in Eph. 6, 12. Evil spirits are there said to be 'in heavenly places,' i. e. in heaven. That is, they do not belong to this earth; they are heavenly in their nature, as spirits without the trammels of flesh and blood. Such at least is one interpretation of Eph. 6, 12. By powers of the air, according to this view, we are to understand, unearthly, superhuman, incorporeal, spiritual beings over whom Satan reigns. This interpretation seems to have been the one generally adopted in the early church.

The spirit that now worketh in the children of disobedience, τοῦ πνεύματος τοῦ νῦν ἐνεργοῦντος, κτλ. This again is a difficult clause. Our version assumes that the word πνεύματος, *spirit,* is in apposition with the word ἄρχοντα, *prince.* ' *The prince* of the power of the air, i. e. *the spirit,* who now works in the children of disobedience.' The objection to this is that πνεύματος is in the genitive and ἄρχοντα in the accusative. This interpretation therefore cannot be adopted without assuming an unusual grammatical irregularity. Others prefer taking πνεύματος as in apposition to ἐξουσίας. The sense is then either: 'Prince of the power of the air, i. e. prince of the spirit, i. e. spirits, who now work;' or, 'Prince of the spirit, which controls the children of disobedience.' The former of these expositions gives a good sense. Satan is the prince of those spirits who are represented in Scripture as constantly engaged in leading men into sin. But it does violence to the text, as there is no other case where the singular πνεῦμα is thus used collectively for the plural. To the latter interpretation it may be objected that the sense thus obtained is feeble and obscure, if the word *spirit* is made to mean 'disposition of men;' which, to say the least, is a very vague and indefinite expression, and furnishes no proper parallelism to the preceding clause " powers of the air." But by *spirit* may be meant the evil principle which works in mankind. Compare 1 Cor. 2, 12. Luther and Calvin both give the same interpretation that is adopted by our translators. Beza, Bengel, and most of the moderns make *spirit* mean the spirit of the world as opposed to the Spirit of God.

The phrase *children of disobedience* (ἐν τοῖς υἱοῖς τῆς ἀπειθείας) does not mean disobedient children—for that would imply that those thus designated were represented as the children of God, or children of men, who were disobedient. The word *children* expresses their relation, so to speak, to disobedience, which is the source of their distinctive character. The word *son* is often used in Scripture to express the idea of derivation or dependence in any form. Thus the 'sons of famine' are the famished; the 'sons of Belial' are the worthless; the 'sons of disobedience' are the disobedient. The word ἀπείθεια means, unwillingness to be persuaded, and is expressive either of disobedience in general, or of unbelief which is only one form of disobedience. In this case the general sense is to be preferred, for the persons spoken of are not characterized as unbelievers, or as obstinately rejecting the gospel, but as disobedient or wicked. The fact asserted in this clause, viz., that Satan and evil spirits work in men, or influence their opinions, feelings and conduct, is often elsewhere taught in Scripture. Matt. 13, 38. John 12, 31; 8, 44. Acts 26, 18. 2 Cor. 4, 4. The fact is all that concerns us, we need not understand how they exert this influence. We do not know how the intercourse of disembodied spirits is conducted, and therefore cannot tell how such spirits have access to our minds to control their operations. The influence, whatever it is, and however effectual it may be, does not destroy our freedom of action, any more than the influence of one man over his fellows. Still it is an influence greatly to be dreaded. These spirits of wickedness are represented as far more formidable adversaries than those who are clothed in flesh and blood. Blessed are those for whom Christ prays, as he did for Peter, when he sees them surrounded by the wiles of the devil.

V. 3. *Among whom also we all had our conversation in times past.* It appears not only from ch. 1 : 11, 13, and from the connection in this place, but still more clearly from v. 11 and those following, in this chapter, that by *you* in this whole epistle, the apostle means Gentiles; and by *we*, when the pronouns are contrasted as here, the Jews. The spiritual condition of the Ephesians before their conversion was not peculiar to them as Ephesians or as heathen. All men, Jews and Gentiles, are by nature in the same state. Whatever differences of individual character, whatever superiority of one age or nation over another may exist, these are but subordinate diversities. There is as to the main point, as this apostle elsewhere teaches, no difference; for all have sinned and come short of the glory of God. There is also no essential difference as to the way in which different communities or individuals manifest the depravity common to them all. There is very great difference as to the degree and the grossness of such manifestations, but in all the two comprehensive forms under which the corruption of our nature reveals itself, "the desires of the flesh and of the mind," are clearly exhibited. The apostle therefore does not hesitate to associate his countrymen with the Gentiles in this description of their moral condition, although the former were in many respects so superior to the latter. Nay, he does not hesitate to include himself, though he was before his conversion as 'touching the righteousness which is of the law blameless.' All men, whatever their outward conduct may be, in their natural state have "a carnal mind" as opposed to "a spiritual mind." See Rom. 8, 5–7. They are all governed by the things which are seen and temporal, instead of those which are not seen and eternal. Paul therefore says of himself and fellow Jews that they all had their conversation among the children of disobedience. They were not separated from them as a distinct and superior class, but were associated with them, congenial in character and life.

Wherein this congeniality consisted is stated in the following clauses. As the Gentiles so also the Jews had their conversation, i. e. they lived *in the lusts of the flesh*. The word ἐπιθυμία, *lust*, means strong desire, whether good or bad. In Scripture most commonly it is taken in a bad sense, and means inordinate desire of any kind. The 'lusts of the flesh' are those irregular desires which have their origin in the flesh. By the flesh, however, is not to be understood merely our sensuous nature, but our whole nature considered as corrupt. The scriptural usage of the word σάρξ is very extensive. It means the material flesh, then that which is external, then that which is governed by what is material, and in so far sinful; then that which is sinful without that limitation; whatever is opposed to the Spirit, and in view of all these senses it means mankind. See Phil. 3, 4, where the apostle includes under the word flesh, his descent from the Hebrews, his circumcision, and his legal righteousness. Gal. 3, 3. 5, 19–21. In this latter passage, envy, hatred, heresy, are included among the works of the flesh, as well as revellings and drunkenness. It depends on the immediate context whether the word, in any given place, is to be understood of our whole nature considered as corrupt, or only of the sensuous or animal part of that nature. When it stands opposed to what is divine, it means what is human and corrupt; when used in opposition to what is intellectual or spiritual in our nature, it means what is sensuous. In the present case it is to be taken in its wide sense because there is nothing to limit it, and because in the following clause it is defined as including both,—" the desires of the flesh (in the restricted sense of the word) and of the mind." The word θελήματα rendered *desires*, means rather

behests, commands. The things done were those which
the flesh and the mind willed to be done. They were
the governing principles to whose will obedience was
rendered. *Διανοία, mind,* is used here for the whole
thinking and sentient principle, so far as distinguished
from the animal principle. Frequently it means the
intellect, here it refers more to the affections. Comp.
Col. 1, 21, "Enemies in your mind." Lev. 19, 7,
"Thou shalt not hate thy brother in thy mind." Numbers 15, 39, "Follow not after your own minds."
Jews and Gentiles, all men, therefore, are represented
in their natural state as under the control of evil. They
fulfil the commands of the flesh and of the mind.

*And were by nature the children of wrath even as
others,* καὶ ἦμεν τέκνα φύσει ὀργῆς. The expression
"children of wrath," agreeably to a Hebrew idiom
above referred to, means 'the objects of wrath,' ob-
noxious to punishment. Compare Deut. 25, 2, 'son
of stripes,' one to be beaten. 1 Sam. 20, 31. 2 Sam.
12, 5, 'son of death,' one certainly to die. The idea
of worthiness is not included in the expression, though
often implied in the context. The phrase 'son of
death,' means one who is to die, whether justly or
unjustly. So 'children of wrath,' means simply 'the
objects of wrath.' But as the wrath spoken of is the
displeasure of God, of course the idea of ill-desert is
necessarily implied.

The word φύσις in signification and usage corre-
sponds very nearly to our word nature. When used,
as in this case, to indicate the source or origin of any

thing in the character or condition, it always expresses what is natural or innate, as opposed to what is made, taught, superinduced, or in any way incidental or acquired. This general idea is of course variously modified by the nature of the thing spoken of. Thus when the apostle says, Gal. 2, 15, ἡμεῖς φύσει Ἰουδαῖοι, *we by nature Jews*, he means Jews by birth, in opposition to profession. In Gal. 4, 8, it is said of the heathen deities that they are not by nature gods, they are such only by appointment, or in virtue of the opinions of men. In Rom. 2, 13, men are said to do *by nature* the things of the law, i. e. the source of these moral acts is to be sought in their natural constitution, not in the instruction or example of others. In Rom. 2, 27, uncircumcision is said to be *by nature*, i. e. natural, not acquired. This usage is common in the classic writers. Thus Plato, de Legibus, lib. 10, says, 'Some teach that the gods are οὐ φύσει, ἀλλὰ τισὶ νόμοις,' i. e. that they owe their divinity not to nature but to certain laws. Afterwards he says, 'Some things are right by nature, others by law.' In another place, he says, of certain persons, 'They were φύσει barbarians, νόμῳ Greeks;' by birth barbarians, but by law Greeks. In these writers the expressions, 'by nature selfish,' 'by nature swift to anger,' 'by nature avaricious,' &c., are of very frequent occurrence. In all such cases the general sense is the same. The thing predicated is affirmed to be natural. It is referred to the natural constitution or condition as opposed to what is acquired. According to this uniform usage the expression, 'We were by nature the children of wrath,' can only mean, 'We were born in that condition.' It was something natural. We did not become the children of wrath, but were already such as we were born.* The simple fact is asserted, not the reason of it. It is *by nature*, not *on account of nature* that we are here declared to be the children of wrath. The Scriptures do indeed teach the doctrine of inherent, hereditary depravity, and that that depravity is of the nature of sin, and therefore justly exposes us to the divine displeasure. And this doctrine may be fairly implied in the text, but it is not asserted. In other words, φύσις does not mean *natural depravity*, and the dative (φύσει) does not here mean *on account of*. The assertion is that men are born in a state of condemnation, and not that their nature is the ground of that condemnation. This is, indeed, an old and widely extended interpretation;

* In this interpretation commentators of all classes agree. RUECKERT, one of the ablest and most untrammelled of the recent German commentators, says: " It is perfectly evident from Rom. 5, 12–20, that Paul was far from being opposed to the view expressed in Ps. 51, 7, that men are born sinners ; and as we interpret for no system, so we will not attempt to deny that the thought, ' we were born children of wrath,' i. e. such as we were from our birth we were exposed to the divine wrath, is the true sense of the words."

HARLESS, a commentator of higher order, says: " Unless we choose to explain the word φύσει in a senseless and inconsistent manner, we can account for its use only by admitting that Paul proceeds on the assumption of an enmity to God at present natural and indwelling. And since such a native condition is not a fatuity, we can properly acknowledge no other explanation of the fact here incidentally mentioned, than that which in perfect consistency with the whole apostolic system of doctrine, is given in Rom. 5th."

but it does violence to the force of the word φύσις, which means simply *nature*, and not either holy or corrupt nature. The idea of moral character may be implied in the context, but is not expressed by the word. When we say, ' a man is by nature kind,' it is indeed implied that his nature is benevolent, but nature does not signify ' natural benevolence.' Thus when it is said, men are ' by nature corrupt,' or, ' by nature the children of wrath,' all that is asserted is that they are born in that condition.

Others take φύσις to mean in this place simply disposition, character, inward state of mind ; very much as we often use the word heart. According to this view, the word means not *quod nascenti inest, sed quod consuetudo in naturam vertit.* The sense then is : ' We, as well as others are, as to our inward disposition or state of mind, children of wrath.' All the expressions quoted by Clericus and other advocates of this interpretation, are really proofs that the word φύσις has not the signification which they assign to it. When it is said that Barbarians are by nature rapacious, the Syrians by nature fickle, the Lacedemonians taciturn, more is meant than that such is the actual character of these people. The characteristic trait asserted of them is referred to what is innate or natural. In other words φύσις does not mean, in such cases, simply disposition, but innate disposition.

Still more remote from the proper meaning of the terms is the interpretation which renders φύσει *truly*, *really*. This is substituting an idea implied in the

context for the signification of the word. When Paul
says, the heathen deities are not *by nature* gods, he
does indeed say they are not really gods; but this
does not prove that *by nature* means *truly.*

Another exposition of this passage is, that the
apostle here refers to the incidental cause of our being
the children of wrath. Our exposure to the divine
displeasure is due to our nature, because that nature
being what it is, filled with various active principles
innocent or indifferent, leads us into sin, and we thus
become children of wrath. It is not by nature, but
durch Entwickelung natürlicher Disposition, 'through
the development of natural disposition,' as Meyer
expresses this idea. This is a theological hypothesis
rather than an interpretation. When it is said men
are by nature desirous of truth, by nature honest, by
nature cruel, more is affirmed than that they become
such, under the influence of natural principles of which
these characteristics cannot be predicated. The very
reverse is the thing asserted. It is affirmed that love
of truth, honesty, or cruelty are attributes of the
nature of those spoken of. In like manner when it is
said, 'We are by nature the children of wrath,' the
very thing denied is, that we become such by a process
of development. The assertion is that we are such by
nature, as we were born. The truth here taught, therefore, is that which is so clearly presented in other parts
of Scripture, and so fully confirmed by the history of
the world and faith of the church, viz. that mankind
as a race are fallen; they had their probation in Adam,

and therefore are born in a state of condemnation. They need redemption from the moment of their birth; and therefore the seal of redemption is applied to them in baptism, which otherwise would be a senseless ceremony.

V. 4. The apostle having thus described the natural state of men, in this and the following verses, unfolds the manner in which those to whom he wrote had been delivered from that dreadful condition. It was by a spiritual resurrection. God, and not themselves, was the author of the change. It was not to be referred to any goodness in them, but to the abounding love of God. The objects of this love were not Jews in distinction from the Gentiles, nor the Gentiles as such, nor men in general, but *us*, i. e. Christians, the actual subjects of the life-giving power here spoken of. All this is included in this verse.

Ὁ δὲ Θεὸς, *but God*, i. e. notwithstanding our guilt and corruption, God, *being rich in mercy*, πλούσιος ὢν ἐν ἐλέει, i. e. because he is rich in mercy. Ἔλεος is, *ipsum miseris succurrendi studium*, 'the desire to succour the miserable;' οἰκτιρμός is *pity*. *Love* is more than either. It was not merely *mercy* which has all the miserable for its object; but *love* which has definite individual persons for its objects, which constrained this intervention of God for our salvation. Therefore the apostle adds, διὰ τὴν πολλὴν ἀγάπην αὐτοῦ. Διά is not to be rendered *through*, but *on account of*. It was to satisfy his love, that he raised us from the death of sin.

V. 5. *Καὶ ὄντας ἡμᾶς.* The conjunction *καί* does not serve merely to resume the connection; nor is it to be referred to *ἡμᾶς, us also,* us as well as others; but it belongs to the participle.—'And being,' i. e. *even when we were* dead in trespasses. Notwithstanding our low, and apparently helpless condition, God interfered for our recovery.

Συνεζωοποίησε τῷ Χριστῷ, he quickened us together with Christ. Ζωοποιεῖν means, to make alive, to impart life. In the New Testament it is almost always used of the communication of the life of which Christ is the author. It either comprehends every thing which is included in salvation, the communication of life in its widest scriptural sense; or it expresses some one point or moment in this general life-giving process. As the death from which the Christian is delivered includes condemnation (judicial death), pollution, and misery; so the life which he receives comprehends forgiveness (justification), regeneration, and blessedness. Thus in 2 Cor. 2, 12. 13, the apostle says, " And you being dead in your sins and the uncircumcision of your flesh, hath he quickened together with him, having forgiven you all trespasses." As, however, in the passage before us, the words " hath raised us up," and " hath made us to sit in heavenly places," are connected with the word " he hath quickened," the latter must be limited to the commencement of this work of restoration. That is, it here expresses deliverance from death and the imparting of life, and not the whole work of salvation.

We are said to be 'quickened together with Christ.' This does not mean merely that we are quickened *as* he was, that there is an analogy between his resurrection from the grave, and our spiritual resurrection; but the truth here taught is that which is presented in Rom. 6, 6. 8. Gal. 2, 19. 20. 2 Cor. 5, 14. 1 Cor. 15, 22. 23, and in many other passages, viz. that in virtue of the union, covenant and vital, between Christ and his people, his death was their death, his life is their life, and his exaltation is theirs. Hence all the verbs used in this connection, συνεζωοποίησε, συνήγειρε, συνεκάθισε, are in the past tense. They express what has already taken place, not what is future; not what is merely in prospect. The resurrection, the quickening and raising up of Christ's people were in an important sense accomplished, when he rose from the dead and sat down at the right hand of God. Εἰ γὰρ ἡ ἀπαρχὴ ζῇ, καὶ ἡμεῖς, is the pregnant comment of Chrysostom. The life of the whole body is in the head, and therefore when the head rose, the body rose. Each in his order however; first Christ, and then they that are Christ's.

The apostle says, by way of parenthesis, *by grace are ye saved*. The gratuitous nature of salvation is one of the most prominent ideas of the context and of the epistle. The state of men was one of helplessnes and ill-desert. Their deliverance from that state is due to the power and the unmerited love of God. They neither deserved to be saved, nor could they redeem themselves. This truth is so important and enters so deeply into the very nature of the Gospel, that Paul brings it forward on every fit occasion. And if the mode in which he speaks of our deliverance, does not of itself show it to be gratuitous, he introduces the declaration parenthetically, lest it should be for a moment forgotten.

V. 6. *And hath raised us up and caused us to sit together in heavenly places in Christ Jesus.* This is an amplification of what precedes. In its widest sense the life, which in v. 5 is said to be given to us, includes the exaltation expressed in this verse. It is, therefore, only by way of amplification that the apostle, after saying we are made partakers of the life of Christ, adds that we are raised up and enthroned with him in heaven. To understand this we must know what is here meant by "heavenly places," and in what sense believers are now the subjects of the exaltation here spoken of. Throughout this epistle the expression "heavenly places" means heaven. But the latter phrase has in Scripture a wide application. It means not only the atmospheric heavens in which the clouds have their habitation; and the stellar heavens in which the sun, moon and stars dwell; and the third heavens, i. e. the place where God specially manifests his presence and where the glorified body of Christ now is, but also the state into which believers are introduced by their regeneration. In this last sense it coincides with one of the meanings of the phrase "kingdom of heaven." It is that state of purity, exaltation and favour with God, into which his children are even in this world introduced. The opposite state is called "the kingdom of Satan;" and hence men are said to be translated from "the kingdom of darkness into the kingdom of God's dear Son." It is in this sense of the word that we are said, Phil. 3, 20, to be the citizens of heaven. We, if Christians, belong not to the earth, but heaven; we are within the pale of God's kingdom; we are under its laws; we have in Christ a title to its privileges and blessings, and possess, alas! in what humble measure, its spirit. Though we occupy the lowest place of this kingdom, the mere suburbs of the heavenly city, still we are in it. The language of the apostle in the context will appear the less strange, if we apprehend aright the greatness of the change which believers, even in this life, experience. They are freed from the condemnation of the law, from the dominion of Satan, from the lethargy and pollution of spiritual death; they are reconciled to God, made partakers of his Spirit, as the principle of everlasting life; they are adopted into his family and have a right to all the privileges of the sons of God both in this life and in that which is to come. This is a change worthy of being expressed by saying: "He hath quickened us, and raised us up, and made us to sit together with Christ in heavenly places."—All this is *in Christ*. It is in virtue of their union with Christ that believers are partakers of his life and exaltation. They are to reign with him. The blessings then of which the apostle here speaks, are represented as already conferred for two reasons: first, because they are in a measure already enjoyed; and secondly, be-

cause the continuance and consummation of these
blessings are rendered certain by the nature of the
union between Christ and his people. In him they are
already raised from the dead and seated at the right
hand of God.

V. 7. Why has God done all this? Why from eternity
has he chosen us to be holy before him in love? Why
has he made us accepted in the Beloved? Why when
dead in trespasses and sins hath he quickened us, raised
us up and made us to sit together in heavenly places in
Christ? The answer to these questions is given in this
verse. It was, *in order that, in the ages to come, he
might show the exceeding riches of his grace in his
kindness towards us, through Christ Jesus,* ἵνα ἐνδείξηται—τὸν πλοῦτον τῆς χάριτος—ἐν χρηστότητι ἐφ᾽ ἡμᾶς.
The manifestation of the grace of God, i. e. of his unmerited love, is declared to be the specific object of
redemption. From this it follows that whatever clouds
the grace of God, or clashes with the gratuitous nature
of the blessings promised in the gospel, must be inconsistent with its nature and design. If the salvation of
sinners be intended as an exhibition of the grace of
God, it must of necessity be gratuitous.

The words, *in the ages to come,* ἐν τοῖς αἰῶσι τοῖς
ἐπερχομένοις, are by many understood to refer to the
future generations in this world; secula, aetates seu
tempora inde ab apostolicis illis ad finem mundi secu-
turas, as Wolf expresses it. Calvin, who understands
the apostle to refer specially to the calling of the Gentiles in the preceding verses, gives the same explana-

tion. Gentium vocatio mirabile est divinae bonitatis opus, quod filiis parentes et avi nepotibus tradere per manus debent, ut nunquam ex hominum animis silentio deleatur. As however there is nothing in the context to restrict the language of the apostle to the Gentiles, so there is nothing to limit the general expression *ages to come* to the present life. Others, restricting verse 6th to the resurrection of the body, which is to take place at the second advent of Christ, understand the phrase in question to mean the 'world to come,' or the period subsequent to Christ's second coming. Then, when the saints are raised up in glory, and not before, will the kindness of God towards them be revealed. But the preceding verse does not refer exclusively to the final resurrection of the dead, and therefore this phrase does not designate the period subsequent to that event. It is better therefore to take it without limitation, for all future time.

The simplest construction of the passage supposes that ἐν χρηστότητι is to be connected with ἐνδείξηται ; ἐφ' ἡμᾶς with χρηστότητι, and ἐν Χριστῷ with the words immediately preceding. God's grace is manifested through his kindness towards us, and that kindness is exercised through Christ and for his sake. The ground of this goodness is not in us but in Christ, and hence its character as grace, or unmerited favour.

Vs. 8, 9. These verses confirm the preceding declaration. The manifestation of the grace of God is the great end of redemption. This is plain, *for* salva-

tion is entirely of grace. Ye are saved by grace; ye
are saved by faith and not by works; and even faith is
not of yourselves, it is the gift of God. We have then
here a manifold assertion, affirmative and negative, of
the gratuitous nature of salvation. It is not only said
in general, 'ye are saved by grace,' but further that
salvation is by faith, i. e. by simply receiving or appre-
hending the offered blessing. From the very nature
of faith, as an act of assent and trust, it excludes the
idea of merit. If by faith, it is of grace; if of works,
it is of debt; as the apostle argues in Rom. 4, 4. 5.
Faith, therefore, is the mere *causa apprehendens*, the
simple act of accepting, and not the ground on which
salvation is bestowed. *Not of works.* The apostle
says *works*, without qualification or limitation. It is
not, therefore, ceremonial, as distinguished from good
works; or legal, as distinguished from evangelical or
gracious works; but works of all kinds as distinguished
from faith, which are excluded. Salvation is in no
sense, and in no degree, of works; for to him that
worketh the reward is a matter of debt. But salvation
is of grace and therefore not of works lest any man
should boast. That the guilty should stand before God
with self-complacency, and refer his salvation in any
measure to his own merit, is so abhorrent to all right
feeling that Paul assumes it (Rom. 4, 2) as an intuitive
truth, that no man can boast before God. And to all
who have any proper sense of the holiness of God and
of the evil of sin, it is an intuition; and therefore a
gratuitous salvation, a salvation which excludes with

works all ground of boasting, is the only salvation suited to the relation of guilty men to God.

The only point in the interpretation of these verses of any doubt, relates to the second clause. What is said to be the gift of God? Is it salvation, or faith? The words καὶ τοῦτο only serve to render more prominent the matter referred to. Compare Rom. 13, 11. 1 Cor. 6, 6. Phil. 1, 28. Heb. 11, 12. They may relate to *faith* (τὸ πιστεύειν), or to the salvation spoken of (σεσωσμένους εἶναι). Beza, following the fathers, prefers the former reference; Calvin, with most of the modern commentators, the latter. The reasons in favour of the former interpretation are, 1. It best suits the design of the passage. The object of the apostle is to show the gratuitous nature of salvation. This is most effectually done by saying, ' Ye are not only saved by faith in opposition to works, but your very faith is not of yourselves, it is the gift of God.' 2. The other interpretation makes the passage tautological. To say: ' Ye are saved by faith; not of yourselves; your salvation is the gift of God; it is not of works,' is saying the same thing over and over without any progress. Whereas to say : ' Ye are saved through faith (and that not of yourselves it is the gift of God), not of works,' is not repetitious; the parenthetical clause instead of being redundant does good service and greatly increases the force of the passage. 3. According to this interpretation the antithesis between faith and works, so common in Paul's writings, is preserved. ' Ye are saved by faith, not by works, lest any man should

boast.' The middle clause of the verse is therefore
parenthetical, and refers not to the main idea *ye are
saved*, but to the subordinate one *through faith*, and is
designed to show how entirely salvation is of grace,
since even faith by which we apprehend the offered
mercy, is the gift of God. 4. The analogy of Scripture is in favor of this view of the passage, in so far
that elsewhere faith is represented as the gift of God.
1 Cor. 1, 26–31.   Eph. 1, 19.   Col. 2, 12, *et passim*.

V. 10. That salvation is thus entirely the work of
God, and that good works cannot be the ground of our
acceptance with him, is proved in this verse—1st. By
showing that we are God's workmanship.   He, and not
ourselves, has made us what we are.   And 2d. By the
consideration that we are created unto good works.   As
the fact that men are elected unto holiness, proves that
holiness is not the ground of their election; so their
being created unto good works shows that good works
are not the ground on which they are made the subjects
of this new creation, which is itself incipient salvation.

Αὐτοῦ γάρ ἐσμεν ποίημα.   The position of the pronoun at the beginning of the sentence renders it em-
phatic. *His* workmanship are we.   He has made us
Christians.   Our faith is not of ourselves.   It is of God
that we are in Christ Jesus.   The sense in which we
are the workmanship of God is explained in the following clause, *created in Christ Jesus ;* for if any man is
in Christ he is a new creature.   Union with him is a
source of a new life, and a life unto holiness ; and
therefore it is said created *unto good works*.   Holiness

is the end of redemption, for Christ gave himself for us that he might redeem us from all iniquity, and purify unto himself a peculiar people zealous of good works. Titus 2, 14. Those therefore who live in sin are not the subjects of this redemption.

Οἷς προητοίμασε, is variously interpreted. The verb signifies properly *to prepare beforehand*. As this previous preparation may be in the mind, in the form of a purpose, the word is often used in the sense of pre-ordaining, or appointing. Compare Gen. 24, 14. Matt. 25, 34. 1 Cor. 2, 9. Rom. 9, 23. This however is rather the idea expressed in the context than the proper signification of the word. The relative is by Bengel and others connected, agreeably to a common Hebrew idiom, with the following pronoun, οἷς ἐν αὑτοῖς, *in which*, and the verb taken absolutely. The sense then is, ' In which God has preordained that we should walk.' By the great majority of commentators οἷς is taken for ἅ, by the common attraction, 'which God had pre-pared beforehand, in order that we should walk in them.' Before our new creation these works were in the purpose of God prepared to be our attendants, in the midst of which we should walk. A third interpretation supposes οἷς to be used as a proper dative, and supposes ἡμᾶς as the object of the verb. ' To which God has pre-destined *us*, that we should walk in them.' The second of these explanations is obviously the most natural.

Thus has the apostle in this paragraph clearly taught that the natural state of man is one of con-demnation and spiritual death; that from that condition

believers are delivered by the grace of God in Christ
Jesus ; and the design of this deliverance is the manifestation, through all coming ages, of the exceeding
riches of his grace.

SECTION II.—Vs. 11–22.

11.   Wherefore remember, that ye *being* in time past Gentiles in
the flesh, who are called Uncircumcision by that which is called
12. the Circumcision in the flesh made by hands ; that at that time
ye were without Christ, being aliens from the commonwealth
of Israel, and strangers from the covenants of promise, having
13. no hope, and without God in the world ; but now, in Christ
Jesus, ye, who sometimes were far off, are made nigh by the
14. blood of Christ. For he is our peace, who hath made both
one, and hath broken down the middle wall of partition
15. *between us ;* having abolished in his flesh the enmity, *even* the
law of commandments *contained* in ordinances : for to make
16. in himself of twain one new man, *so* making peace ; and that
he might reconcile both unto God in one body by the cross,
17. having slain the enmity thereby : and came and preached
peace to you which were afar off, and to them that were nigh.
18. For through him we both have an access by one Spirit unto the
19. Father.   Now therefore ye are no more strangers and foreigners, but fellow-citizens with the saints, and of the household of
20. God ; and are built upon the foundation of the apostles and
prophets, Jesus Christ himself being the chief corner *stone ;*
21. in whom all the building, fitly framed together, groweth unto
22. a holy temple in the Lord : in whom ye also are builded together, for a habitation of God through the Spirit.

ANALYSIS.

In the preceding paragraph the apostle had set
forth—1. The moral and spiritual condition of the

Ephesians by nature. 2. The spiritual renovation and exaltation which they had experienced. 3. The design of God in this dispensation. In this paragraph he exhibits the corresponding change in their relations. In doing this he sets forth :—

I. Their former relation—1st. To the church as foreigners and aliens. 2d. To God as those who were far off, without any saving knowledge of him, or interest in his promises, vs. 11. 12.

II. The means by which this alienation from God and the church had been removed, viz. by the blood of Christ. His death had a twofold effect.—1. By satisfying the demands of justice, it secured reconciliation with God. 2. By abolishing the law in the form of the Mosaic institutions, it removed the wall of partition between the Jews and Gentiles. A twofold reconciliation was thus effected; the Jews and Gentiles are united in one body, and both are reconciled to God, vs. 13–18.

III. In consequence of this twofold reconciliation, the Ephesians were intimately united with God and his people. This idea is set forth under a threefold figure.—1. They are represented as fellow-citizens of the saints. 2. They are members of the family of God. 3. They are constituent portions of that temple in which God dwells by his Spirit, vs. 19–22.

The idea of the church which underlies this paragraph, is that which is every where presented in the New Testament. The church is the body of Christ. It consists of those in whom he dwells by his Spirit.

To be alien from the church, therefore, is to be an alien from God. It is to be without Christ and without hope. The church of which this is said is not the nominal, external, visible church as such, but the true people of God. As, however, the Scriptures always speak of men according to their profession, calling those who profess faith, believers, and those who confess Christ, Christians ; so they speak of the visible church as the true church, and predicate of the former what is true only of the latter. The Gentiles while aliens from the church were without Christ, without God, and without hope ; when amalgamated with the church they became the habitation of God through the Spirit. Such many of them truly were, such they all professed to be, and they are therefore addressed in that character. But union with the visible church no more made them real partakers of the Spirit of Christ, than the profession of faith made them living believers.

COMMENTARY.

V. 11. *Wherefore remember*, i. e. since God has done such great things for you, call to mind your former condition, as a motive both for humility and gratitude. *That ye being in time past Gentiles in the flesh*, ἔθνη ἐν σαρκί, i. e. uncircumcised heathen. This gives in a word the description of their former state. All that follows, in this and the succeeding verse, is but amplification of this idea. The words *in the flesh*, do not mean *origine carnali*, *natalibus*, *by birth*; nor *as to external condition*, which would imply that spiritually, or as to their internal state, they were not heathen. The context shows that it refers to circumcision, which being a sign in the flesh, is designated with sufficient clearness by the expression in the text. As circumcision was a rite of divine appointment, and the seal of God's covenant with his people, to be uncircumcised was a great misfortune. It showed that those in that condition were without God and without hope. The apostle therefore adds, as explanatory of the preceding phrase, οἱ λεγόμενοι ἀκροβυστία, *who are called Uncircumcision.* This implied that they did not belong to the covenant people of God; and in the lips of the Jews it was expressive of a self-righteous abhorrence of the Gentiles as unclean and profane. This feeling on their part arose from their supposing that the mere outward rite of circumcision conveyed holiness and secured the favour of God. As the apostle knew that the circumcision of the flesh was in itself of no avail, and as he was far from sympathizing in the contemptuous feeling which the Jews entertained for the Gentiles, he tacitly reproves this spirit by designating the former as the so *called circumcision in the flesh, made with hands.* This is a description of the Israel κατὰ σάρκα, the external people of God, who were Jews outwardly, but who were destitute of the true circumcision which was of the heart. They were the concision, as the apostle elsewhere says, we are the circumcision, which worship God in the Spirit, and rejoice in Christ Jesus, and have no confidence in the flesh, Phil.

3, 3. The Jews were a striking illustration of the effect of ascribing to external rites objective power, and regarding them as conveying grace and securing the favour of God, irrespective of the subjective state of the recipient. This doctrine rendered them proud, self-righteous, malignant, and contemptuous, and led them to regard religion as an external service compatible with unholiness of heart and life. This doctrine the apostle every where repudiates and denounces as fatal. And therefore in this connection, while speaking of the real advantage of circumcision, and of the covenant union with God of which it was the seal, he was careful to indicate clearly that it was not the circumcision in the flesh, made with hands, which secured the blessings of which he speaks. Compare Rom. 2, 25–29. 1 Cor. 7, 19. Phil. 3, 3–6. Col. 2, 11.

V. 12. The sentence begun in verse 11 is here resumed. Remember, ὅτι ἦτε ἐν τῷ καιρῷ ἐκείνῳ χωρὶς Χριστοῦ, *that at that time ye were without Christ*. This means more than that they were as heathen, destitute of the knowledge and expectation of the Messiah. As Christ is the only redeemer of men, and the only mediator between God and man, to be without Christ, was to be without redemption and without access to God. To possess Christ, to be in Him, is the sum of all blessedness; to be without Christ includes all evil.

What follows is a confirmation of what precedes. They were without Christ because *aliens from the commonwealth of Israel*. The idea of separation and estrangement is strongly expressed by the word ἀπηλ-

λοτριωμένοι. They stood as ἄλλοι, as *others*, distinguished as a separate class from the people of God.
The word πολιτεία means — 1. Citizenship. 2. The
order or constitution of the state. 3. The community
or state itself. The last signification best suits the connection. Ἰσραήλ means the theocratical people; and
πολιτεία τοῦ Ἰσραήλ is that community or commonwealth which was Israel. This includes the other
senses, for in being aliens from the community of God's
people, they were of course destitute of citizenship
among them, and outside of the theocratical constitution.

And strangers from the covenants of promise, καὶ
ξένοι τῶν διαθηκῶν τῆς ἐπαγγελίας. The word *cove-*
nants is in the plural because God entered repeatedly
into covenant with his people. It is called a *covenant*
of promise, or rather of *the* promise, because the promise of redemption was connected therewith. That
the promise meant is that great promise of a redeemer
made to Abraham, and so often afterwards repeated,
is plain not only from the context, but from other passages of Scripture. "The promise made to the fathers,"
says the apostle, in Acts 13, 32, "hath God fulfilled in
that he hath raised up Jesus." Comp. Rom. 4, 14–16.
Gal. 3, 16. As the heathen were not included in the
covenant God made with his people, they had no interest in the promise, the execution of which that covenant secured. Their condition was therefore most
deplorable. They were *without hope*—ἐλπίδα μὴ ἔχον-
τας, *not having hope*. They had nothing to hope, be-

cause shut out of the covenant of promise. The promise of God is the only foundation of hope, and therefore those to whom there is no promise, have no hope. And having no hope of redemption, the great blessing promised, they were, in the widest sense of the word, hopeless. They were moreover without God, ἄθεοι. This may mean that they were atheists, in so far that they were destitute of the knowledge of the true God, and served those who by nature were no gods. Jehovah was not their God; they had no interest in him, they were without him. This includes the idea that they were forsaken of him—he had left them *in the world*. They stood outside of that community which belonged to God, who knew and worshipped him, to whom his promises were made, and in the midst of whom he dwelt. In every point, therefore, their condition as heathen afforded a melancholy contrast to that of the true people of God, and to that into which they had been introduced by the Gospel. Their alienation from the theocracy or church involved in it, or implied, a like alienation from God and his covenant.

V. 13. *But now in Christ Jesus,* i. e. in virtue of union with Christ; ὑμεῖς οἱ τοτὲ ὄντες μακρὰν, ἐγγὺς ἐγενήθητε, *ye who sometime were afar off, are made nigh.* As under the old dispensation God dwelt in the temple, those living near his abode and having access to him, were his people. Israel was near; the Gentiles were afar off. They lived at a distance, and had no liberty of access to the place where God revealed his presence. Hence in the prophets, as in Isaiah 49, 1.

57, 19, by those near are meant the Jews, and by those afar off the Gentiles. This form of expression passed over to the New Testament writers. Acts 2, 39, "The promise is to you and to your children, and to all that are far off." Eph. 2, 17, "Preached peace to you that were far off, and to them that were nigh." Among the later Jews the act of receiving a proselyte, was called "making him nigh."* As being far from God included both separation from his people, and spiritual distance or alienation from himself; so to be brought nigh includes both introduction into the church and reconciliation with God. And these two ideas are clearly presented and intended by the apostle in this whole context. This twofold reconciliation is effected, ἐν τῷ αἵματι τοῦ Χριστοῦ, by the blood of Christ. This clause is explanatory of the words at the beginning of the verse. 'In Christ Jesus, i. e. by the blood of Christ, ye are made nigh.' Without shedding of blood there is no remission and no reconciliation of sinners with God. When Moses ratified the covenant between God and his people, "He took the blood of calves and of goats and sprinkled both the book and all the people, saying, This is the blood of the covenant which God hath enjoined unto you. It was necessary that the patterns of things in the heavens should be purified with these; but the heavenly things themselves with better sacrifices than these." Heb. 9, 19–23. As under

---

* The Rabbins said : Quicunque gentilem appropinquare facit, et proselytum facit, idem est ac si ipsum creâsset. WETSTEIN.

the typical and ritual economy of the Old Testament the people were brought externally nigh to God, by the blood of calves and goats, through which temporal redemption was effected and the theocratical covenant was ratified; so we are brought spiritually nigh to God by the blood of Christ, who has obtained eternal redemption for us, being once offered to bear the sins of many, and to ratify by his death the covenant of God with all his people, whether Jews or Gentiles.

Vs. 14. 15. These verses contain a confirmation and illustration of what precedes. 'Ye who were far off are made nigh by the blood of Christ. *For* he is our peace. He has effected the twofold reconciliation above referred to.' This he has accomplished by abolishing the law. The law, however, is viewed in a twofold aspect in this connection. First, it was that original covenant of works, demanding perfect obedience, whose conditions must be satisfied in order to the reconciliation of men with God. Christ by being made under the law, Gal. 4, 4, and fulfilling all righteousness, has redeemed those who were under the law. He delivered them from the obligation of fulfilling its demands as the condition of their justification before God. In this sense they are not under the law. Comp. Rom. 6, 14. 7, 4. 6. Gal. 5, 18. Col. 2, 14. But secondly, as Christ abolished the law as a covenant of works by fulfilling its conditions, so he abolished the Mosaic law by fulfilling all its types and shadows. He was the end of the law in both these aspects, and therefore, it ceased to bind the people of God in either of these forms. Of this doctrine the whole of the New Testament is full. The epistles especially are in large measure devoted to proving that believers are not under the law in either of these senses, but under grace. Thus it is that Christ is our peace. The abolition of the law as a covenant of works reconciles us to God; the abolition of the Mosaic law removes the wall between the Jews and Gentiles. This is what is here taught. By abolishing the law of commandments, i. e. the law in both its forms, the apostle says, Christ has, first, of the twain made one new man, v. 15; and secondly, he has reconciled both unto God in one body by the cross, v. 16.

Though the general sense of this passage is plain, there is no little diversity as to the details of the interpretation. The Greek is printed for the convenience of the reader. Αὐτὸς γάρ ἐστιν ἡ εἰρήνη ἡμῶν, ὁ ποιήσας τὰ ἀμφότερα ἕν, καὶ τὸ μεσότοιχον τοῦ φραγμοῦ λύσας, τὴν ἔχθραν, ἐν τῇ σαρκὶ αὐτοῦ, τὸν νόμον τῶν ἐντολῶν ἐν δόγμασι καταργήσας. Our translators, by assuming that ἔχθραν depends on καταργήσας, and of course that νόμον is in apposition with it, have in a great measure determined thereby the interpretation of the whole passage. The words μεσότοιχον, ἔχθραν, and νόμον must all refer to the same thing. The sense would then be, 'For he is our peace, having made the two one by having destroyed the middle wall of partition, that is, by having destroyed, by his flesh, the enmity, viz., the law of commandments with ordinances.' The preferable construction is to make ἔχθραν depend on λύσας. It is

then in apposition with μεσότοιχον, but not with νόμον ;
and καταργήσας τὸν νόμον, instead of being a mere repetition of λύσας τὸ μεσότοιχον, is an independent
clause explaining the manner in which the reconciliation of the Jews and Gentiles had been effected. The
passage then means, 'He is our peace because he has
made the two one by removing the enmity or middle
wall which divided the Jews and Gentiles, and this was
done by abolishing the law.' The reconciliation itself
is expressed by saying, 'He made the two one, having
removed the wall or enmity between them.' The mode
in which this was done, is expressed by saying, ' He
abolished the law.'

In the phrase μεσότοιχον τοῦ φραγμοῦ, *middle wall
of partition*, the latter noun is explanatory of the
former, i. e. φραγμοῦ is the genitive of apposition.
The middle wall which consisted in the hedge, which
separated the two parties. What that hedge was is
immediately expressed by the word ἔχθραν. It was
the enmity subsisting between them. 'Having removed the middle wall, i. e. the enmity, or their mutual
hatred.' By enmity, therefore, is not to be understood
the law, as the cause of this alienation, but the alienation itself; because in what follows the removal of the
enmity and the abolition of the law are distinguished
from each other, the latter being the means of accom-
plishing the former.

That ἔχθραν is to be connected with λύσας and not, as
our translation assumes, with καταργήσας, is argued first
from the position of the words, which favours this con-

struction; secondly, because the expression λύειν ἔχθραν is common, and καταργεῖν ἔχθραν never occurs; and thirdly, because the sense demands this construction, inasmuch as the ambiguous phrase middle wall of partion thus receives its needed explanation. The apostle first states, what it was that divided the Jews and Gentiles, viz., their mutual hatred, and then how that hatred had been removed.

The words ἐν τῇ σαρκὶ αὐτοῦ, are not to be connected with λύσας. That is, the apostle does not mean to say that Christ has removed the enmity between the Jews and Gentiles *by his flesh*. They are to be connected with the following participle (καταργήσας). " Having by his flesh, i. e. by his death, abolished the law." This is the great truth which Paul had to teach. Christ by his death has freed us from the law. We are no longer under the law but under grace. Rom. 6, 14. We are no longer required to seek salvation on the ground of obedience to the law, which says: " Do this, and live," and " Cursed is every one that continueth not in all things written in the book of the law to do them." Christ has freed us from the law as a covenant of works, by being himself made subject to it, Gal. 4, 5; by bearing its penalty, Gal. 3, 13; by his body, Rom. 7, 4; by the body of his flesh, Col. 1, 22; by his cross, Col. 2, 14. In this connection the expressions, " by the blood of Christ," v. 13; " by his flesh," v. 14; " by his cross," all mean the same thing. They are but different modes of expressing his sacrificial, or atoning death, by which the law was satisfied and our recon-

ciliation to God is effected. The "abolishing," therefore, of which the apostle speaks, does not consist in
setting the law aside, or suspending it by a sovereign,
executive act. It is a causing it to cease; or rendering
it no longer binding by satisfying its demands, so that
we are judicially free from it; free not by the act of a
sovereign but by the sentence of a judge; not by mere
pardon, but by justification. Who is he that condemns,
when God justifies? Rom. 8, 34. The law which
Christ has thus abolished is called "the law of commandments in ordinances." This may mean the law
of commandments with ordinances—referring to the
two classes of laws (ἐντολή and δόγμα), moral and
positive; or it may refer to the form in which the pre-
cepts are presented in the law, as positive statutes, or
commands, τῶν ἐντολῶν giving the contents of the law,
and ἐν δόγμασι the form. The idea probably is that the
law in all its compass, and in all its forms, so far as it
was a covenant prescribing the conditions of salvation,
is abolished. The law of which the apostle here speaks
is not exclusively the Mosaic law. It is so described
in various parallel passages, as holy, just and good, as
taking cognizance of the inward feelings, as to make
it evident it is the law of God in its widest sense.
It is the law which binds the heathen and which is
written on their hearts. It is the law from which
the death of Christ redeems men. But redemption
is not mere deliverance from Judaism, and therefore
the law from which we are freed by the death of
Christ is not merely the law of Moses. Deliverance

from the Mosaic institutions could not have the effects ascribed to the freedom from the law of which Paul speaks. It could not secure reconciliation to God, justification, and holiness, all of which, according to the apostle, flow from the redemption effected by Christ. The antithetical ideas always presented in Paul's writings, on this subject, are the law and grace, the law and the gospel, the system which says: "Do and live,"—and the system which says: "Believe and live;"—as, however, the form in which the law was ever present to the minds of the early Christians was that contained in the Mosaic institutions; as all, who in that day were legalists, were Judaizers, and as the Mosaic economy was included in the law which Christ abolished, in many cases (as in the passage before us), special reference is had to the law in that particular form. But in teaching that men cannot be saved by obedience to the law of Moses, Paul taught that we cannot be saved by obedience to the law in any form. Or rather, by teaching that salvation is not of works of any kind, but of grace and through faith, he teaches it is not by the specific, ceremonial works enjoined in the law of Moses.

It is objected to the above interpretation of this passage, which is the common one, that in order to justify connecting ἐν δόγμασι with ἐντολῶν (*the law of commandments in ordinances*), the article should be used. It is therefore urged that ἐν δόγμασι must be connected with καταργήσας and the passage read, " having abolished by doctrine the law of commandments." To this, however, it is answered—1. That the connecting article is frequently omitted in cases where the qualifying word is intimately connected with the word to be qualified, so as to form one idea with it. See Eph. 2, 11. 2 Cor. 7, 7. Col. 1, 4. 2. That καταργήσας has its qualifying clause in the words ἐν τῇ σαρκί. It would be incongruous to say that Christ abolished the law by his death, by doctrine. 3. The word δόγμα never means *doctrine* in the New Testament, and therefore cannot have that meaning here. 4. And finally the sense is bad, contrary to the whole analogy of Scripture. The law was not abolished by Christ as a teacher; but by Christ as a sacrifice. It was not by his doctrine, but by his blood, his body, his death, his cross, that our deliverance from the law was effected. The doctrine of the passage, therefore, is that the middle wall of partition between the Jews and Gentiles, consisting in their mutual enmity, has been removed by Christ's having, through his death, abolished the law in all its forms, as a rule of justification, and thus, opening one new way of access to God, common to Jews and Gentiles.

The design of Christ in thus abolishing the law was two-fold. First, the union of the Jews and Gentiles in one holy, Catholic church. And, Secondly, the reconciliation of both to God. The former is expressed, by saying: "In order that he might create the two, in himself, one new man, making peace." *The two*, τοὺς δύο, are of course the two spoken of above, the Jews and Gentiles. They were separate, hostile bodies, alike

dead in trespasses and sins, equally the children of
wrath. They are created anew, so as to become one
body of which Christ is the head. And, therefore, it
is said, ἐν ἑαυτῷ, *in himself*, i. e. in virtue of union
with him. Union with Christ being the condition at
once of their unity and of their holiness. They are
created εἰς ἕνα καινὸν ἄνθρωπον. They are one, and
they are *new*, i. e. renewed. Καινός means newly
made, uninjured by decay or use; and in a moral sense
renewed, *pure*. See 4, 24. 2 Cor. 5, 17. Gal. 6. 15.
Col. 3, 10. *Making peace, ποιῶν εἰρήνην.* The present
participle is here used, because the effect or operation
is a continuous one. The union or peace which flows
from the abrogation of the law by the death of Christ,
is progressive, so far as it is inward or subjective. The
outward work is done. The long feud in the human
family is healed. The distinction between Jew and
Gentile is abolished. All the exclusive privileges of
the former are abrogated. The wall which had so long
shut out the nations is removed. There is now one fold
and one shepherd. Since the abrogation of the law there
is neither Jew nor Greek, there is neither bond nor
free, there is neither male nor female; for all believers
are one in Christ Jesus. Gal. 3, 28.

V. 16. The second part of Christ's purpose is expressed in this verse. It was that he might reconcile
(ἀποκαταλλάξῃ) the two, united in one body, unto God,
by means of the cross, having thereby slain the enmity.
The end effected was reconciliation with God;—the
subjects of this reconciliation are the church, the one

body into which Jews and Gentiles are merged (so that the one is σύσσωμα with the other, Eph. 3, 6); the means of this reconciliation is the cross, because the crucifixion of our Lord removes the enmity which prevented the reconciliation here spoken of.

To reconcile is to effect peace and union between parties previously at variance. Neither the English nor Greek terms (διαλλάσσειν, καταλλάσσειν) indicate whether the change effected is mutual or only on one side. A child is reconciled to an offended father who receives him into favour, though the father's feelings only have been changed. Whether the reconciliation effected by Christ between man and God results from an inward change in men, or from the propitiation of God—or whether both ideas are to be included, is determined not by the signification of the word, but by the context and the analogy of Scripture. When Christ is said to reconcile men to God, the meaning is that he propitiated God, satisfied the demands of his justice, and thus rendered it possible that he might be just and yet justify the ungodly. This is plain, because the reconciliation is always said to be effected by the death, the blood, the cross of Christ; and the proximate design of a sacrifice is to propitiate God, and not to convert the offerer or him for whom the offering is made. What in one place is expressed by saying Christ reconciled us to God, is in another place expressed by saying, he was a propitiation, or made propitiation for our sins.

The subjects of this reconciliation are the Jews and

Gentiles united in one body, i. e. the church—τοὺς ἀμφοτέρους ἐν ἑνὶ σώματι. His death had not reference to one class to the exclusion of the other. It was de· signed to bring unto God, the whole number of the redeemed, whether Jews or Gentiles, as one living body, filled with his Spirit as well as washed in his blood.

Many commentators understand the words "in one body" to refer to Christ's own body, and the words "by the cross," at the close of the sentence, to be merely explanatory. The sense would then be, "That he might reconcile both unto God, by one body, i. e. by the one offering of himself, i. e. by his cross." The obvious objection to this interpretation is, that "one body" cannot naturally be explained to mean "one offering of his body." Besides this, the passage, vs. 13–16, would then repeat five times the idea : the sacrifice of Christ reconciled us to God. The natural opposition between " *the two* " and " *the one body*," favours the common interpretation. Christ created the two into one new man, and as thus united in one body, he reconciled both unto God.

The means by which this reconciliation was effected is the cross—because on it he slew the enmity which separated us from God. The latter clause of the verse is therefore explanatory of what precedes. 'He reconciled both to God, having, by the cross, slain the enmity.' *The enmity* in this place, as in v. 15, many understand to be the enmity between the Jews and Gentiles, and make the apostle say : 'Christ by his crucifixion has destroyed the enmity between the Jews and Gentiles and then reconciled them thus united in one body to God.' It is urged in favour of this interpretation that it is unnatural to make the word *enmity* in this verse and in verse 15 refer to different things. The great doctrine in the whole context is the unity of all believers, and therefore, that is to be kept in view. It is the enmity between the Jews and Gentiles and their union of which the apostle is treating. But that idea had just before been expressed. It is perfectly pertinent to the apostle's object to show that the union between the Jews and Gentiles was effected by the reconciliation of both, by his atoning death, to God. The former flows from the latter. In this connection the words "having slain the enmity on it," serve to explain the declaration that the cross of Christ reconciles us to God. His death satisfied justice, it propitiated God, i. e. removed his wrath, or his enmity to sinners; not hatred, for God is love, but the calm and holy purpose to punish them for their sins. This view is sustained by the constantly recurring representations of Scripture. In Col. 1, 20–22, we have a passage which is exactly parallel to the one before us. It is there said, that God, having made peace by the blood of the cross, reconciled by Christ all things unto himself, and "you," the apostle adds, "that were sometime alienated and enemies in *your* mind by wicked works, yet now hath he reconciled in the body of his flesh through death." Here it is obvious that the peace intended is peace between God and man.

So too in Col. 2, 13. 14, it is said: "You being dead ...
hath he quickened together with him, having forgiven
you all trespasses; blotting out the handwriting of
ordinances that was against us, which was contrary to
us, and took it out of the way, nailing it to his cross."
Here again the reconciliation is between man and God;
the means, the cross—the mode, the abrogation or
satisfaction of the law. The epistles to the Ephesians
ánd to the Colossians are so much a reflection the one
of the other, that they serve for mutual illustration.
As there can be no doubt as to what Paul meant in the
passages addressed to the Colossians, they serve to
determine his meaning in the parallel passages to the
Ephesians. The context, so far from opposing, favours
the interpretation given above. Reconciliation involves the removal of enmity; the reconciliation is to
God, therefore the enmity is that which subsisted
between God and man—the peace announced in consequence of this reconciliation, verse 17, is peace with
God; it consists in the liberty of access to him spoken
of in verse 18. Thus all is natural in the relation of the
several clauses to each other.

V. 17. *And having come, he preached peace, for
you afar off, and peace* for those near.* The connection is not with verse 14, but with verses 14–16. Christ
having effected peace, announced it. This is the burden of the Gospel, Peace on earth, and good-will to-

---

* The repetition of εἰρήνην before τοῖς ἐγγύς, has in its favour many
of the oldest MSS. and versions, and is adopted by Lachmann, Meyer, and
others.

ward man. God is reconciled. Being justified by faith we have peace with God. Christ having redeemed us from the curse of the law; having reconciled us to God by his death, came and preached peace. To what preaching does the apostle refer? Some say to Christ's personal preaching while here on earth. *Having come*, i. e. in the flesh, he preached. This supposes the connection is not with what immediately precedes, but with verse 14.—'He is our peace, and having come into the world he preached peace.' But this breaks the concatenation of the ideas. The reconciliation is represented as preceding the annunciation of it. Having died, he came and preached. The preaching is, therefore, the annunciation of the favour of God, made by Christ, either in person, or through his apostles and his Spirit. *Having come*, ἐλθών, is not redundant, nor does it refer to his coming into the world, but to that reappearing which took place after his resurrection, which was temporarily in person and continuous in his Spirit. He is with the church always, even to the end of the world; and it is his annunciation of peace which is made, by the word and Spirit, through the church. The peace meant, according to one interpretation, is peace between Jews and Gentiles, according to another, peace with God. The decision between the two depends on the view taken of the context. If the interpretation given above of the preceding verses be correct, then the peace here mentioned can only be peace with God. The dative ὑμῖν does not depend immediately on the verb, and point out the object to which the preaching was directed. It indicates those for whose benefit this peace has been procured. Christ announced that peace with God had, by the cross, been secured for those afar off, viz. the Gentiles, as well as for the Jews, or those who were nigh.

V. 18. The proof that peace has thus been obtained for both is, that both have equally free access to God. The ὅτι at the beginning of the verse is not to be rendered *that*, as indicating the nature of the peace; but *since*, as introducing the evidence that such peace was procured. That evidence is found in the fact that we have access to God. Had not his wrath been removed, Rom. 5, 10, the enmity been slain, we could have no access to the divine presence. And since Gentiles have as free access to God as the Jews, and upon the same terms and in the same way, it follows that the peace procured by the death of Christ, was designed for the one class as well as for the other.

Access is not mere liberty of approach; it is προσαγωγή, *introduction*. Christ did not die simply to open the way of access to God, but actually to introduce us into his presence and favour. This all Scripture teaches, and this the context demands. Those for whom the death of Christ has procured peace, are declared in what follows to be fellow-citizens of the saints; members of the family of God, constituent parts of that temple in which God dwells by his Spirit. It is a real not a mere potential redemption and reconciliation which the blood of Christ effects. He died, the just for the unjust, to bring us nigh unto God. This introduction

into a state of grace, Rom. 5, 3, is not identical with
the peace procured by Christ, but the effect or sequence of it. Having made propitiation, or secured
peace, he introduces us as our mediator and advocate
into the divine presence.

As to this access we are taught that it is—1. To the
Father. 2. It is through Christ. 3. It is by the Spirit.
The doctrine of the Trinity as involved in the whole
scheme of redemption, evidently underlies the representation contained in this passage. In the plan of
salvation as revealed in Scripture, the Father represents the Godhead, or God absolutely. He gave a
people to the Son, sent the Son for their redemption,
and the Spirit to apply to them that redemption.
Hence, in the beginning of this epistle, it is said that
God as the God and Father of our Lord Jesus Christ,
hath blessed us with all spiritual blessings, chose us
before the foundation of the world to be holy, having
predestinated us to be his children. He, therefore,
has made us acceptable in the Beloved, in whom we
have redemption through his blood. It is the Father,
therefore, as the apostle says, who has made known to
us his purpose to reconcile all things unto himself by
Jesus Christ. Thus also in Col. 1, 19. 20, it is said it
pleased the Father that in him all fulness should dwell,
and having made peace through the blood of the cross
by him to reconcile all things unto himself. In 1 Cor.
8, 6, it is said there is to us one God even the Father,
by whom are all things, and we in him; and one Lord,
Jesus Christ, through whom are all things, and we by

him. This representation will be recognized as pervading the Scripture. It is the Father as representing the Godhead, to whom we are said to be reconciled, to be brought near, into whose family we are adopted, and of whose glory we are heirs.

Secondly, this access is through Christ. This means, 1st, as explained in the context, by his blood, his flesh, his cross. That is, it is by his vicarious death. It is by his dying, the just for the unjust, that he brings us near to God. 2. It is by his intercession, for he has not only died for us, but he has passed through the heavens there to appear before God for us. It is, therefore, *through him*, as our mediator, intercessor, introducer, forerunner, that we draw near to God. This is a truth so plainly impressed on the Scriptures and so graven on the hearts of believers, that it gives form to all our modes of approach to the throne of God. It is in the name of Christ, all our praises, thanksgivings, confessions, and prayers are offered, and for his sake alone do we hope to find them accepted.

Thirdly, this access to the Father is by the Spirit. The inward change by which we are enabled to believe in Christ, the feelings of desire, reverence, filial confidence which are essential to our communion with God, are the fruits of the Spirit. Hence we are said to be drawn or led by the Spirit, and the Spirit also as well as Christ is called our advocate, or paraclete ; and God, it is said, because we are sons, hath sent forth the Spirit of his Son into our hearts, crying, Abba, Father, Gal. 4, 6. The words ἐν ἑνὶ πνεύματι, *by one spirit*, are not to be understood as expressing the inward concord or fellowship of the Jews and Gentiles in drawing near to God, nor simply that we are influenced by a common spirit of life, but the words are to be understood of the Holy Ghost.—1. Because the word πνεῦμα, without as well as with the article so generally refers to the Spirit in the New Testament. 2. Because the obvious reference to the Trinity in the passage, ("to the Father, through Christ, by the Spirit,") demands this interpretation. And 3. Because the same office is elsewhere characteristically referred to the Spirit. The other interpretations are included in this. If Jews and Gentiles are led by the Spirit to draw near to God, it follows that they come with one heart; and are animated by one principle of life. The preposition ἐν may be taken instrumentally, and rendered *by*, as in the following verse. Or it may mean *in communion with*. The Holy Ghost is designated here as *one* Spirit, in opposition to the two classes, Jews and Gentiles. Both have access by one and the same Spirit. The two, therefore, are not only one body as stated in verse 16, but they are inhabited and controlled by one Spirit. Thus in 1 Cor. 12, 11, "one and the self-same Spirit," is said to divide to every man severally as he wills; and in verse 12, it is, "By one Spirit we are all baptized into one body." Thus has the divine purpose of which the apostle spoke in the first chapter—his purpose to unite all his people in one harmonious body—been consummated. Christ by his cross has reconciled them, both Jews and Gentiles, unto God; the distinction between the two classes is abolished; united in one body, filled and guided by one Spirit, they draw near to God as his common children.

V. 19. The consequences of this reconciliation are that the Gentiles are now fellow-citizens of the saints, members of the family of God, and part of that temple in which God dwells by his Spirit. Formerly they were ξένοι, *strangers*, now they are συμπολῖται, *fellow-citizens*. Formerly the Gentiles stood in the same relation to the theocracy or commonwealth of Israel, that we do to a foreign State. They had no share in its privileges, no participation in its blessings. Now they are " fellow-citizens of the saints." By *saints* are not to be understood the Jews, nor the ancient patriarchs, but the people of God. Christians have become, under the new dispensation, what the Jews once were, viz. *saints*, men selected and separated from the world, and consecrated to God as his peculiar people. They now constitute the theocracy—which is no longer confined to any one people or country, but embraces all in every country who have access to God by Christ Jesus. In this spiritual kingdom the Gentiles have now the right of citizenship. They are on terms of perfect equality with all other members of that kingdom. And that kingdom is the kingdom of heaven. The same terms of admission are required, and neither more nor less, for membership in that kingdom, and for admission into heaven; all who enter the one enter the other; the one is but the infancy of the other; we are now, says Paul, the citizens of heaven. It is not, there-

fore, to the participation of the privileges of the old,
external, visible theocracy, nor simply to the pale of
the visible Christian church, that the apostle here
welcomes his Gentile brethren, but to the spiritual
Israel, the communion of saints ; to citizenship in that
kingdom of which Christ is king, and membership in
that body of which he is the head. It is only a change
of illustration without any essential change of sense,
when the apostle adds, they are no longer πάροικοι but
οἰκεῖοι. The family is a much more intimate brotherhood than the State. The relation to a father is much
more sacred and tender than that which we bear to a civil
ruler ; and therefore, there is an advance in this clause
beyond what is said in the former. If in the former
we are said to be fellow-citizens with the saints, here
we are said to be the children of God ; whose character and privileges belong to all those in whom God
dwells by his Spirit.

V. 20. As οἶκος means both a family and a house,
the apostle passes from the one figure to the other.
The Gentiles are members of the family of God, and
they are parts of his house. They are built, ἐπὶ τῷ
θεμελίῳ τῶν ἀποστόλων καὶ προφητῶν, on the foundation of the apostles and prophets, Christ himself being
the chief corner-stone.

That the prophets here mentioned are those of the
new dispensation, is evident—first from the position of
the terms. It would more naturally be prophets and
apostles if the Old Testament prophets had been intended. As God has set in the church, ' first apostles,

and second, prophets,' it is obvious that these are the classes of teachers here referred to. 2. The statement here made that the apostles and prophets are, or have laid, the foundation of that house of which the Gentiles are a part, is more obviously true of the New, than of the Old Testament prophets. 3. The passage in ch. 3, 5, in which it is said, "The mystery of Christ is now revealed to holy apostles and prophets by the Spirit," is also strongly in favour of this interpretation.

On account of the omission of the article before $\pi\rho o$ $\phi\eta\tau\hat{\omega}\nu$ some render the clause thus: 'The apostle-prophets—or apostles who are prophets.' But this is unnecessary, because the repetition of the article is often dispensed with, when the connected nouns belong to one category, and constitute one class. Both apostles and prophets belong to the class of Christian teachers. This interpretation is not only unnecessary, it is also improbable; because apostles and prophets were not identical. There were many prophets who were not apostles. The latter were the immediate messengers of Christ, invested with infallible authority as teachers, and supreme power as rulers in his church. The pro-phets were a class of teachers who spoke by inspira-tion as the Spirit from time to time directed.

The principal difference of opinion as to the inter-pretation of this clause, is whether "the foundation of the apostles and prophets" means the foundation which they constitute—or, which they laid. In favour of the latter view, it is urged that Christ, and not the apostles, is the foundation of the church; that Paul, 1 Cor. 3,

10, speaks of himself as having laid the foundation, and not as being part of it; and that it is derogatory to Christ to associate him with the apostles on terms of such apparent equality, he being one part and they another of the foundation.   On the other hand, however, it may be said, that there is a true and obvious sense in which the apostles are the foundation of the church; secondly, they are expressly so called in Scripture—as in Rev. 21, 14, besides the disputed passage, Matt. 16, 18; and thirdly, the figure here demands this interpretation.   In this particular passage Christ is the corner stone, the apostles the foundation, believers the edifice.   The corner stone is distinguished from the foundation.   To express the idea that the church rests on Christ, he is sometimes called the foundation and sometimes the corner stone of the building; but where he is called the one, he is not represented as the other. This representation no more implies the equality of Christ and the apostles, than believers being represented as constituting with him one building, implies their equality with him.

As the corner stone of a building is that which unites and sustains two walls, many suppose that the union and common dependence on Christ of the Jews and Gentiles, are intended in the application of this term to the Redeemer.   But as the same figure is used where no such reference can be assumed, it is more natural to understand the apostle as expressing the general idea that the whole church rests on Christ.   This Isaiah predicted should be the case, when he represents

Jehovah as saying: "Behold I lay in Zion for a foundation, a stone, a tried stone, a precious corner stone, a
sure foundation; he that believeth shall not make
haste." Isaiah 28, 16. Ps. 118, 22. Matt. 21, 42.
Acts 4, 11. 1 Cor. 3, 11. 1 Pet. 2, 6-8.

V. 21. Christ being the corner stone, every thing
depends on union with him. Therefore the apostle
adds, "In whom all the building fitly framed together
groweth unto a holy temple in the Lord." Christ is the
principle at once of support and of growth. He not
only sustains the building, but carries it on to its con-
summation. The words $\dot{\epsilon}\nu$ $\dot{\hat{\omega}}$ are not to be rendered, *on
which*, referring to the foundation, but, *in whom*, refer-
ring to Christ. Union with him is the sole essential
condition of our being parts of that living temple of
which he is the corner stone.

The words $\pi\hat{a}\sigma a$ $\dot{\eta}$ $o\grave{\iota}\kappa o\delta o\mu\dot{\eta}$, even without the article,
which, because wanting in the oldest manuscripts, many
critics omit, must here mean "the whole," and not
"every building." It would destroy the whole consistency of the figure to represent "every congregation," as a temple by itself resting on Christ as the
corner stone. Christ has but one body, and there is but
one temple composed of Jews and Gentiles, in which
God dwells by his Spirit.

All the parts of this temple are "fitly framed
together," $\sigma\nu\nu a\rho\mu o\lambda o\gamma o\nu\mu\dot{\epsilon}\nu\eta$. Intimate union by faith
with Christ is the necessary condition of the increase
spoken of immediately afterwards. The building however is not only thus united with the corner stone, but

the several parts one with another, so as to constitute a well compacted whole. This union, as appears from the nature of the building, is not external and visible, as a worldly kingdom under one visible head, but spiritual.

"Groweth unto a holy temple," αὔξει εἰς ναὸν ἅγιον, i. e. increases so as to become a holy temple. A temple is a building in which God dwells. Such a temple is holy, as sacred to him. It belongs to him, is consecrated to his use, and can neither be appropriated by any other, nor used for any thing but his service, without profanation. This is true of the church as a whole, and of all its constituent members. The money-changers of the world cannot, with impunity, make the church a place of traffic, or employ it in any way to answer their sordid or secular ends. The church does not belong to the state, and cannot lawfully be controlled by it. It is " sacred," set apart for God. It is his house in which he alone has any authority.

The words ἐν Κυρίῳ, in the Lord, at the end of this verse, admit of different constructions. They may be connected with the word temple immediately preceding, and be taken as equivalent to the genitive 'Temple in the Lord,' for 'Temple of the Lord.' But as the word Lord must refer to Christ, and as the temple is the house of God, this explanation produces confusion. They may be connected with the word holy; 'holy in the Lord,' i. e. holy in virtue of union with the Lord, which gives a very good sense. Or they may be referred to the verb, 'Grows by,' or better, 'in union

with the Lord.' This has in its favour the parallel
passage, 4, 16. The church compacted together in him,
grows in him, in virtue of that union, into a holy
temple.

V. 22. What was said of the whole body of believers, is here affirmed of the Ephesian Christians.
"In whom ye also are builded together for an habitation of God through the Spirit." *Builded together*,
συνοικοδομεῖσθε, may mean either, 'you together with
other believers;' or, 'you severally are all united in
this building.' The former appears more consistent
with the context. *Habitation of God*, κατοικητήριον τοῦ
Θεοῦ, is only an equivalent expression to the phrase
"holy temple" of the preceding verse. There seems
to be no sufficient reason, for considering that the κατοικητήριον of this verse refers to individual believers,
and ναὸς ἅγιος in the preceding, to the united body.
So that the sense were, 'God, by dwelling in each of
you by his Spirit, makes you collectively his temple.'
This confuses the whole figure. The two verses are
parallel. The whole building grows to a holy temple.
And you Ephesians are builded together with other
believers so as to form with them this habitation of
God.

The words ἐν πνεύματι, at the end of the verse, are
variously explained. Some make them qualify adjectively the preceding word. 'Habitation in the Spirit,'
for 'Spiritual habitation.' Others express the sense
paraphrastically, thus : 'Habitation of God in virtue
of the indwelling of the Spirit.' This is in accordance

with other passages in which the church is called the temple of God because he dwells therein by the Spirit. The Spirit being a divine person, his presence is the presence of God. Finally, the words may be connected with the verb, and the preposition have an instrumental force. 'Ye are builded by the Spirit into an habitation of God.' This is perhaps the best explanation. The church increases in the Lord, v. 21, and is builded by the Spirit, v. 22. It is in union with the one, and by the agency of the other this glorious work is carried on.

CHAPTER III

SECTION I.—Vs. 1–13.

1. For this cause, I Paul, the prisoner of Jesus Christ for you
2. Gentiles, if ye have heard of the dispensation of the grace of
3. God which is given me to you-ward: how that by revelation
   he made known unto me the mystery, as I wrote afore in few
4. words; whereby, when ye read, ye may understand my knowl-
5. edge in the mystery of Christ, which in other ages was not
   made known unto the sons of men, as it is now revealed unto
6. his holy apostles and prophets by the Spirit; that the Gentiles
   should be fellow-heirs, and of the same body, and partakers of
7. his promise in Christ by the gospel: whereof I was made a
   minister, according to the gift of the grace of God given unto
8. me by the effectual working of his power. Unto me, who am
   less than the least of all saints, is this grace given, that I should
   preach among the Gentiles the unsearchable riches of Christ;
9. and to make all *men* see what *is* the fellowship of the mystery,
   which from the beginning of the world hath been hid in God,
10. who created all things by Jesus Christ: to the intent that now
    unto the principalities and powers in heavenly *places* might be

11. known by the church the manifold wisdom of God, according
to the eternal purpose which he purposed in Christ Jesus our
12. Lord: in whom we have boldness and access with confidence
13. by the faith of him. Wherefore I desire that ye faint not at
my tribulations for you, which is your glory.

ANALYSIS.

The office which Paul had received was that of an
apostle to the Gentiles, vs. 1–2. For this office he was
qualified by direct revelation from Jesus Christ, concerning the purpose of redemption, of his knowledge
of which the preceding portions of his epistle, were
sufficient evidence, vs. 3, 4. The special truth, now
more plainly revealed than ever before, was the union
of the Gentiles with the Jews as joint partakers of the
promise of redemption, by means of the gospel, vs. 5,
6. As the gospel is the means of bringing the Gentiles
to this fellowship with the saints, Paul was, by the
special grace and almighty power of God, converted
and made a minister of the gospel, vs. 7, 8. The object
of his ministry was to make known the unsearchable
riches of Christ, and enlighten men as to the purpose
of redemption which had from eternity been hid in the
divine mind, v. 9. And the object or design of redemption itself is the manifestation of the wisdom of
God to principalities and powers in heaven, v. 10. This
glorious purpose has been executed in Christ, in whom
we as redeemed have free access to God. Afflictions
endured in such a cause were no ground of depression,
but rather of glory, vs. 11–13.

COMMENTARY.

V. 1. *For this cause,* i. e. because you Gentiles are fellow-citizens of the saints, and specially because you Ephesians are included in the temple of God.

As there is no verb of which the words, ἐγὼ Παῦλος, *I Paul,* are the nominative, there is great diversity of opinion as to the proper construction of the passage. The most common view is that the sentence here begun is recommenced and finished in v. 14, where the words, "For this cause" are repeated. The apostle intended saying at the beginning of the chapter what he says in v. 14. "For this cause, I Paul, bow my knees," i. e. 'because you Ephesians have been brought to God, I pray for your confirmation and growth in grace.'

Others supply simply the substantive verb (εἰμὶ). 'For this cause I am the prisoner of Jesus Christ.' But in this case to say the least, the article (ὁ δέσμιος) before the predicate is unnecessary. Others make the clause, the prisoner of Christ, to be in apposition to *I Paul,* and supply the predicate *I am a prisoner.* The sense would then be, 'I Paul, the prisoner of Jesus Christ, am a prisoner, and in bonds for you Gentiles.' This is better than any of the various modes of explanation which have been proposed, except the one first mentioned, which gives a far better sense. It is far more elevated and more in keeping with Paul's character, for him to say, 'Because you are now part of God's spiritual temple, I pray for your confirmation and growth;' than, 'Because you are introduced into the communion of saints, I am a prisoner of Jesus Christ.'

The expression, ὁ δέσμιος τοῦ Χριστοῦ, *the prisoner of Christ*, does not mean *prisoner on account of Christ.* Those for whom he suffered bonds are immediately afterwards said to be the Gentiles. It means Christ's prisoner. As he was Christ's servant, apostle, and minister, so he was Christ's prisoner. In all his relations he belonged to Christ. He was a prisoner, ὑπὲρ ὑμῶν τῶν ἐθνῶν, *for you Gentiles.* It was preaching the Gospel to the Gentiles which brought down upon him the hatred of his countrymen, and led them to accuse him before the Roman magistrates, and to his being sent a prisoner to Rome.

V. 2. This verse is connected with the immediately preceding words.—' My apostolic mission is to the Gentiles ; I am a prisoner for your sake, since ye have heard of the office which God has given me for your benefit.' The word εἴγε rendered in our version by *if*, does not necessarily express doubt. Paul knew that the Ephesians were aware that he was an apostle to the Gentiles. The word is often used where the thing spoken of is taken for granted. Eph. 4, 21. 2 Cor. 5, 3. In such cases, it may properly be rendered, *since, inasmuch as.* It is only a more refined or delicate form of assertion. It is unnecessary, therefore, to assume either that this epistle was not addressed to the Ephesians particularly ; or that ἀκούειν is to be taken in the sense of *bene intelligere* (if so be ye have well understood) ; or that Paul, when preaching at Ephesus, had preserved silence on his apostleship. He speaks of himself as a prisoner for their sake, inasmuch as they had heard he was the apostle to the Gentiles.

The expression, *dispensation of the grace given unto me*, is the designation of his office. It was an οἰκονομία, *a stewardship*. A stewardship of the grace given, τῆς χάριτος τῆς δοθείσης, means either a stewardship which is a grace, or favour, or which flows from grace, i. e. was graciously conferred. Compare verse 8, in which he says, " To me was this grace given." Not unfrequently the office itself is called χάρις, a grace or favour. Rom. 12, 3. 15, 15. 1 Cor. 3, 10. Gal. 2, 9. Paul esteemed the office of a messenger of Christ as a manifestation of the undeserved kindness of God towards him, and he always speaks of it with gratitude and humility. It was not its honours, nor its authority, much less any emolument connected with it, which gave it value in his eyes; but the privilege which it involved of preaching the unsearchable riches of Christ.

Instead of understanding οἰκονομία in the sense above given, of *office*, it may refer to the act of God, and be rendered, *dispensation*. 'If, or since, ye have heard how God dispensed the grace given unto me,' i. e. if ye understand the nature of the gift I have received. In Col. 1, 25, Paul speaks of the οἰκονομία as given; here it is χάρις which is said to be given. In both cases the general idea is the same, the form alone is different. His office and the grace therewith connected, including all the gifts ordinary and extraordinary, which went to make him an apostle, were both

an οἰκονομία and a χάρις. The apostleship was not a
mere office like that of a prelate or prince, conferring
certain rights and powers; it was an inward grace,
including plenary and infallible knowledge. You
could no more appoint a man an apostle, than you
could appoint him a saint. Neither inspiration nor
holiness come by appointment. An apostle without
inspiration is as much a solecism as a saint without
holiness. Rome, here as every where, retains the sem-
blance without the reality ; the form without the
power. She has apostles without inspiration, the office
without the grace of which the office was but the expression. Thus she feeds herself and her children upon
ashes.

To you-ward. Paul's mission was to the Gentiles.
It was in special reference to them that he had received
his commission and the gifts therewith connected.
When Christ appeared to him on his journey to Damas-
cus, he said to him, "I have appeared unto thee for
this purpose, to make thee a minister and witness both
of these things which thou hast seen, and of those
things in the which I will appear unto thee ; delivering thee from the people and from the Gentiles, unto
whom now I send thee, to open their eyes, and to
turn them from darkness to light, and from the power
of Satan unto God, that they may receive forgiveness of sins, and inheritance among them which are
sanctified by faith that is in me." Acts 26, 16–18.
Here we have an authentic account of Paul's mission.
He was appointed a witness of what had been and of

what should be made known to him by revelation
He was sent to the Gentiles, to turn them from Satan
to God in order that they might be saved.

V. 3. *How that by revelation was made known unto
me*, &c. This clause is connected with what precedes
and explains it.—' Ye have heard of the grace which I
have received, i. e. ye have heard how that by revelation was made known to me.' Κατὰ ἀποκάλυψιν,
after the manner of a revelation, i. e. δι' ἀποκαλύψεως,
Gal. 1, 12. He was not indebted for his knowledge
of the Gospel to the instructions of others, as he proves
in his epistle to the Galatians by a long induction
of facts in his history. This was one of the indispensable qualifications for the apostleship. As the
apostles were witnesses, their knowledge must be direct
and not founded on hearsay. The thing made known
was a " mystery;" i. e. a secret, something undiscoverable by human reason, the knowledge of which
could only be attained by revelation. This revelation
was a grace or favour conferred on the apostle himself.

The mystery of which he here speaks is that of
which the preceding chapters treat, viz. the union of
the Gentiles with the Jews. Of that subject he had
just written *briefly;* ἐν ὀλίγῳ, *with little*, i. e. few
words.

V. 4. By reading what he had written, they could
judge of his knowledge of the mystery of Christ.
πρὸς ὅ, *according to which*. What he had written
might be taken as the standard or evidence of his
knowledge. *Mystery of Christ*, may mean the mystery

or revelation concerning Christ; or of which he is the author (i. e. of the secret purpose of redemption), or which is Christ. Christ himself is the great mystery of godliness, God manifest in the flesh. He is the revelation of the μυστήριον or secret purpose of God, which had been hid for ages. Thus the apostle in writing to the Colossians says: "God would make known the riches of the glory of the mystery among the Gentiles; which (i. e. the mystery) is Christ in you, the hope of glory." Col. 1, 27.

What Paul had written respecting the calling of the Gentiles in the preceding chapter, was an indication of his knowledge of the whole plan of salvation—here designated as "the mystery of Christ," which includes far more than the truth that the Gentiles were fellow-citizens of the saints. It has the same extensive meaning in Col. 4, 3, where Paul prays that God would open a door of utterance for him "to speak the mystery of Christ." This verse is, therefore, virtually a parenthesis, in so far as the relative ὅ at the beginning of the next verse refers to the word μυστήριον in v. 3; or if referred to that word as used in v. 4, it is to it as including the more limited idea expressed in v. 3.

V. 5. God by revelation had made known to Paul a mystery, or purpose, *which* was not revealed as it now was to the apostles. That the Gentiles were to partake of the blessings of the Messiah's reign, and to be united as one body with the Jews in his kingdom, is not only frequently predicted by the ancient prophets, but Paul himself repeatedly and at length quotes their declarations on this point to prove that what he taught was in accordance with the Old Testament; see Rom. 9, 25–33. The emphasis must, therefore, be laid on the word *as*. This doctrine was not formerly revealed *as*, i. e. not so fully or so clearly as under the Gospel.

The common text reads ἐν ἑτέραις γενεαῖς, *in* other generations. But most editors, on the authority of the older MSS., omit the preposition. Still the great majority of commentators interpret the above phrase as determining the time, and render it, *during other ages*. To this, however, it is objected that γενεά never means, an age in the sense of period of time, but always *a generation*, the men of any age, those living in any one period. If this objection is valid γενεαῖς must be taken as the simple dative, and υἱοῖς τῶν ἀνθρώπων be regarded as explanatory. The passage would then read, "Which was not made known to other generations, i. e. to the sons of men," &c. But in Acts 14, 16. 15, 21, and especially in Col. 1, 26 (ἀπὸ τῶν αἰώνων καὶ ἀπὸ τῶν γενεῶν), γενεά is most naturally taken in the sense of age, or period of duration. In the same sense it is used in the Septuagint, Ps. 72, 5. 102, 25. Is. 51, 8.

As it is now revealed to his holy apostles and to the prophets by the Spirit, ὡς νῦν ἀπεκαλύφθη . . . . ἐν πνεύματι. The apostles and prophets of the new dispensation were the only classes of inspired men; the former being the permanent, the latter the occasional organs of the Spirit. They therefore were the only recipients of direct revelations. They are here called *holy* in the sense of *sacred, consecrated*. They were men set apart for the peculiar service of God. In the same sense the prophets of the old economy are called holy. Luke 1, 70. 2 Peter 1, 21. The pronoun *his* in connection with *apostles* may refer to God as the author of the revelation spoken of, or to Christ whose messengers the apostles were. 'My knowledge of the mystery of Christ, which, in former ages, was not made known, as it is now revealed to *his* apostles,' &c. *By the Spirit*, i. e. revealed by the Spirit. Πνεύματι, though without the article, refers to the Holy Spirit, the immediate author of these divine communications. It follows from the scriptural doctrine of the Trinity, which teaches the identity as to substance of the Father, Son, and Spirit, that the act of the one is the act of the others. Paul, therefore, refers the revelations which he received sometimes to God, as in verse 3 ; sometimes to Christ as in Gal. 1, 12 ; sometimes to the Spirit.

V. 6. The mystery made known to the apostles and prophets of the new dispensation, was εἶναι τὰ ἔθνη συγκληρονόμα, κτλ., i. e. that the Gentiles *are*, in point of right and fact, fellow-heirs, of the same body, and partakers of this promise. The form in which the calling of the Gentiles was predicted in the Old Testament led to the general impression that they were to partake of the blessings of the Messiah's reign by becoming Jews, by being as proselytes merged into the old theocracy, which was to remain in all its peculiarities. It seems never to have entered into any human mind until the day of Pentecost, that the theocracy itself was to be abolished, and a new form of religion was to be introduced, designed and adapted equally for all mankind, under which the distinction between Jew and Gentile was to be done away. It was this catholicity of the Gospel which was the expanding and elevating revelation made to the apostles, and which raised them from sectarians to Christians.

The Gentiles *are fellow-heirs.* They have the same right to the inheritance as the Jews. The inheritance is all the benefits of the covenant of grace; the knowledge of the truth, all church privileges, justification, adoption, and sanctification; the indwelling of the Spirit, and life everlasting; an inheritance so great that simply to comprehend it requires divine assistance, and elevates the soul to the confines of heaven. Hence Paul prays (1, 17. 18), that God would give the Ephesians the Spirit of revelation that they might know what is the riches of the glory of the inheritance to which they had been called.

They are σύσσωμα; i. e. they are constituent portions of the body of Christ; as nearly related to him, and as much partakers of his life as their Jewish brethren. The hand is not in the body by permission of the eye, nor the eye by permission of the hand. Neither is the Gentile in the church by courtesy of the Jews, nor the Jew by courtesy of the Gentiles. They are one body.

What in the preceding terms is presented figuratively

is expressed literally, when it is added, *they are partakers of his* (God's) *promise.* The promise is the promise of redemption ; the promise made to our first parents, repeated to Abraham, and which forms the burden of all the Old Testament predictions. Gal. 3, 14. 19. 22, 29.

The only essential and indispensable condition of participation in the benefits of redemption is union with Christ. The Gentiles are fellow-heirs, and of the same body and partakers of the promise, says the apostle, *in Christ,* i. e. in virtue of their union with him. And this union is effected or brought about, *by the Gospel.* It is not by birth nor by any outward rite, nor by union with any external body, but by the Gospel, received and appropriated by faith, that we are united to Christ, and thus made heirs of God. This verse teaches therefore—1. The nature of the blessings of which the Gentiles are partakers, viz. the inheritance promised to the people of God. 2. The condition on which that participation is suspended, viz. union with Christ ; and 3. The means by which that union is effected, viz. the Gospel. Hence the apostle enlarges on the dignity and importance of preaching the Gospel. This is the subject of the verses which follow.

V. 7. *Of which* (Gospel) *I was made a minister ;* a διάκονος, *a runner, servant, minister.* Minister of the Gospel, means one whose business it is to preach the Gospel. This is his service ; the work for which he is engaged, and to which he is bound to devote himself. There are two things which Paul here and in the verse

following says in reference to his introduction into the
ministry ; first, it was a great favour ; and secondly,
it involved the exercise of divine power.

He was made a minister, κατὰ τὴν δωρεὰν τῆς χάριτος τοῦ Θεοῦ, *according to the gift of the grace of God
given* to him. According to the common text (δωρεὰν—
δοθεῖσαν), *the gift was given.* "The gift of the grace of
God," may mean the gracious gift, i. e. the gift due to
the grace of God ; or, the gift which is the grace of
God ; so that the χάρις, *grace*, as Paul often calls his
apostleship, is the thing given. In either way the gift
referred to was his vocation to be an apostle. That he
who was a persecutor and blasphemer should be called
to be an apostle, was in his view a wonderful display
of the grace of God.

The gift in question was given, κατὰ τὴν ἐνέργειαν
τῆς δυνάμεως αὐτοῦ, *by the effectual working of his*
(God's) *power*. Paul's vocation as an apostle involved
his conversion, and his conversion was the effect of the
power of God. This refers to the nature of the work,
and not to its mere circumstances. It was not the
blinding light, nor the fearful voice, which he refers to
the power of God, but the inward change, by which
he, a malignant opposer of Christ, was instantly converted into an obedient servant. The regeneration of
the soul is classed among the mighty works of God,
due to the exceeding greatness of his power. See ch.
1, 19.

V. 8. *To me*, adds the apostle, *who am less than the
least of all saints, is this grace given, that I should*

preach among the Gentiles, the unsearchable riches of Christ.

By the word *saints* is to be understood not the apostles, but the people of God, who are "called to be saints," 1 Cor. 1, 7. Rom. 1, 7. *Less than the least,* ἐλαχιστοτέρος, a comparative formed from a superlative. It was not merely the sense of his sinfulness in general, which weighed so heavily on the apostle's conscience. It was the sin of persecuting Christ, which he could never forgive himself. As soon as God revealed his Son in him, and he apprehended the infinite excellence and love of Christ, the sin of rejecting and blaspheming such a Saviour appeared so great that all other sins seemed as comparatively nothing. Paul's experience in this matter is the type of the experience of other Christians. It is the sin of unbelief; the sin of rejecting Christ, of which, agreeably to our Saviour's own declaration, the Holy Spirit is sent to convince the world. John 16, 9.

To one thus guilty it was a great favour to be allowed to preach Christ. The expression τὸν ἀνεξιχνίαστον πλοῦτον τοῦ Χριστοῦ, *unsearchable riches of Christ ; riches which cannot be traced ; past finding out,* may mean either the riches or blessings which Christ bestows, or the riches which he possesses. Both ideas may be included, though the latter is doubtless the more prominent. The unsearchable riches of Christ, are the fulness of the Godhead, the plenitude of all divine glories and perfections which dwell in him ; the fulness of grace to pardon, to sanctify and save ; every thing in short, which renders him the satisfying portion of the soul.

V. 9. It was Paul's first duty to preach the unsearchable riches of Christ among the Gentiles, for he was especially the " apostle of the Gentiles." But his duty was not confined to them. He was commissioned both to preach to the Gentiles, *and to make all see,* &c. This is the common interpretation of the passage. Others, however, insist that the *all* is here limited by the context to the Gentiles. But the force of *and,* which marks the accession of a new idea, is thus in a great measure lost. And the following verse favours the widest latitude that can be given to the words in question.

The word φωτίζειν properly means, *to shine,* as any luminous body does, and then *to illuminate,* to impart light to, as a candle does to those on whom it shines, and as God does to the minds of men, and as the Gospel does, which is as a light shining in a dark place, and hence the apostle, 2 Cor. 4, 4, speaks of the φωτισμὸς τοῦ εὐαγγελίου. Utitur apta similitudine, says Calvin, quum dicit, φωτίσαι πάντας, quasi plena luce effulgeat Dei gratia in suo apostolatu. The Church is compared to a candlestick, and ministers to stars. Their office is to dispense light. The light imparted by the Gospel was knowledge, and hence to illuminate is, in fact, to teach ; which is the idea the word is intended here to express.

The thing taught was, ἡ οἰκονομία τοῦ μυστηρίου τοῦ ἀποκεκρυμμένου, *the economy of the mystery which*

from the beginning of the world hath been hid in God.
The common text in this clause reads κοινωνία, *fellow-*
ship, but all the corrected editions of the New Testament, on the authority of the ancient MSS., read οἰκονομία, *plan*, or, *economy.* The mystery or secret, is not
the simple purpose to call the Gentiles into the church,
but the mystery of redemption. This mystery, ἀπὸ
τῶν αἰώνων, *from ages*, from the beginning of time,
had been hid in God. Compare Rom. 16, 25, "The
mystery which was kept secret since the world began."
1 Cor. 2, 7, "The wisdom of God in a mystery, the
hidden *wisdom*, which God ordained before the world."
Col. 1, 26, "The mystery which hath been hid from
ages and from generations." In all these places
the mystery spoken of is God's purpose of redemption, formed in the counsels of eternity, impenetrably
hidden from the view of men until revealed in his
own time. It was this plan of redemption thus formed,
thus long concealed, but now made known through the
Gospel, that Paul was sent to bear as a guiding and
saving light to all men.

Who created all things by Jesus Christ. The words
διὰ Ἰησοῦ Χριστοῦ, (*by Jesus Christ*,) being wanting
in the great majority of oldest MSS., are generally
regarded as spurious. The *all things* here referred to
are by some restricted to every thing pertaining to the
Gospel dispensation. For this interpretation there is
no necessity in the context; and it is contrary to the
common usage and force of the terms. There must be
some stringent necessity to justify making "creator

of all things," mean "author of the new dispensation." Others restrict the terms to all men : ' He who created all men now calls all.'* This however is arbitrary and uncalled for. The words are to be taken in their natural sense, as referring to the universe. It was in the bosom of the Creator of all things that this purpose of redemption so long lay hid. The reference to God as creator in this connection, may be accounted for as merely an expression of reverence. We often call God the Infinite, the Almighty, the Creator, &c., without intending any special reference of the titles to the subject about which we may be speaking. So Paul often calls God, *blessed*, without any special reason for the appellation. Some however think that in the present case the apostle uses this expression in confirmation of his declaration that the plan of redemption was from ages hid in God—for he who created all things must be supposed to have included redemption in his original purpose. Others suppose the association of the ideas is—he who created, redeems—the same God who made the universe has formed the plan of redemption. None but the creator can be a redeemer.

V. 10. *To the intent that now might be made known*, ἵνα γνωρισθῇ νῦν. If this clause depend on the immediately preceding, then the apostle teaches that creation is in order to redemption. God created all things *in order that* by the church might be made known his

---

* Unus Deus omnes populos condidit, sic etiam nunc omnes ad se vocat. BEZA.

manifold wisdom. This is the supralapsarian view of the order of the divine purposes, and as it is the only passage in Scripture which is adduced as directly asserting that theory, its proper interpretation is of special interest. It is objected to the construction just mentioned—1. That the passage would then teach a doctrine foreign to the New Testament, viz. that God created the universe in order to display his glory in the salvation and perdition of men; which supposes the decree to save to precede the decree to create, and the decree to permit the fall of men. 2. Apart from the doctrinal objections to this theory, this connection of the clauses is unnatural, because the words 'who created all things,' is entirely subordinate and unessential, and therefore not the proper point of connection for the main idea in the whole context. That clause might be omitted without materially affecting the sense of the passage. 3. The apostle is speaking of his conversion and call to the apostleship. To him was the grace given to preach the unsearchable riches of Christ, and teach all men the economy of redemption, *in order that* through the church might be made known the manifold wisdom of God. It is only thus that the connection of this verse with the main idea of the context is preserved. It is not the design of creation, but the design of the revelation of the mystery of redemption of which he is here speaking. 4. This interpretation is further sustained by the force of the particle *now* as here used. *Now* stands opposed to 'hid from ages.' God sent Paul to preach the Gospel, *in order that* what

had been so long hid might *now* be made known.
It was the design of preaching the Gospel, and not the
design of creation of which the apostle had occasion to
speak. The natural connection of ἵνα, therefore, is
with the verbs εὐαγγελίσασθαι and φωτίσαι, which
express the main idea in the context. "Paul," says
Olshausen, "contrasts the greatness of his vocation
with his personal nothingness, and he therefore traces
the design of his mission through different steps. First,
he says, he had to preach to the heathen; then, to
enlighten all men concerning the mystery of redemption, and both, in order to manifest even to angels the
infinite wisdom of God."

The Bible clearly teaches not only that the angels
take a deep interest in the work of redemption, but
that their knowledge and blessedness are increased by
the exhibition of the glory of God in the salvation
of men.

The expression, ἡ πολυποίκιλος σοφία, "manifold
wisdom," refers to the various aspects under which
the wisdom of God is displayed in redemption; in
reconciling justice and mercy; in exalting the unworthy while it effectually humbles them; in the person
of the Redeemer, in his work; in the operations of the
Holy Spirit; in the varied dispensations of the old and
new economy, and in the whole conduct of the work
of mercy and in its glorious consummation. It is by
the church redeemed by the blood of Christ and sanctified by his Spirit, that to all orders of intelligent beings
is to be made, through all coming ages, the brightest

display of the divine perfections. It is ταῖς ἀρχαῖς καὶ ταῖς ἐξουσίαις ἐν τοῖς ἐπουρανίοις that this exhibition of the manifold wisdom of God is to be made διὰ τῆς ἐκκλησίας. This gives us our highest conception of the dignity of the church. The works of God manifest his glory by being what they are. It is because the universe is so vast, the heavens so glorious, the earth so beautiful and teeming, that they reveal the boundless affluence of their maker. If then it is through the church God designs specially to manifest to the highest order of intelligence, his infinite power, grace and wisdom, the church in her consummation, must be the most glorious of his works. Hence preaching the Gospel, the appointed means to this consummate end, was regarded by Paul as so great a favour. To me, less than the least, was this grace given.

V. 11. This exhibition of the manifold wisdom of God was contemplated in the original conception of the plan of redemption; for the apostle adds, it was *according to the eternal purpose which he purposed in Christ Jesus our Lord.* Πρόθεσις τῶν αἰώνων, *purpose* formed in eternity—which existed through all past ages—not, purpose concerning the ages, or different periods of the world. Compare 2 Tim. 1, 9, πρόθεσιν—πρὸ χρόνων αἰωνίων. The words ἣν ἐποίησε may be rendered either, as by our translators, *which he purposed,* or, *which he executed.* The latter method is preferred by the majority of commentators, as better suited to the context, and especially to the words *in Christ Jesus our Lord,* as the title Christ *Jesus* always refers to the historical

Christ, the incarnate Son of God. The purpose of God to make provision for the redemption of men has been fulfilled in the incarnation and death of his Son.

V. 12. Hence, as the consequence of this accomplished work, *we have*, in him, τὴν παῤῥησίαν καὶ τὴν προσαγωγὴν ἐν πεποιθήσει, *boldness and access with confidence*, i. e. free and unrestricted access to God, as children to a father. We come with the assurance of being accepted, because our confidence does not rest on our own merit, but on the infinite merit of an infinite Saviour. It is *in Him* we have this liberty. WE have this free access to God; we believers; not any particular class, a priesthood among Christians to whom alone access is permitted, but all believers without any priestly intervention, other than that of one great High Priest who has passed through the heavens, Jesus the Son of God. Παῤῥησία as used in Scripture, is not merely *freespokenness*, nor yet simple *frankness*, but *fearlessness*, freedom from apprehension of rejection or of evil. It is this Christ has procured for us. Even the vilest may, in Christ, approach the infinitely holy, who is a consuming fire, with fearlessness. Nothing short of an infinite Saviour could effect such a redemption. The accumulation of substantives in this sentence, *boldness, access, confidence*, shows that there was no word which could express what Paul felt in view of the complete reconciliation of men to God through Jesus Christ.

We have this free access to God with full confidence of acceptance *through faith of Him*, i. e. by

faith in Christ.   This is explanatory of the first clause
of the verse, ἐν ᾧ—διὰ τῆς πίστεως αὐτοῦ, *in whom,*
i. e. *by faith of Him ;* faith of which he is the object.
Comp. 2, 13.   It is the discovery of the dignity of his
person, confidence in the efficacy of his blood, and
assurance of his love, all of which are included, more
or less consciously, in faith, that enables us joyfully to
draw near to God.   This is the great question which
every sinner needs to have answered.—How may I
come to God with the assurance of acceptance ?   The
answer given by the apostle and confirmed by the
experience of the saints of all ages is, ' By faith in
Jesus Christ.'   It is because men rely on some other
means of access, either bringing some worthless bribe
in their hands, or trusting to some other mediator,
priestly or saintly, that so many fail who seek to enter
God's presence.

V. 13.   *Wherefore,* i. e. because we have this access
to God, the sum of all good, we ought to be superior
to all the afflictions of this life, and maintain habitually
a joyful spirit.   Being the subjects of such a redemption and having this liberty of access to God, believers
ought not to be discouraged by all the apparently ad-
verse circumstances attending the propagation of the
Gospel.   As neither the object of the verb αἰτοῦμαι,
nor the subject of the verb ἐκκακεῖν is expressed, this
verse admits of different explanations.   It may mean,
' I pray *you* that *you* faint not ;' or, ' I pray *God* that
I faint not ;' or, ' I pray *God* that *ye* faint not.'
Whether the object of the verb be " *God* " or " *you,*"

it is hard to decide; as it would be alike appropriate
and agreeable to usage to say, 'I pray God,' or, 'I
pray you,' i. e. I beseech you not to be discouraged.
The latter is on the whole to be preferred, as there is
nothing in the context to suggest God as the object
of address, and as the verb αἰτεῖν, though properly sig-
nifying simply to *ask*, whether of God or man, is often
used in a stronger sense, *to require*, or *demand*, Luke
23, 23. Acts 25, 3. 15. Paul might well require of the
Ephesians, in view of the glories of the redemption of
which they had become partakers, not to be discouraged. As to the second point, viz. the subject of the
verb ἐκκακεῖν, there is less room to doubt. It is far
more in keeping with the whole tone of the passage,
that Paul should refer to their fainting than to his own.
There was far more danger of the former than of the
latter. And what follows ("which is your glory"),
is a motive by which his exhortation to them is enforced.

The relative ἥτις in the next clause, admits of a
twofold reference. It may relate to θλίψεσι, *afflictions;*
or to μὴ ἐκκακεῖν, *not fainting*. In the one case the
sense would be : 'The afflictions which I suffer for you
instead of being a ground of discouragement are a
glory to you.' In the other : 'Not fainting is an honour to you.' The latter is flat, it amounts to nothing
in such a context. It is perfectly in keeping with the
heroic character of the apostle, who himself gloried in
his afflictions, and with the elevated tone of feeling
pervading the context, that he should represent the

afflictions which he endured for the Gentiles as an honour and not as a disgrace and a cause of despondency.

SECTION II.—Vs. 14–21.

14.   For this cause I bow my knees unto the Father of our Lord
15. Jesus Christ, of whom the whole family in heaven and earth
16. is named, that he would grant you, according to the riches
      of his glory, to be strengthened with might by his Spirit in
17. the inner man; that Christ may dwell in your hearts by faith:
18. that ye, being rooted and grounded in love, may be able to
      comprehend with all saints what *is* the breadth, and length,
19. and depth, and height; and to know the love of Christ,
      which passeth knowledge, that ye might be filled with all the
20. fulness of God. Now unto him that is able to do exceeding
      abundantly above all that we ask or think, according to the
21. power that worketh in us, unto him *be* glory in the church by
      Christ Jesus throughout all ages, world without end. Amen.

ANALYSIS.

The prayer of the apostle is addressed to the Father of our Lord Jesus Christ, who is also in him our Father.   He offers but one petition, viz. that his readers might be strengthened by the Holy Ghost in the inner man; or that Christ might dwell in their hearts by faith. The consequence of this would be, that they would be confirmed in love, and thus enabled in some measure to comprehend the infinite love of Christ, which would enlarge their capacity unto the fulness of God; that is, ultimately render them, in their measure, as full of holiness and blessedness, as God is in his.

COMMENTARY.

V. 14. This verse resumes the connection interrupted in verse 1st. The prayer which the apostle there commenced, he here begins anew. *For this cause,* τούτου χάριν, repeated from v. 1, and therefore the connection is the same here as there, i. e. because you Ephesians are made partakers of the redemption purchased by Christ. *I bow my knees.* The posture of prayer, for prayer itself. *Unto the Father of our Lord Jesus Christ.** The peculiar Christian designation of God, as expressing the covenant relation in which he stands to believers. It is because he is the Father of our Lord Jesus Christ, our incarnate God and Saviour, that he is our Father, and accessible to us in prayer. We can approach him acceptably in no other character than as the God who sent the Lord Jesus to be our propitiation and mediator. It is therefore by faith in him as reconciled, that we address him as the Father of our Lord Jesus Christ.

V. 15. *Of whom the whole family in heaven and earth is named.* The word πατριά is a collective term for the descendants of the same father, immediate or remote. In Luke 2, 4, we read of the house and family

---

* The MSS. A. B. C. 17. 67, the Coptic-Æthiopic, and Vulgate versions, and many of the Fathers omit the words τοῦ Κυρίου ἡμῶν 'Ιησοῦ Χριστοῦ. As however important external authorities and the context are in their favour, the majority of recent editions and commentators retain them.

of David, and in Acts 3, 25, of all the families of the
earth. The most important question here is, whether
πᾶσα πατριά is to be rendered *every family*, or, *the
whole family*. In favour of the latter are the considerations that the omission of the article, which usage
doubtless demands, is not unfrequent where either
the substantive has acquired the character of a proper
name, or where the context is so clear as to prevent
mistake. (See Winer's Gram. p. 131.) And secondly,
the sense is better suited to the whole context. If Paul
intended to refer to the various orders of angels, and
the various classes of men, as must be his meaning if
πᾶσα πατριά is rendered *every family*, then he contemplates God as the universal Father, and all rational
creatures as his children. But the whole drift of the
passage shows that it is not God in his relation as creator, but God in his relation as a spiritual father—who
is here contemplated. He is addressed as the "Father
of our Lord Jesus Christ," and therefore our Father.
It is plain therefore that those who are here contemplated as children, are those who are by Jesus Christ
brought into this relation to God. Consequently the
word πατριά cannot include any but the subjects of
redemption. The whole family in heaven therefore
cannot mean the angels, but the redeemed already
saved, and the family on earth, the company of believers still living.

As children derive their name from their father and
their relation to him is thereby determined, so the
apostle says, the whole family of God derive their

name from him and are known and recognized as his children.

V. 16. This verse contains the apostle's prayer in behalf of the Ephesians. He prays that God, according to the riches of his glory, would strengthen them with might by his Spirit in the inner man.

The riches of his glory, πλοῦτος τῆς δόξης, means the plenitude of divine perfection. It is not his power to the exclusion of his mercy, nor his mercy to the exclusion of his power, but it is every thing in God that renders him glorious, the proper object of adoration. The apostle prays that God would deal with his people according to that plenitude of grace and power, which constitutes his glory and makes him to his creatures the source of all good.

δυνάμει κραταιωθῆναι. Δυνάμει may be rendered adverbially, "*powerfully* strengthened," or it may be rendered *as to power*, indicating the principle which was to be confirmed or strengthened; or, "*with power*," as expressing the gift to be communicated. They were to receive power communicated through the Holy Spirit. This is to be preferred, because the subject of this invigorating influence is not any one principle, but the whole "inner man."

There are two interpretations of the phrase κραταιω-θῆναι εἰς τὸν ἔσω ἄνθρωπον, *to be strengthened as to the inner man*, the choice between which must depend on the analogy of Scripture. According to one theory of human nature, the higher powers of the soul, the reason, the mind, the spirit, the inner man, retain their integrity since the fall, but in themselves are too weak to gain the victory over the animal or lower principles of our nature, designated as the flesh, or outward man. There is a perpetual struggle, even before regeneration, between the good and evil principles in man, between the reason, or πνεῦμα, and the flesh, or σάρξ.· The former being the weaker needs to be strengthened by the divine Spirit. "*The inner man*," says Meyer, "is the νοῦς, the rational moral Ego, the rational soul of man which harmonizes with the divine will, but needs to be strengthened by the Spirit of God (δυνάμει κρατιω-θῆναι διὰ τοῦ πνεύματος), in order not to be overcome by the sinful lusts of the σάρξ, whose animating or life principle is the ψυχή, the animal soul." This is the theory of semi-Pelagianism, embodied and developed in the theology of the church of Rome. The opposite, or Augustinian theory, adopted by the Lutheran and Reformed churches, is that of total depravity, i. e. that the whole soul, the higher, as well as lower powers of our nature, are the seat and subject of original sin, and that the natural man is thereby disabled and made opposite to all spiritual good. Consequently the conflict of which the Scriptures speak is not between the higher and lower powers of our nature,—but between nature and what is not nature, between the old and new man. The new principle is something supernatural communicated by the Spirit of God. The classical passages of Scripture relating to this subject, are Rom. 7, 14–25. 1 Cor. 2, 14. 15. Gal. 5, 17–26. In none of these passages does πνεῦμα designate the reason as opposed to the sensual principle, but the Spirit of God as dwelling in the renewed soul and giving it its own character, and therefore also its own name. It is the soul as the subject of divine influence, or as the dwelling place of the Holy Ghost, that is called Spirit. By the "inner man," therefore, in this passage is not to be understood the soul as opposed to the body, or the rational, as distinguished from the sensual principle; but the interior principle of spiritual life, the product of the almighty power of the Spirit of God—as is clearly taught in ch. 1, 19 of this epistle. Even in 2 Cor. 4, 16, where the apostle says : "Though our outward man perish, our inward man is renewed day by day," the meaning is the same. That language could not be used of an unrenewed man. It does not mean simply that though the body was wasted, the mind was constantly refreshed. The inner man that was renewed day by day was the renewed or spiritual man; the soul as the organ and temple of the Spirit of God.

V. 17. *That Christ may dwell in your hearts by faith,* κατοικῆσαι τὸν Χριστὸν διὰ τῆς πίστεως ἐν ταῖς καρδίαις ὑμῶν. Christ dwells in his people—he dwells in their hearts ; he dwells in them through faith. These are the truths contained in this passage.

As to the first, viz. the indwelling of Christ, it does not differ from what is expressed in the preceding verse, further than as indicating the source or nature of that spiritual strength of which that verse speaks. When Paul prayed that his readers might be strengthened in the inner man, he prayed that Christ might dwell in them. The omnipresent and infinite God is said to dwell wherever he specially and permanently manifests his presence. Thus he is said to dwell in heaven, Ps. 123, 1; to dwell among the children of Israel, Numb. 35, 34; in Zion, Ps. 9, 11; with him that is of an humble and contrite spirit, Is. 57, 11; and in his people, 2 Cor. 6, 16. Sometimes it is God who is said to dwell in the hearts of his people, sometimes the Spirit of God, sometimes, as in Rom. 8, 9, it is the Spirit of Christ; and sometimes, as Rom. 8, 10, and in the passage before us, it is Christ himself. These varying modes of expression find their solution in the doctrine of the Trinity. In virtue of the unity of the divine substance, he that had seen the Son, hath seen the Father also; he that hath the Son hath the Father; where the Spirit of God is, there God is; and where the Spirit of Christ is, there Christ is. The passage in Rom. 8, 9. 10 is specially instructive. The apostle there says, "The Spirit of God dwelleth in you. Now, if any man have not the Spirit of Christ, he is none of his; and if Christ be in you, &c." From this it is plain that Christ's being in us, means that we have his Spirit; and to have his Spirit means that the Spirit of God dwells in us. When, therefore, the apostle speaks of Christ dwelling in our hearts, he refers to the indwelling of the Holy Ghost, for Christ dwells in his people by his Spirit. They thus become partakers of his life, so that it is Christ that liveth in them, Gal. 2, 20. This is the true and abiding source of spiritual strength and of all other manifestations of the divine life.

Christ is said to dwell in ἐν ταῖς καρδίαις, *the hearts* of his people. The two common figurative senses of the word heart in Scripture, are, the feelings as distinguished from the understanding, and the whole soul, including the intellect and affections. It is in this latter sense the Scriptures speak of an understanding heart, 1 Kings 3, 9. 12. Prov. 8, 5; and of the thoughts, devices and counsels of the heart. Judges 5, 15. Prov. 19, 21; 20, 5. According to the Bible religion is not a form of feeling to the exclusion of the intellect, nor a form of knowledge to the exclusion of the feelings. Christ dwells in the heart, in the comprehensive sense of the word. He is the source of spiritual life to the whole soul; of spiritual knowledge as well as of spiritual affections.

By faith, διὰ τῆς πίστεως, *by means of faith.* There are two essential conditions of this indwelling of Christ; a rational nature, and, so far as adults are concerned, faith. The former is necessarily presupposed in all communion with God. But it is not with every rational nature that God enters into fellowship. The indwelling of Christ includes more than the communion of spirit with spirit. It implies congeniality. This faith produces or involves; because it includes spiritual apprehension—the perception of the truth and excellence of "the things of the Spirit;" and because it works by love; it manifests itself in the exercise of complacency, desire and delight. The most beautiful object might be in the apartment of a blind man, and he not be sensible of its presence; or if by any means

made aware of its nearness, he could have no delight
in its beauty. Christ dwells in us by faith, because it
is by faith we perceive his presence, his excellence, and
his glory, and because it is by faith we appropriate and
reciprocate the manifestations of his love. Faith is to
this spiritual communion, what esteem and affection
are to the fellowships of domestic life.

V. 18. The construction of the clause, ἐν ἀγάπῃ
ἐρριζωμένοι καὶ τεθεμελιωμένοι ἵνα, κτλ, is a matter of
doubt. By many of the older and later commentators,
it is connected with the preceding clause. The sense
would then be: 'That thus Christ may dwell in the
hearts of you, ἐν ταῖς καρδίαις ὑμῶν, ἐρριζωμένοι, rooted
and grounded in love.' This supposes the grammatical
construction to be irregular, as ἐρριζ. does not agree with
ὑμῶν. The only reason urged for this interpretation is,
that as Paul contemplates his readers as regenerated,
he could not pray that Christ should dwell in their
hearts, for such indwelling is inseparable from the new-
birth which they already enjoyed. To pray for the
indwelling of Christ would be to pray for their regeneration. The inward sense, therefore, despite the grammatical form of the words, requires such a construction
as shall harmonize with that idea. Paul prays, not
that Christ may dwell in their hearts, but that he may
dwell in their hearts as confirmed in love. It is not,
therefore, for the indwelling of Christ, but for their
confirmation in love, for which he prays. There does
not seem to be much force in this reasoning. The indwelling of Christ, is a thing of degrees. God mani-

fests himself more fully and uniformly in the hearts of his people at one time than at another. Any Christian may pray for the presence of God, and what is his indwelling but the manifestation of his presence? The majority of commentators, therefore, assuming merely a trajection of the particle ἵνα (comp. Acts 19, 4. Gal. 2, 10. 2 Thess. 2, 7), connect the clause in question with what follows; *in order that, being rooted and grounded in love, ye may understand,* &c. The effect of the inward strengthening by the Spirit, or of the indwelling of Christ, is this confirmation of love; and the effect of the confirmation of love, is ability to comprehend (in our measure) the love of Christ.

The love in which we are to be rooted is not the love of God or of Christ toward us, but either brotherly love or love as a Christian grace without determining its object. It is that love which flows from faith, and of which both God and the brethren are the objects. It is for the increase and ascendency of this grace through the indwelling of Christ, till it sustains and strengthens the whole inner man, so that the believer may stand as a well-rooted tree or as a well-founded building, that the apostle here prays.

ἐξισχύσητε καταλαβέσθαι, *may be fully able* (as the ἐκ is intensive) *to comprehend.* Without being strengthened by the Spirit in the inner man, without the indwelling of Christ, without being rooted and grounded in love, it is impossible to have any adequate apprehension of the gospel or of the love of Christ therein revealed. The apostle therefore prays that his readers may be thus strengthened, *in order that*, with all saints, they may be able to comprehend the truth of which he speaks. The knowledge in question is peculiar to *the holy*, i. e. the saints. It is a spiritual knowledge, both because of its origin and of its nature. It is derived from the Spirit, and it consists in those views which none but the spiritual can experience. The object of this knowledge is infinite. "It is high as heaven; what canst thou do? deeper than hell; what canst thou know? The measure thereof is longer than the earth, and broader than the sea?" Job 11, 8. 9. This language is used to express the infinitude of God. The apostle employs a similar mode of representation to indicate the boundless nature of the object of the believer's knowledge. To know what is infinite, and which therefore passes knowledge, can only mean to have some due appreciation of its nature, and of the fact that it is infinite. It is only thus that we can know space, immensity, eternity or God. Paul therefore would have us understand that the subject of which he speaks has a length and breadth, a depth and height, which pass all understanding. But what is this immeasurable theme? The answers given to this question are too numerous to be detailed. The main point is, whether the additional particular indicated by τέ, in the phrase γνῶναι τε, is to be sought in the difference between καταλαβέσθαί and γνῶναι (between comprehending and knowing), or in the difference of the objects. In the former case, the sense of the passage would be: 'That ye may comprehend and know the length and breadth, the depth and height of the love of Christ which passes knowledge.' Just as we would say, 'That ye may know and feel.' In *knowing*, according to Scriptural usage, the idea of experimental knowledge, or knowledge united with appropriate feeling, may well be included. This is the simpler explanation and gives a very good sense. According to the other view, the meaning is: 'That ye may comprehend the length and breadth, the depth and height of —— and also know the love of Christ;' something different from the love of Christ, being the object intended in the first clause. The great body of commentators, who adopt this view, suppose the reference is to the economy of redemption spoken of in v. 9. Paul prays that his hearers may comprehend the immensity of that plan of mercy, and know the love of Christ. Others refer to the manifold wisdom displayed in the salvation of men. Others to the unsearchable riches of Christ. All these subjects are indeed spoken of in the preceding context; but not in the prayer. At v. 14, there is such a change of the subject and in the progress of the discourse, as to make it harsh to go back of that verse to seek for an object. It is more natural to look for it in the following clause, where one is found which makes further search unnecessary. It is the love of Christ, i. e. his love to us which passes knowledge. It is infinite; not only because it inheres in an infinite subject, but because the condescension and sufferings to which it led, and the blessings which it secures for its objects, are beyond our comprehension. This love of Christ, though it surpasses the power of our understanding to comprehend, is still a subject of experimental knowledge. We may know how excellent, how wonderful, how free, how disinterested, how long-suffering, how manifold and constant, it is, and that it is infinite. And this is the highest and most sanctifying of all knowledge. Those who thus know the love of Christ towards them, purify themselves even as he is pure.

That ye might be filled with all the fulness of God. The words, εἰς πᾶν τὸ πλήρωμα τοῦ Θεοῦ, are not properly translated, *with all the fulness of God;* but *unto the complete fulness of God.* That is the standard which is to be reached. Πλήρωμα may have its ordinary signification, 'that by which any thing is filled,'— or its secondary meaning, *abundance,* as we would say, 'the fulness of a stream.' If the latter sense of the word be retained, Θεοῦ is the genitive of the object,— and 'the fulness of God' is that fulness, or plenitude which flows from him, and which he communicates. If the former and ordinary sense be adhered to, then Θεοῦ is the genitive of the subject, and the 'fulness of God' is that fulness of which God is full. It is the plenitude of the divine perfection, as in Col. 2, 9, where the fulness of the Godhead is said to dwell in Christ bodily. The majority of commentators take the phrase here in the same general sense. The fulness of God is that excellence, says Chrysostom, of which God himself is full. The expression is then parallel to that in Matt. 5, 48, "Be ye perfect even as your Father which is in heaven is perfect." And the truth presented is the same substantially as that in Eph. 4, 13, " Until we all come—unto a perfect man, unto the measure of the stature of the fulness of Christ;" and 1 Cor. 13, 12, " Then shall I know even as also I am known." Absolute perfection is the standard to which the believer is to attain. He is predestinated to be conformed to the image of the Son of God, Rom. 8, 29. He is to be perfect as man, as God is perfect as God; and the perfection of man consists in his being full of God; God dwelling in him so as absolutely to control all his cognitions, feelings, and outward actions. This is expressed in Theodoret's interpretation of the phrase in question: ἵνα τελείως αὐτὸν ἔνοικον δέξησθε.

If, however, the other view be adopted the result is nearly the same. " The fulness of God," is then the abundance of gifts and grace which flows from God; and the meaning of the whole clause is: ' That ye may be filled until the whole plenitude of the divine beneficence has passed over to you.' The end contemplated is the reception of the *donorum plenitudo*, or the *donorum Dei perfectio*. " He who has Christ," says Calvin, " has every thing that is required to our perfection in God, for this is what is meant by the *fulness of God*."

In favour, however, of the former view is the ordinary meaning of the word πλήρωμα, the meaning of the phrase fulness of God, in other passages, the analogy of Scripture as exhibited in the parallel passages above quoted, and the simplicity of the interpretation, no paraphrase being necessary to bring out the sense. We are to grow to the stature of Christ; to be perfect as our Father is perfect; to be filled unto the measure of the fulness of God. When we are thus filled the distance between us and God will still be infinite. This is the culminating point of the apostle's prayer. He prays that they may be strengthened in order to comprehend the infinite love of Christ; and that they might comprehend the love of Christ, in order that they might be filled unto the measure of God's fulness.

Vs. 20, 21. Paul's prayer had apparently reached a height beyond which neither faith, nor hope, nor even imagination could go, and yet he is not satisfied. An immensity still lay beyond. God was able to do not only what he had asked, but infinitely more than he knew how either to ask or think. Having exhausted all the forms of prayer, he casts himself on the infinitude of God, in full confidence that he can and will do all that omnipotence itself can effect. His power, not our prayers nor our highest conceptions, is the measure of the apostle's anticipations and desires. This idea he weaves into a doxology, which has in it more of heaven than of earth.

There are two forms of expression here united; Paul says, τῷ ὑπὲρ πάντα ποιῆσαι δυναμένῳ, *to him who is able to do more than all things;* and as though this were not enough, he adds, ὑπὲρ ἐκπερισσοῦ ὧν αἰτούμεθα ἤ νοοῦμεν, *exceeding abundantly above all we ask or think.* God is not only unlimited in himself,

but is unrestricted by our prayers or knowledge. No
definite bounds, therefore, can be set to what they may
expect in whom Christ dwells, and who are the objects
of his infinite love.

Κατὰ τὴν δύναμιν τὴν ἐνεργουμένην ἐν ἡμῖν, *according to the power that worketh in us.* The infinite power
of God from which so much may be expected, is the
same of which we are now the subjects. It is that
power which wrought in Christ when it raised him
from the dead, and set him at the right hand of God,
ch. 1, 19–20; and which has wrought an analogous
change in the believer in raising him from the death
of sin, and making him to sit in heavenly places in
Christ Jesus; and which still sustains and carries on
the work of salvation in the soul. The past is a foretaste and pledge of the future. Those who have been
raised from the dead, who have been transformed by
the renewing of their minds, translated from the kingdom of darkness into the kingdom of God's dear Son,
and in whom God himself dwells by his Spirit, having
already experienced a change which nothing but omnipotence could effect, may well join in the doxology to
Him who is able to do exceeding abundantly above all
we can ask or think.

The glory; ἡ δόξα is either the glory that is due,
or the glory which God has. To give glory to God, is
either to praise him, or to reveal his glory, i. e. cause
it to be seen and acknowledged. Thus the doxology,
To Him be glory—may mean either, ' Let Him be
praised;' or, ' Let His glory be acknowledged.'

*In the church by Christ Jesus.** The original is, ἐν τῇ ἐκκλησίᾳ ἐν Χριστῷ Ἰησοῦ, which Luther renders, *in the church which is in Christ*, i. e. the Christian church. This interpretation is adopted by several modern commentators. But in that case the article τῇ before ἐν Χριστῷ ought not to. be omitted. Besides, as the Christian church is the only church which could be thought of, the addition of the words *in Christ* would be unnecessary. The ordinary interpretation, therefore, is to be preferred. Glory is to be rendered to God in the church, and in and through Christ Jesus, as her head and representative. The *church* is the company of the redeemed here and in heaven; which constitutes one body through which God is to manifest his manifold wisdom, and which is through all ages to ascribe unto him glory, honour, and dominion.

The idea of eternity or of endless duration is variously expressed in Scripture. Sometimes eternity is conceived of as one, and the singular αἴων is used; sometimes as an endless succession of periods or ages, and then the plural αἰῶνες is used. Thus εἰς τὸν αἰῶνα, *to eternity*, and εἰς τοὺς αἰῶνας, or εἰς τοὺς αἰῶνας τῶν αἰώνων, *to the ages indefinitely*, i. e. endless ages, alike mean, *for ever*. So βασιλεὺς τοῦ αἰῶνος, *king of eternity*, and βασιλεὺς τῶν αἰώνων, *king of endless ages*,

---

* The Text here varies considerably. The Uncial MSS., A and C, several of the later ones, the Coptic and Vulgate, Jerome and Pelagius read, ἐν τῇ ἐκκλησίᾳ καὶ ἐν Χριστῷ Ἰησοῦ; D, F, G invert the order and read, ἐν Χριστῷ Ἰησοῦ καὶ ἐν τῇ ἐκκλησίᾳ. The majority of editors retain the common Text.

both mean *the king eternal*. The peculiarity of the case before us is, that the apostle combines these two forms : εἰς πάσας τὰς γενεὰς τοῦ αἰῶνος τῶν αἰώνων, *to all the generations of an eternity of ages*. This is in keeping with the cumulative character of the whole context. Finding no ordinary forms of expression suited to his demands, the apostle heaps together terms of the largest import to give some vent to thoughts and aspirations which he felt to be unutterable. These things belong to the στεναγμοὶ ἀλαλήτοι of which he speaks in Rom. 8, 26.

CHAPTER IV

SECTION I.—Vs. 1–16.

1. I therefore, the prisoner of the Lord, beseech you that ye
2. walk worthy of the vocation wherewith ye are called, with
all lowliness and meekness, with long-suffering, forbearing one
3. another in love; endeavouring to keep the unity of the Spirit
4. in the bond of peace. *There is* one body, and one Spirit, even
5. as ye are called in one hope of your calling; one Lord, one
6. faith, one baptism, one God and Father of all, who *is* above
7. all, and through all, and in you all. But unto every one of us
is given grace according to the measure of the gift of Christ.
8. Wherefore he saith, When he ascended up on high, he led cap-
9. tivity captive, and gave gifts unto men. Now that he ascended, what is it but that he also descended first into the lower
10. parts of the earth? He that descended is the same also that
ascended up far above all heavens, that he might fill all things.
11. And he gave some, apostles; and some, prophets; and some,
12. evangelists; and some, pastors and teachers; for the perfecting of the saints, for the work of the ministry, for the edifying
13. of the body of Christ; till we all come in the unity of the
faith, and of the knowledge of the Son of God, unto a perfect

man, unto the measure of the stature of the fulness of Christ :

14. that we *henceforth* be no more children, tossed to and fro, and carried about with every wind of doctrine, by the sleight of men, *and* cunning craftiness, whereby they lie in wait to de-

15. ceive : but speaking the truth in love, may grow up into him

16. in all things, which is the head, *even* Christ : from whom the whole body fitly joined together and compacted by that which every joint supplieth, according to the effectual working in the measure of every part, maketh increase of the body unto the edifying of itself in love.

ANALYSIS.

The apostle exhorts his readers to walk worthy of their vocation. Such a walk should be characterized by humility, meekness, long-suffering, and zeal to promote spiritual unity and peace, vs. 1–3. The church is one because it is one body, has one Spirit, one hope, one Lord, one faith, one baptism, and one God and Father who is over, through, and in all its members, vs. 4–6.

This unity, however, is consistent with great diversity of gifts, which Christ distributes according to his own will, v. 7. This is confirmed by a passage from the Psalms which speaks of the Messiah as giving gifts to men ; which passage it is shown must refer to Christ, since it speaks of a divine person ascending to heaven, which necessarily implies a preceding descent to the earth, vs. 9–10. The gifts which Christ bestows on his church are the various classes of ministers, apostles, prophets, evangelists, and pastors who are teachers,

v. 11. The design of the ministry is the edification of the church, and to bring all its members to unity of faith and knowledge, and to the full stature of Christ; that they should no longer have the instability of children, but be a firm, compact, and growing body in living union with Christ its head, vs. 12–16.

COMMENTARY.

V. 1. Παρακαλῶ οὖν ὑμᾶς ἐγὼ ὁ δέσμιος ἐν Κυρίῳ. The exhortation is a general one; it flows from the preceding doctrines, and is enforced by the authority, and the sufferings of him who gave it. As you are partakers of the redemption purchased by Christ, "*I therefore* beseech you." I the prisoner, not of, but *in* the Lord, ἐν Κυρίῳ. He was a prisoner because he was in the Lord and for his sake. It was as a Christian and in the cause of Christ he suffered bonds. Compare the frequently occurring expressions, συνεργὸς ἐν Χριστῷ, ἀγαπητὸς ἐν Κυρίῳ, δόκιμος ἐν Χριστῷ, ἐκλεκτὸς ἐν Κυρίῳ. He speaks as a prisoner not to excite sympathy, not merely to add weight to his exhortation, but rather as exulting that he was counted worthy to suffer for Christ's sake. This is in accordance with the beautiful remark of Theodoret: τοῖς διὰ τὸν Χριστὸν δεσμοῖς ἐναβρύνεται μᾶλλον ἢ βασιλεὺς διαδήματι, he glories in his chains more than a king in his diadem. 'I, the martyr Paul, the crowned apostle, exhort you,' &c. All is thus in keeping with the elevated tone of feeling which marks the preceding passage.

The exhortation is, ἀξίως περιπατῆσαι τῆς κλήσεως ἧς ἐκλήθητε, to walk worthy of the vocation wherewith they were called. That vocation was to sonship; ch. 1, 5. This includes three things—holiness, exaltation, and unity. They were called to be conformed to the image of Christ, to share in his exaltation and glory, and to constitute one family as all are the children of God. A conversation becoming such a vocation, therefore, should be characterized by holiness, humility, and mutual forbearance and brotherly love. The apostle, therefore, immediately adds, with all lowliness and meekness. Undeserved honour always produces these effects upon the ingenuous. To be raised from the depths of degradation and misery and made the sons of God, and thus exalted to an inconceivable elevation and dignity, does and must produce humility and meekness. Where these effects are not found, we may conclude the exaltation has not taken place. Lowliness of mind, ταπεινοφροσύνη, includes a low estimate of one's self, founded on the consciousness of guilt and weakness, and a consequent disposition to be low, unnoticed, and unpraised. It stands opposed not only to self-complacency and self-conceit, but also to self-exaltation, and setting one's self up to attract the honour which comes from men. This is taught in Rom. 12, 16, where τὰ ὑψηλὰ φρονοῦντες, seeking high things, is opposed to the lowliness of mind here inculcated. There is a natural connection between humility and meekness, and therefore they are here joined together as in so many other places. Πραότης is softness, mild-

ness, gentleness, which when united with strength, is one of the loveliest attributes of our nature. The blessed Saviour says of himself, "I am meek (πρᾶος) and lowly in heart," Matt. 11, 29; and the apostle speaks of "the gentleness of Christ," 2 Cor. 10, 1. Meekness is that unresisting, uncomplaining disposition of mind, which enables us to bear without irritation or resentment the faults and injuries of others. It is the disposition of which the lamb, dumb before the shearers, is the symbol, and which was one of the most wonderful of all the virtues of the Son of God. The most exalted of all beings was the gentlest.

The third associated virtue which becomes the vocation wherewith we are called, is *long-suffering; μακρο-θυμία,* a disposition which leads to the suppression of anger, 2 Cor. 6, 6. Gal. 3, 22. Col. 3, 12; to deferring the infliction of punishment, and is therefore often attributed to God, Rom. 2, 4; 9, 22. 1 Pet. 3, 10; and to patient forbearance towards our fellow men, 2 Tim. 4, 2. 1 Tim. 1, 16. It is explained by what follows, *forbearing one another in love.* Or, rather, the three virtues, humility, meekness, and long-suffering, are all illustrated and manifested in this mutual forbearance. Ἀνέχω, is *to restrain,* ἀνέχομαι, *to restrain oneself,* ἀνεχόμενοι ἀλλήλων ἐν ἀγάπῃ, therefore, means *restraining yourselves in reference to each other in love.* Let love induce you to be forbearing towards each other.

The construction of the passage adopted by our translators is preferable to either connecting μετὰ μακροθ. with ἀνεχ. "*with long-suffering forbearing,*" or

detaching ἐν ἀγάπῃ from this clause and connecting it
with the following one, so as to read ἐν ἀγάπῃ σπουδάζοντες. The participle σπουδάζοντες is of course connected with what precedes. They were to walk worthy
of their vocation, forbearing one another, endeavouring
to keep the unity of the Spirit. Of the phrase *unity
of the spirit*, there are three interpretations. 1. Ecclesiastical unity, so Grotius : unitatem ecclesiae, quod
est corpus spirituale. Instead of that discordance manifested in the church of Corinth, for example, not only
in their division into parties, but in the conflict of
" spirits," or contentions among those endowed with
spiritual gifts, the apostle would have the Ephesians
manifest in the church that they were animated by one
spirit. But this is foreign not only to the simple meaning of the terms, but also to the context. 2. The word
spirit is assumed to refer to the human spirit, and the
unity of the spirit to mean, *concordia animorum*, or
harmony. 3. The only interpretation in accordance
with the ordinary usage of the words and with the context, is that which makes the phrase in question mean
that unity of which the Spirit is the author. Every
where the indwelling of the Holy Ghost is said to be
the principle of unity in the body of Christ. This
unity may be promoted or disturbed. The exhortation
is that the greatest zeal should be exercised in its pre-
servation ; and the means by which it is to be preserved is *the bond of peace*. That is, that bond which
is peace. The peace which results from love, humility,
meekness, and mutual forbearance, is essential to the

union and communion of the members of Christ's body, which is the fruit and evidence of the Spirit's presence. As hatred, pride and contention among Christians cause the Spirit to withdraw from them, so love and peace secure his presence. And as his presence is the condition and source of all good, and his absence the source of all evil, the importance of the duty enjoined cannot be over-estimated. Our Lord said: "Blessed are the peace-makers." Blessed are those who endeavour to preserve among the discordant elements of the church, including as it does men of different nations, manners, names and denominations, that peace which is the condition of the Spirit's presence. The apostle labours in this, as in his other epistles, to bring the Jewish and Gentile Christians to this spirit of mutual forbearance, and to convince them that we are all one in Christ Jesus.*

As in Col. 3, 14, love is said to be "the bond of perfectness," many commentators understand "the bond of peace" in this passage to be love. So Bengel: *Vinculum quo pax retinetur est ipse amor.* But as the passages are not really parallel, and as in Colossians

---

* O si animis nostris insideret haec cogitatio, hanc legem nobis esse propositam, ut non magis dissidere inter se possint filii Dei, quam regnum coelorum dividi, quanto in colenda fraterna benevolentia essemus cautiores? quanto nobis horrori essent omnes simultates, si reputaremus, ut decet, eos omnes se alienare a regno Dei, qui a fratribus se disjungunt? sed nescio qui fit, ut secure nos esse filios Dei gloriemur, mutuae inter nos fraternitatis obliti. Discamus itaque ex Paulo, ejusdem hereditatis minime esse capaces, nisi qui unum corpus sunt et unus spiritus.—CALVIN.

love is mentioned and here it is not; and as the sense is simple and good without any deviation from the plain meaning of the words, the great majority of interpreters adopt the view given above.

V. 4. Having urged the duty of preserving unity, the apostle proceeds to state both its nature and grounds. It is a unity which arises from the fact—there is and can be but one body, one Spirit, one hope, one Lord, one faith, one baptism, and one God.

One body, ἐν σῶμα. This is not an exhortation, but a declaration. The meaning is not, Let us be united in one body, or in soul and body; but, as the context requires, it is a simple declaration. There is one body, viz. one mystical body of Christ. All believers are in Christ; they are all his members; they constitute not many, much less conflicting bodies, but one. "We, being many, are one body in Christ, and every one members one of another." Rom. 12, 5. 1 Cor. 10, 17; 12, 27. In ch. 1, 23, the church is said "to be his body, the fulness of him that filleth all in all." As all true believers are members of this body, and as all are not included in any one external organization, it is obvious that the one body of which the apostle speaks, is not one outward visible society, but a spiritual body of which Christ is the head and all the renewed are members. The relation, therefore, in which believers stand to each other, is that which subsists between the several members of the human body. A want of sympathy is evidence of want of membership.

One spirit, ἐν πνεῦμα. This again does not mean

one heart. It is not an exhortation to unanimity of
feeling, or a declaration that such unanimity exists.
*Quasi diceret, nos penitus corpore et anima, non ex parte
duntaxat, debere esse unitos.* The context and the
analogy of Scripture, as a comparison of parallel passages would evince, prove that by *spirit* is meant the
Holy Spirit. As there is one body, so there is one
Spirit, which is the life of that body and dwells in all
its members. "By one Spirit," says the apostle, "are
we all baptized into one body, whether we be Jews or
Gentiles, whether we be bond or free; and have all
been made to drink into one Spirit." 1 Cor. 12, 13.
Of all believers, he says, "The Spirit of God dwelleth
in you." 1 Cor. 3, 16; 6, 19. Rom. 8, 9. 11. There
is no doctrine of Scripture more plainly revealed than
that the Spirit of God dwells in all believers, and that
his presence is the ultimate ground of their unity as
the body of Christ. As the human body is one because
pervaded by one soul; so the body of Christ is one because it is pervaded by one and the same Spirit, who
dwelling in all is a common principle of life. All sins
against unity, are, therefore, sins against the Holy
Ghost. They dissever that which he binds together.
Our relation to Christ as members of his body; and
our relation to the Holy Spirit who is our life, demands
of us that we love our brethren and live at peace with
them.

Even as ye are called in one hope of your calling.
καθὼς καὶ ἐκλήθητε ἐν μιᾷ ἐλπίδι τῆς κλήσεως ὑμῶν. *Inasmuch as.* That is, believers are one body and have

one spirit, because they have one hope. The fact that they all have the same high destiny, and are filled with the same expectations, proves that they are one. The unity of their hope is another evidence and element of the communion of saints. The Holy Ghost dwelling in them gives rise to the same aspirations, to the same anticipations of the same glorious inheritance, to a participation of which they had been called. The word *hope* is sometimes used for the things hoped for, as when the apostle speaks of the hope laid up in heaven. Col. 1, 5. See also Titus 2, 13. Heb. 6, 18. Most frequently of course it has its subjective sense, viz. the expectation of future good. There is no reason for departing from that sense here, though the other is intimately allied with it, and is necessarily implied. It is because the object is the same, that the expectation is the same. *Hope of your calling*, is the hope which flows from your vocation. The inward, effectual call of the Holy Spirit gives rise to this hope for two reasons. First, because their call is to the inheritance of the saints in light. They naturally hope to obtain what they are invited to receive. They are invited to reconciliation and fellowship with God, and therefore they hope for his salvation ; and in the second place, the nature of this call makes it productive of hope. It is at once an earnest and a foretaste of their future inheritance. See ch. 1, 14, and 1 Cor. 1, 22. It assures the believer of his interest in the blessings of redemption, Rom. 8, 16; and as a drop of water makes the thirsty traveller long for the flowing stream, so the first fruits of the Spirit, his first sanctifying operations on the heart, cause it to thirst after God. Ps. 42, 1. 2. Hope includes both expectation and desire, and therefore the inward work of the Spirit being of the nature both of an earnest and a foretaste, it necessarily produces hope.

Another ground of the unity of the church is, that all its members have ONE LORD. Lordship includes the ideas of possession and authority. A lord, in proper sense, is both owner and sovereign. When used in reference to God or Christ, the word expresses these ideas in the highest degree. Christ is THE LORD, i. e. omnium rerum summus dominus et possessor. He is our Lord, i. e. our rightful owner and absolute sovereign. This proprietorship and sovereignty pertain to the soul and to the body. We are not our own, and should glorify him in our body and spirit which are his. Our reason is subject to his teaching, our conscience to his commands, our hearts and lives to his control. We are his slaves. And herein consists our liberty. It is the *felix necessitas boni* of which Augustin speaks. It is analogous to absolute subjection to truth and holiness, only it is to a person who is infinite in knowledge and in excellence. This lordship over us belongs to Christ not merely as God, or as the Logos, but as the Theanthropos. It is founded not simply on his divinity, but also and specially on the work of redemption. We are his because he has bought us with his own most precious blood. 1 Cor. 6, 20. 1 Pet. 1, 1. For this end he both died and rose again, that he might be Lord both of dead and of living. Rom. 14, 9. Such being the nature and the grounds of the sovereignty of Christ, it necessarily binds together his people. The slaves of one master and the subjects of the same sovereign are intimately united among themselves, although the ownership and authority are merely external. But when, as in our relation to Christ, the proprietorship and sovereignty are absolute, extending to the soul as well as to the body, the union is unspeakably more intimate. Loyalty to a common Lord and master animates with one spirit all the followers of Christ.

One faith. This is the fifth bond of union enumerated by the apostle. Many commentators deny that the word πίστις is ever used for the object of faith, or the things believed; they therefore deny that *one faith* here means one creed. But as this interpretation is in accordance with the general usage of language, and as there are so many cases in which the objective sense of the word is best suited to the context, there seems to be no sufficient reason for refusing to admit it. In Gal. 1, 23, Paul says, "He preached the faith;" in Acts 6, 7, men, it is said, "were obedient to the faith." The apostle Jude speaks of "the faith once delivered to the saints." In these and in many other instances the objective sense is the natural one. In many cases both senses of the word may be united. It may be said of speculative believers that they have one faith, so far as they profess the same creed, however they may differ in their real convictions. All the members of the Church of England have one faith, because they all profess to adopt the Thirty-Nine Articles, although the greatest diversity of doctrine prevails among them. But true believers have one faith, not only because they profess the same creed, but also because they really and inwardly embrace it. Their union, therefore, is not merely an external union, but inward and spiritual. They have the same faith objectively and subjectively. This unity of faith is not perfect. That, as the apostle tells us in a subsequent part of this chap ter, is the goal towards which the church contends. Perfect unity in faith implies perfect knowledge and perfect holiness. It is only as to fundamental doctrines, those necessary to piety and therefore necessary to salvation, that this unity can be affirmed of the whole church as it now exists on earth. Within these limits all the true people of God are united. They all receive the Scriptures as the word of God, and acknowledge themselves subject to their teachings. They all recognize and worship the Lord Jesus as the Son of God. They all trust to his blood for redemption and to his Spirit for sanctification.

One baptism. Under the old dispensation when a Gentile became a Jew, he professed to accede to the covenant which God had made with his people, and he received the sign of circumcision not only as a badge of discipleship but as the seal of the covenant. All the circumcised therefore were *foederati*, men bound together by the bonds of a covenant which united them to the same God and to each other. So under the new dispensation the baptized are *foederati;* men bound together in covenant with Christ and with each other. There is but one baptism. All the baptized make the same profession, accept the same covenant, and are consecrated to the same Lord and Redeemer. They are, therefore, one body. "For as many as have been baptized into Christ, have put on Christ. There is neither Jew nor Greek, there is neither bond nor free, there is neither male ι,or female, for ye are all one in Christ Jesus." Gal. 3, 27. 28.

V. 6. *One God and Father of all, who is over all, and through all and in us all,* εἷς Θεὸς καὶ Πατὴρ πάντων, ὁ ἐπὶ πάντων καὶ διὰ πάντων καὶ ἐν πᾶσιν ἡμῖν. As the church is one because pervaded by one Spirit, and because it is owned and governed by one Lord, so it is one because it has one God and Father; one glorious Being to whom it sustains the twofold relation of creature and child. This God is not merely *over* us, as afar off, but through all and in us all, i. e. pervading and filling all with his sustaining and life-giving presence. There are many passages to which the doctrine of the Trinity gives a sacred rhythm, though the doctrine itself is not directly asserted. It is so here. There is one Spirit, one Lord, one God and Father. The unity of the church is founded on this doctrine. It is one because there is to us one God the Father, one Lord, one Spirit. It is a truly mystical union; not a mere union of opinion, of interest, or of feeling; but something supernatural arising from a common principle of life. This life is not the natural life which belongs to us as creatures; nor intellectual, which belongs to us as rational beings; but it is spiritual life, called elsewhere the life of God in the soul. And as this life is common, on the one hand, to Christ and all his members—and on the other, to Christ and God, this union of the church is not only with Christ, but with the Triune God. Therefore in Scripture it is said that the Spirit dwells in believers, that Christ dwells in them, and that God dwells in them. And, therefore, also our Lord prays for his people, " That they all may be one; as thou, Father, art in me, and I in thee, that they also may be one in us." John 17, 21.

It is obvious from the whole connection that the word πάντων (" of all," and " through all "), is not neuter. The apostle does not refer to the dominion of God over the universe, or to his providential agency throughout all nature. Neither is the reference to his dominion over rational creatures or over mankind. It is the relation of God to the church, of which the whole passage treats. God as Father is over all its members, through them all and in them all. The church is a habitation of God through the Spirit. It is his temple in which he dwells and which is pervaded in all its parts by his presence. The preposition διά, therefore, does not here express instrumentality, but diffusion. It is not that God operates " through all " (διὰ πάντων), but that he pervades all and abides in all. This is the climax. To be filled with God; to be pervaded by his presence, and controlled by him, is to attain the summit of all created excellence, blessedness and glory.

V. 7. This unity of the church, although it involves the essential equality of all believers, is still consistent with great diversity as to gifts, influence, and honour. According to the apostle's favourite illustration, it is like the human body, which is composed of many members with different functions. It is not all eye nor all ear. This diversity of gifts is not only consistent with unity, but is essential to it. The body is not one member but many. In every organism a diversity of parts is necessary to the unity of the whole. If all were one member, asks the apostle, where were the body? Summa praesentis loci est, says Calvin, quod Deus in neminem omnia contulerit; sed quisque certam mensuram receperit; ut alii aliis indigeant et in commune conferendo quod singulis datum est, alii alios mutuo juvent. The position, moreover, of each member in the body, is not determined by itself, but by God. The eye does not make itself the eye, nor the ear, the ear. It is thus in the church. The different positions, gifts, and functions of its members, are determined not by themselves but by Christ. All this is taught by the apostle when he says, "But (i. e. notwithstanding the unity of the church) unto every one of us is given grace, according to the measure of the gift of Christ." There is this diversity of gifts, and the distribution of these gifts is in the hand of Christ. The *grace* here spoken of includes the inward spiritual gift, and the influence, function or office, as the case might be, flowing from it. Some were apostles, some prophets, some evangelists. The *grace* which made them such, was the inward gift and the outward office.

The giver is Christ; he is the source of the spiritual influence conferring power, and the official appointment conferring authority. He, therefore, is God, because the source of the inward life of the church and of its authority and that of its officers. He is sovereign in the distribution of his gifts. They are distributed, κατὰ τὸ μέτρον τῆς δωρεᾶς τοῦ Χριστοῦ, *according to the measure of the gift of Christ;* that is, as he sees fit to give. The rule is not our merit, or our previous capacity, nor our asking, but his own good pleasure. Paul was made an apostle, who before was a blasphemer and injurious. The duty, as the apostle teaches, which arises from all this is, that every one should be contented with the position assigned him; neither envying those above, nor despising those below him. To refuse to occupy the position assigned us in the church, is to refuse to belong to it at all. If the foot refuses to be the foot, it does not become the hand, but is cut off and perishes. Sympathy is the law of every body having a common life. If one member suffers, all suffer; and if one rejoices, all rejoice. We can tell, therefore, whether we belong to the body of Christ, by ascertaining whether we have this contentment with our lot, and this sympathy with our fellow members.

V. 8. The position which the preceding verse assigns to the Lord Jesus as the source of all life and power in the church, is so exalted, that the apostle interrupts himself to show that this representation is in accordance with what the Scriptures had already taught on this subject. The seventh verse speaks of Christ giving gifts. As this was his office, the Scriptures speak of him as a conqueror laden with spoils, enriched by his victories, and giving gifts to men. That the Psalmist had reference to the Messiah, is evident, because the passage speaks of his ascending. But for a divine person to ascend to heaven, supposes a previous descent to the earth. It was the Son of God, the Messiah, who descended, and therefore it was the Son of God who ascended, and who is represented by the sacred writer as enriched by his triumphant work on earth, and distributing the fruits of his conquest as he pleased. This seems to be the general sense of the passage in the connection, although it is replete with difficulties. The great truth is, that Christ's exaltation is the reward of his humiliation. By his obedience and sufferings he conquered the Prince of this world, he redeemed his people, and obtained the right to bestow upon them all needed good. He is exalted to give the Holy Ghost, and all his gifts and graces, to grant repentance and remission of sins. This great truth is foreshadowed and foretold in the Old Testament Scriptures. *Wherefore he saith,* διὸ λέγει, i. e. God, or the Scriptures. "Having ascended up on high, he led captivity captive, and gave gifts unto men." That is, what I have said respecting Christ being the distributor of spiritual gifts, is in accordance with the prophetic declaration, that the ascended Messiah should give gifts to men. The Messiah is represented by the Psalmist as a conqueror, leading captives in triumph, and laden with spoils which he distributes to his fol-

lowers. Thus Christ conquered. He destroyed him
that hath the power of death, i. e. the devil. He delivered those who through the fear of death were subject to bondage. Heb. 2, 15. Having spoiled principalities and powers, he made a show of them openly,
triumphing over them. Col. 2. 15. When a strong
man armed keepeth his palace, his goods are in peace;
but when a stronger than he cometh upon him, and
overcometh him, he taketh from him all his armour
wherein he trusted, and divideth his spoil. Luke, 11,
21. 22. Such is the familiar mode of representation
respecting the work of Christ. He conquered Satan.
He led captivity captive. The abstract is for the concrete—captivity for captives—αἰχμαλωσία for αἰχμά-
λωτοι as συμμαχία for σύμμαχοι. Compare Judges 5,
12, "Awake, awake, Deborah, awake, awake, utter a
song: arise, Barak, and lead thy captivity captive, thou
son of Abinoam." These captives thus led in triumph
may be either the enemies of Christ, Satan, sin, and
death, which is the last enemy which shall be destroyed;
or his people, redeemed by his power and subdued by
his grace. The former is perhaps the more consistent
with the figure, and with the parallel passages quoted
above. Both are true; that is, it is true that Christ
has conquered Satan, and leads him captive; and it is
also true that he redeems his people and subdues them
to himself, and leads them as willing captives. They
are made willing, in the day of his power. Calvin,
therefore, unites both representations: Neque enim
Satanam modo et peccatum et mortem totosque inferos

prostravit, sed ex rebellibus quotidie facit sibi obse-
quentem populum, quum verbo suo carnis nostræ lasci-
viam domat; rursus hostes suos, h. e. impios omnes
quasi ferreis catenis continet constrictos, dum illorum
furorem cohibet sua virtute, ne plus valeant, quam illis
concedit. This clause of the quotation is, however,
entirely subordinate. The stress lies on the last clause,
"He gave gifts to men."

There are two serious difficulties connected with
this citation. The first is, that the quotation does not
agree with the original. In the Ps. 68, 18, the passage
is, "Thou hast received gifts among men." Paul has
it, "He gave gifts to man." To get over this difficulty
some have supposed that the apostle does not quote the
Psalm, but some Hymn which the Ephesians were in
the habit of using. But this is not only contrary to
the uniform usage of the New Testament writers, but
also to the whole context, for the apostle argues from
the passage quoted as of divine authority. Others
have assumed an error in the Hebrew text. Ration-
alists say it is a misquotation from failure of memory.
Others argue that the word לָקַח, used by the Psalmist,
means to give as well as to take. Or, at least, it often
means to bring; and therefore, the original passage
may be translated, "Thou hast brought gifts among
men;" the sense of which is, 'Thou hast given gifts to
men.' The difference is thus reduced to a mere verbal
alteration, the sense remaining the same. It is a strong
confirmation of this view that the Chaldee Paraphrase
expresses the same sense: *dedisti dona filiis hominum.*

Dr. Addison Alexander in his comment on Ps. 68, 18. remarks, "To *receive gifts* on the one hand and *bestow gifts* on the other are correlative ideas and expressions, so that Paul, in applying this description of a theocratic triumph to the conquests of our Saviour, substitutes one of these expressions for the other." This is perhaps the most natural solution. The divine writers of the New Testament, filled with the same Spirit, which moved the ancient prophets, are not tied to the mere form, but frequently give the general sense of the passages which they quote. A conqueror always distributes the spoils he takes. He receives to give. And, therefore, in depicting the Messiah as a conqueror, it is perfectly immaterial whether it is said, He received gifts, or, He gave gifts. The sense is the same. He is a conqueror laden with spoils, and able to enrich his followers.

The second difficulty connected with this quotation is that Ps. 68 is not Messianic. It does not refer to the Messiah, but to the triumphs of God over his enemies. Yet the apostle not only applies it to Christ, but argues to prove that it must refer to him. This difficulty finds its solution in three principles which are applicable not only to this, but also to many similar passages. The first is the typical character of the old dispensation. It was a shadow of good things to come. There was not only a striking analogy between the experience of the ancient people of God, in their descent into Egypt, their deliverance from the house of bondage, their journey through the wilderness, and their entrance into Canaan, and the experience of the church, but this analogy was a designed prefiguration—God's dealings as the head of the ancient theocracy, were typical of his dealings with the church. His delivering his people, his conquering their enemies, and his enriching his followers with their spoil, were all adumbrations of the higher work of Christ. As the passover was both commemorative of the deliverance out of Egypt and typical of the redemption effected by Christ; so, many of the descriptions of the works and triumphs of God under the old economy are both historical and prophetic. Thus the Psalm quoted by the apostle is a history of the conquests of God over the enemies of his ancient people, and a prophecy of the conquests of the Messiah.

The second principle applicable to this and similar cases, is the identity of the Logos or Son manifested in the flesh under the new dispensation with the manifested Jehovah of the old economy. Hence what is said of the one, is properly assumed to be said of the other. Therefore, as Moses says Jehovah led his people through the wilderness, Paul says Christ led them. 1 Cor. 10, 4. As Isaiah saw the glory of Jehovah in the temple, John says he saw the glory of Christ. John 12, 41. As it is written in the prophets, "As I live, saith Jehovah, every knee shall bow to me, and every tongue shall confess to God," Is. 45, 23, Paul says, this proves that we must all stand before the judgment seat of Christ. Rom. 14, 10. 11. What in Ps. 102, 25, &c., is said of God as creator, and as eternal and immutable, is in Hebrews 1, 10, applied to Christ. On the same principle what is said in Ps. 68, 18, of Jehovah as ascending to heaven and leading captivity captive, is here said to refer to Christ.

There is still a third principle to be taken into consideration. Many of the historical and prophetic descriptions of the Old Testament are not exhausted by any one application or fulfilment. The promise that Japheth should dwell in the tents of Shem, was fulfilled every time the descendants of the former were made to share in the blessings temporal or spiritual of the latter. The predictions of Isaiah of the redemption of Israel were not exhausted by the deliverance of the people of God from the Babylonish captivity, but had a direct reference to the higher redemption to be effected by Christ. The glowing descriptions of the blessings consequent on the advent of the Messiah, relate not merely to the consequences of his first advent, but to all that is to follow his coming the second time without sin unto salvation. The prediction that every knee shall bow to God and every tongue confess to him, is a prediction not only of the universal prevalence of the true religion; but also, as the apostle teaches, of a general judgment at the last day. In like manner, what the Old Testament says of Jehovah descending and ascending, of his conquering his enemies and enriching his people, is not exhausted by his figurative descending to manifest his power, nor by such conspicuous theophanies as occurred on Sinai and in the Temple, or in the triumphs recorded in the Hebrew

Scriptures, but refer also to his personal advent in the flesh, to his ascension and his spiritual triumphs. It is, therefore, in perfect accordance with the whole analogy of Scripture, that the apostle applies what is said of Jehovah in Ps. 68 as a conqueror, to the work of the Lord Jesus, who, as God manifested in the flesh, ascended on high leading captivity captive and giving gifts unto men.

Vs. 9. 10. *Now that he ascended, what is it but that he also descended first into the lower parts of the earth ? He that descended is the same also that ascended up far above all heavens, that he might fill all things.*

The obvious design of these verses is to show that the passage quoted from the Psalmist refers to Christ. The proof lies in the fact that ascension in the case of a divine person, a giver of spiritual gifts to men, implies a previous descent. It was Christ who descended, and therefore, it is Christ who ascended. It is true the Old Testament often speaks of God's descending, and therefore, they may speak of his ascending. But according to the apostle, the divine person intended in those representations was the Son, and no previous descent or ascent, no previous triumph over his enemies, included all that the Spirit of prophecy intended by such representations. And, therefore, the Psalmist must be understood as having included in the scope of his language the most conspicuous and illustrious of God's condescensions and exaltations. All other comings were but typical of his coming in the flesh, and all ascensions were typical of his ascension from the grave.

The apostle, therefore, here teaches that God, the subject of the sixty-eighth Psalm, descended " into the lower parts of the earth ;" that "he ascended up above all heavens," and that this was with the design " that he might fill all things."

The Hebrew phrase תַּחְתִּיּוֹת אֶרֶץ to which the apostle's τὰ κατώτερα μέρη τῆς γῆς, (the lower parts of the earth,) answers, is used for the earth in opposition to heaven, Is. 44, 23 ; probably for the grave in Ps. 63, 10 ; as a poetical designation for the womb in Ps. 139, 15 ; and for Hades or the invisible world, Ez. 32, 24. Perhaps the majority of commentators take this last to be the meaning of the passage before us. They suppose the reference is to the *descensus ad inferos*, or to Christ's " descending into hell." But in the first place this idea is entirely foreign to the meaning of the passage in the Psalm on which the apostle is commenting. In the second place, there as here, the only descent of which the context speaks is opposed to the ascending to heaven. ' He that ascended to heaven is he who first descended to earth.' In the third place, this is the opposition so often expressed in other places and in other forms of expression, as in John 3, 13, " No man hath ascended up to heaven, but he that came down from heaven, even the Son of Man who is in heaven." John 6, 38, " I came down from heaven." John 8, 14, " I know whence I came and whither I go." John 16, 28, " I came forth from the Father, and am come into the world ; again, I leave the world, and go to the Father." The expression of the apostle there-

fore means, " the lower parts, viz. the earth." The
genitive τῆς γῆς is the common genitive of apposition.
Compare Acts 2, 19, where the heaven above is opposed to the earth beneath ; and John 8, 23.

He that descended to earth, who assumed our
nature, is the same also that ascended *up far above all
heavens.* Ὑπεράνω, *longe supra,* expressing the highest exaltation. As the Hebrew word for heaven is in
the plural form, the New Testament writers often use
the plural even when the heavens are considered as
one, as in the phrase βασιλεία τῶν οὐρανῶν. But often
there is a reference to a plurality of heavens, as when
the expression " all heavens " is used. The Jews
reckoned seven heavens, and Paul, 2 Cor. 12, 2, speaks
of the third heavens ; the atmosphere, the region of the
stars, and above all the abode of God. *Above all
heavens* plainly means above the whole universe ;
above all that is created visible and invisible ; above
thrones, principalities, and powers. All things, all
created things, are subject to the ascended Redeemer.

He is thus exalted, ἵνα πληρώσῃ τὰ πάντα, *that he
might fill all things.* As the word πληρόω signifies
to fill, to fulfil, to render perfect, and *to accomplish,*
these words may mean—1. That he might fill all
things, i. e. the universe with his presence and power.
2. That he might fulfil all the predictions and promises
of God respecting his kingdom. 3. That he might
render all perfect, replete with grace and goodness.
4. That he might accomplish all things necessary to
the consummation of his work. The first interpreta-

tion is greatly to be preferred. *Tὰ πάντα* properly means the universe; and if taken to mean any thing else, it must be because the context demands it, which is not the case here. Secondly, this passage is evidently parallel with ch. 1, 21, where also it is said of Christ as exalted, that " he fills the universe in all its parts." Thirdly, the analogy of Scripture is in favour of this interpretation. The omnipresence and universal dominion of God are elsewhere expressed in a similar way. " Do I not fill heaven and earth, saith the Lord." Jer. 23, 24. The same grand idea is expressed in Matt. 28, 18, " All power is given unto me in heaven and upon earth;" and in Phil. 2, 9. 10, and in many other places. It is not of the ubiquity of Christ's body of which the apostle speaks, as the Lutherans contend, but of the universal presence and power of the ascended Son of God. It is God clothed in our nature, who now exercises this universal dominion; and, therefore, the apostle may well say of Christ, as the incarnate God, that he gives gifts unto men.

V. 11. *Καὶ αὐτὸς ἔδωκε, and He gave.* He, the ascended Saviour, to whom all power and all resources have been given—he gave, some, apostles; and some, prophets; and some, evangelists; and some, pastors and teachers. These were among the gifts which Christ gave his church; which, though implying diversity of grace and office, were necessary to its unity as an organized whole. These offices are mentioned in the order of their importance. First, the apostles, the immediate messengers of Christ, the witnesses for him, of his doctrines, his miracles, and of his resurrection; infallible as teachers and absolute as rulers in virtue of the gift of inspiration and of their commission. No man, therefore, could be an apostle unless—1. He was immediately appointed by Christ. 2. Unless he had seen him after his resurrection and had received the knowledge of the Gospel by immediate revelation. 3. Unless he was rendered infallible by the gift of inspiration. These things constituted the office and were essential to its authority. Those who without these gifts and qualifications claimed the office, are called " false apostles."

2. *Prophets.* A prophet is one who speaks for another, a spokesman, as Aaron was the prophet of Moses. Those whom God made his organs in speaking to men were prophets, whether their communications were doctrinal, preceptive, or prophetic in the restricted sense of the term. Every one who spoke by inspiration, was a prophet. The prophets of the New Testament differed from the apostles, in that their inspiration was occasional, and therefore their authority as teachers subordinate. The nature of their office is fully taught in 1 Cor. 14, 1–40. As the gift of infallibility was essential to the apostolic office, so the gift of occasional inspiration was essential to the prophetic office. It is inconceivable that God should invest any set of men with the authority claimed and exercised by the apostles and prophets of the New Testament, requiring all men to believe their doctrines and submit to their authority, on the pain of perdition, without giving the

inward gifts qualifying them for their work. This is clearly stated by Calvin in his comment on this verse; to a certain difficulty, he says, "Respondeo, quoties a Deo vocati sunt homines, dona necessarie conjuncta esse officiis; neque enim Deus, apostolos aut pastores instituendo, larvam illis duntaxat imponit; sed dotibus etiam instruit, sine quibus rite functionem sibi injunctam obire nequeunt. Quisquis ergo Dei auctoritate constituitur apostolus, non inani et nudo titulo, sed mandato simul et facultate praeditus est."

And some, evangelists. There are two views of the nature of the office of the evangelists. Some regard them as vicars of the apostles—men commissioned by them for a definite purpose and clothed with special powers for the time being, analogous to the apostolic vicars of the Romanists; or to the temporary superintendents appointed after the Reformation in the Scottish church, clothed for a limited time and for a definite purpose with presbyterial powers, i. e. to a certain extent, with the powers of a presbytery, the power to ordain, install and depose. Evangelists in this sense were temporary officers. This view of the nature of the office prevailed at the time of the Reformation.*

---

* CALVIN in his comment on this verse, says: Apostolis proximi erant *Evangelistae*, et munus affine habebant; tantum gradu dignitatis erant dispares; ex quo genere erant Timotheus et similes. Nam quum in salutationibus illum sibi adjungit Paulus, non tamen facit in apostolatu socium, sed nomen hoc peculiariter sibi vindicat. Ergo, secundum Apostolos, istorum subsidiaria opera usus est Dominus.—And in his Institutes IV, 3, 4, he says: Per *Evangelistas* eos intelligo, qui quum in dignitate

According to the other view, the evangelists were itinerant preachers, οἱ περιἰόντες ἐκήρυττον, as Theodoret and other early writers describe them. They were properly missionaries sent to preach the Gospel where it had not been previously known. This is the commonly received view, in favour of which may be urged—1. The signification of the word, which in itself means nothing more than preacher of the Gospel. 2. Philip was an evangelist, but was in no sense a vicar of the apostles; and when Timothy was exhorted to do the work of an evangelist, the exhortation was simply to be a faithful preacher of the Gospel. Acts 21, 8; Eph. 4, 11; and 2 Tim. 4, 5, are the only passages in which the word occurs, and in no one of them does the connection or any other consideration demand any other meaning than the one commonly assigned to it. 3. Εὐαγγέλισθαι and διδάσκειν are both used to express the act of making known the Gospel; but when as here, the εὐαγγελιστής is distinguished from the διδάσκαλος, the only point of distinction implied or admissible is between one who makes known the Gospel where it had not been heard, and an instructor of those already Christians. The use of εὐαγγέλισθαι in such passages as Acts 8, 4; 14, 7; 1 Cor. 1, 17, and 2 Cor. 10, 16, serves to confirm the commonly received opinion that an evangelist is one who makes known the Gospel. That Timothy and Titus were in some sense apostolic

apostolis minores, officio tamen proximi erant, adeoque vices eorum gerebant. Quales fuerunt, Lucas, Timotheus, Titus, et reliqui similes.

vicars, i. e. men clothed with special powers for a
special purpose and for a limited time, may be admitted, but this does not determine the nature of the office
of an evangelist. They exercised these powers not as
evangelists, but as delegates or commissioners.

And some, pastors and teachers, τοὺς δὲ ποιμένας καὶ
διδασκάλους. According to one interpretation we have
here two distinct offices—that of pastor and that of
teacher. The latter, says Calvin, "had nothing to do
with discipline, nor with the administration of the sacraments, nor with admonitions or exhortations, but simply
with the interpretation of Scripture." Institutes IV,
3, 4. All this is inferred from the meaning of the word
teacher. There is no evidence from Scripture that there
was a set of men authorized to teach but not authorized to exhort. The thing is well nigh impossible. The
one function includes the other. The man who teaches
duty and the grounds of it, does at the same time ad-
monish and exhort. It was however on the ground of
this unnatural interpretation that the Westminster
Directory made *teachers* a distinct and permanent class
of jure divino officers in the church. The Puritans in
New England endeavoured to reduce the theory to
practice, and appointed *doctors* as distinct from preachers. But the attempt proved to be a failure. The two
functions could not be kept separate. The whole
theory rested on a false interpretation of Scripture.
The absence of the article before διδασκάλους proves
that the apostle intended to designate the same persons
as at once pastors and teachers. The former term de-

signates them as ἐπίσκοποι, *overseers*, the latter as
instructors. Every pastor or bishop was required to be
apt to teach. This interpretation is given by Augustin
and Jerome; the latter of whom says: Non enim ait:
alios autem pastores et alios magistros, sed alios pastores et magistros, ut qui pastor est, esse debeat et mag-
ister. In this interpretation the modern commentators
almost without exception concur. It is true the article
is at times omitted between two substantives referring
to different classes, where the two constitute one order
—as in Mark 15, 1, μετὰ τῶν πρεσβυτέρων καὶ γραμ-
ματέων, because the elders and scribes formed one body.
But in such an enumeration as that contained in this
verse, τοὺς μὲν ἀποστόλους, τοὺς δὲ προφήτας, τοὺς δὲ
εὐαγγελιστάς, τοὺς δὲ ποιμένας, the laws of the language
require τοὺς δὲ διδασκάλους, had the apostle intended to
distinguish the διδάσκαλοι from the ποιμένες. *Pastors
and teachers*, therefore, must be taken as a two-fold designation of the same officers, who were at once the
guides and instructors of the people.

V. 12. Having mentioned the officers Christ gave
his church, the apostle states the end for which this gift
was conferred—it was πρὸς τὸν καταρτισμὸν τῶν ἁγίων,
εἰς ἔργον διακονίας, εἰς οἰκοδομὴν τοῦ σώματος τοῦ
Χριστοῦ, *for the perfecting of the saints, for the
work of the ministry, for the edifying of the body of
Christ*.

Both the meaning of the words and the relation of
the several clauses in this verse, are doubtful. The
word καταρτισμός, rendered *perfecting*, admits of dif-

ferent interpretations. The root ἄρω means to unite or bind together. Hence ἄρτιος signifies united, complete, perfect; and the verb καταρτίζω is literally *to mend*, Matt. 4, 21; to reduce to order, to render complete, or perfect, Luke 6, 40; 2 Cor. 13, 11; to prepare or render fit for use, Heb. 10, 5; 13, 21. The substantive may express the action of the verb in the various modifications of its meaning. Hence it has been rendered here—1. To the completion of the saints, i. e. of their number. 2. To their renewing or restoration. 3. To their reduction to order and union as one body. 4. To their preparation (for service). 5. To their perfecting. This last is to be preferred because agreeable to the frequent use of the verb by this apostle, and because it gives the sense best suited to the context.

The word διακόνια, *service*, may express that service which one man renders to another—Luke 10, 40, "with much *serving;*" or specially the service rendered to Christians, 1 Cor. 16, 15, "addicted themselves to *the ministry* of the saints;" or the official service of the ministry. Hence the phrase εἰς ἔργον διακονίας may mean 'to the work of mutual service or kind offices,' or to the work of the ministry—in the official sense. The latter is the common interpretation, and is to be preferred not only on account of the more frequent use of the word in that sense, but also on account of the connection, as here the apostle is speaking of the different classes of ministers of the word.

The principal difficulty connected with this verse concerns the relation of its several clauses. 1. Some

propose to invert the first and second so that the sense
would be, 'Christ appointed the apostles, &c., for the
work of the ministry, the design of which is the perfecting of the saints and the edifying of the body of
Christ.' But although the sense is thus good and pertinent, the transposition is arbitrary. 2. Others regard
the clauses as coordinate. 'These officers were given
for the perfecting of the saints, for the work of the
ministry, for the edifying the body of Christ.' To this is
objected the change in the prepositions (πρὸς, εἰς–εἰς),
and the incongruity of the thoughts—the expressions
not being parallel. 3. The two latter clauses may be
made subordinate to the first. 'Christ has appointed the
ministry with the view of preparing the saints, for the
work of serving one another,' (compare εἰς διακονιαν τοῖς
ἀγίοις, 1 Cor. 16, 15,) and for the edification of his
body. This however assumes διακονία to have a sense
unsuited to the context. 4. Others make the two
clauses with εἰς explanatory of the first clause, 'Christ
appointed these officers for the preparation of the saints,
some for the work of the ministry, and some for the
edifying of his body.' But this is inconsistent with the
structure of the passage. It would require the introduction of τοὺς μὲν—τοὺς δὲ, 'some, for this, and some,
for that.' 5. Others again, give the sense thus, 'For
the sake of perfecting the saints, Christ appointed these
officers to the work of the ministry, to the edification
of his body.' The first clause πρὸς κατ. expresses the
remote, εἰς–εἰς the immediate end of the appointment
in question. The " work of the ministry" is that work

which the ministry perform, viz. the edifying of the body of Christ. This last view is perhaps the best.

"He could not," says Calvin, "exalt more highly the ministry of the Word, than by attributing to it this effect. For what higher work can there be than to build up the church that it may reach its perfection? They therefore are insane, who neglecting this means hope to be perfect in Christ, as is the case with fanatics, who pretend to secret revelations of the Spirit; and the proud, who content themselves with the private reading of the Scripture, and imagine they do not need the ministry of the church." If Christ has appointed the ministry for the edification of his body, it is in vain to expect that end to be accomplished in any other way.

V. 13. The ministry is not a temporary institution, it is to continue until the church has reached the goal of its high calling. This does not prove that all the offices mentioned above are permanent. By common consent the prophets were temporary officers. It is the ministry and not those particular offices, that is to continue. The goal of the church is here described in three equivalent forms—1. Unity of faith and knowledge of the Son of God. 2. A perfect man. 3. The measure of the stature of the fulness of Christ.

1. *Till we all come to the unity*, &c., μέχρι καταντήσωμεν οἱ πάντες. The *all* here mentioned is not all men, but all the people of Christ. The reference is not to the confluence of nations from all parts of the earth, but to the body of Christ, the company of saints of

which the context speaks. The church is tending to the goal indicated.* Our version has *in unity*, but the Greek is εἰς τὴν ἑνότητα, and therefore should be rendered, *to* or *unto*, just as in the following clauses, εἰς ἄνδρα τέλειον and εἰς μέτρον, κτλ. The unity of faith is the end to which all are to attain. The genitive υἱοῦ τοῦ Θεοῦ belongs equally to πίστις and ἐπίγνωσις. The Son of God is the object both of the faith and of the knowledge here spoken of. Many commentators understand knowledge and faith as equivalent, and therefore make the latter member of the clause explanatory of the former : ' to the unity of the faith, that is, to the knowledge of the Son of God.' But this overlooks the καὶ. The apostle says, " faith *and* knowledge." Thus distinguishing the one from the other. And they are in fact different, however intimately related, and however often the one term may be used for the other. Faith is a form of knowledge, and therefore may be expressed by that word. But knowledge is not a form of faith, and therefore cannot be expressed by it. Knowledge is an element of faith ; but faith, in its distinctive sense, is not an element of knowledge. The Greek word here used is not γνῶσις but ἐπίγνωσις. We have no word to express the distinction as the Germans have in their Kennen and Erkennen. It is not merely cognition but recognition. Faith and knowledge, πίστις and ἐπίγνωσις, express or compre-

---

* The ministry is to continue until καταντήσωμεν *we* (all) *shall have attained* to unity of faith.

hend all the elements of that state of mind of which the Son of God, God manifested in the flesh, who loved us and gave himself for us, who died on Calvary and is now enthroned in heaven, is the object. A state of mind which includes the apprehension of his glory, the appropriation of his love, as well as confidence and devotion. This state of mind is in itself eternal life. It includes excellence, blessedness, and the highest form of activity, i. e. the highest exercise of our highest powers. We are like him when we see him. Perfect knowledge is perfect holiness. Therefore when the whole church has come to this perfect knowledge which excludes all diversity, then it has reached the end. Then it will bear the image of the heavenly.

The object of faith and knowledge is *the Son of God.* This designation of our Lord declares him to be of the same nature with the Father, possessing the same attributes and entitled to the same honour. Were this not the case the knowledge of Christ as the Son of God, could not be eternal life; it could not fill, enlarge, sanctify, and render blessed the soul; nor constitute the goal of our high calling; the full perfection of our nature.

It has excited surprise that the apostle should here present unity of faith as the goal of perfection, whereas in ver. 6, Christians are said now to have " one faith," as they have one Lord and one baptism. Some endeavour to get over this difficulty by laying the emphasis upon *all.* The progress of the church consists in bringing *all* to this state of unity. But Paul includes *all* in his assertion in ver. 6.   And if the " one faith" of that verse, and " unity of faith" here are the same, then the starting-point and the goal of the church are identical.   Others say that " the unity of faith and knowledge" means not that all should be united in faith and knowledge, but that all should attain that state in which faith and knowledge are identified—faith is to be lost in knowledge.   The unity, therefore, here intended, is unity between faith and knowledge, and not the unity of believers.   But this is evidently unnatural. " We *all* come to unity," can only mean, " we are all united."   There is no real difficulty in the case.   Unity is a matter of degrees.   The church is now and ever has been one body, but how imperfect is their union! Our Lord's praying that his people may be one, does not prove that they are not now one.   It is here as in other cases.   Holiness is the beginning and holiness is the end.   We must be holy to belong to the church, and yet holiness is the ultimate perfection of the church.   The unity of faith is now confined to the first principles; the unity of faith contemplated in this place is that perfect unity which implies perfect knowledge and perfect holiness.

Unto a perfect man, εἰς ἄνδρα τέλειον.   This clause is explanatory of the former and determines its meaning.   Perfection is the end; perfect manhood.   Τέλειος signifies *ad finem perductus;* when used of a man, it means an adult, one who has reached the end of his development as a man.   When applied to a Christian it means one who has reached the end of his development as a Christian, Heb. 12, 23 ; and the church is perfect when it has reached the end of its development and stands complete in glory. In 1 Cor. 13, 10, τὸ τέλειον stands opposed to τὸ ἐκ μέρους, and there as here indicates the state which is to be attained hereafter when we shall know even as we are known.

The standard of perfection for the church is complete conformity to Christ. It is to attain εἰς μέτρον ἡλικίας τοῦ πληρώματος τοῦ Χριστοῦ. These words are explanatory of the preceding. The church becomes adult, a perfect man, when it reaches the fulness of Christ. However these words may be explained in detail, this is the general idea. Whether ἡλικία means *stature* or *age* depends upon the context. Most commentators prefer the latter signification here, because τέλειος in the preceding clause means *adult*, in reference to age rather than to stature, and νήπιος in the following verse means a child as to age and not as to size.

If the phrase "fulness of Christ," be explained according to the analogy of the phrases "fulness of God," "fulness of the Godhead," &c., it must mean the plenitude of excellence which Christ possesses or which he bestows. And the "age of the fulness of Christ," means the age at which the fulness of Christ is attained. Compare 3, 19, where believers ars said to be filled unto the fulness of God.

If, however, reference is had to the analogy of such expressions as "fulness of the blessing of the Gospel," Rom. 15, 29, which means 'the full or abundant blessing,' then the passage before us means 'the full age

(or stature) of Christ.' The church is to become a perfect man, i. e. it is to attain the measure of the full
maturity of Christ. In other words, it is to be completely conformed to him, perfect as he is perfect. This
interpretation, which supposes πληρώματος to qualify
adjectively ἡλικίας, is in accordance with a familiar
characteristic of Paul's style, who frequently connects
three genitives in this way, the one governing the
others, where one is to be taken adjectively. See Col.
1, 13, εἰς βασιλείαν τοῦ υἱοῦ τῆς ἀγάπης αὐτοῦ, " Son
of his love," for ' his beloved Son ;' "age of fulness,"
for ' full age.' Col. 2, 2. 18. 2 Thess. 1, 9.

Commentators are much divided on the question
whether the goal, the *terminus ad quem* of the church's
progress here spoken of, is to be attained in this world
or the next. Those who say it is to be attained here,
rely principally on the following verse : ' We are to
become men *in order that* we should be no longer
children,' &c. To determine this question it would
seem to be enough to state what the contemplated consummation is. It is perfection, and perfection of the
whole church. We are to become perfect men, we are
to attain complete conformity to Christ ; and we are
all to reach this high standard. The Bible, however,
never represents the consummation of the church as
occurring in this life. Christ gave himself for the
church that he might present it to himself a glorious
church without spot or wrinkle, but this presentation
is not to take place until he comes a second time to be
glorified in the saints and admired in all them that

believe. The context instead of forbidding, demands this view of the apostle's meaning. It would be incongruous to say we must reach perfection in order to grow. But it is not incongruous to say that perfection is made the goal in order that we may constantly strive after it.

V. 14. What has been said may be sufficient to indicate the connection between this and the preceding verses, as indicated by ἵνα (*in order that*). This and the following verses are not subordinate to the 13th, as though the sense were, 'we are to reach perfection in order to grow,'—but they are coördinate—all relating to the design of the ministry mentioned in v. 12. Between the full maturity aimed at, and our present state is the period of growth—and Christ appointed the ministry to bring the church to that end, in order that we should be no longer children but make constant progress. This intermediate design is expressed negatively in this verse and affirmatively in the 15th and 16th. We are not to continue children, v. 13, but constantly to advance toward maturity, vs. 15. 16. The characteristic of children here presented is their instability and their liability to be deceived and led astray. The former is expressed by comparing them to a ship without a rudder, tossed to and fro by the waves, and driven about by every wind—κλυδωνιζόμενοι καὶ περιφερόμενοι παντὶ ἀνέμῳ—or to two unstable things, a restless wave, and something driven by the wind. In the use of much the same figure the apostle in Heb. 13, 9 exhorts believers not "to be carried away with diverse and

strange doctrines." And the apostle James compares
the unstable to "a wave of the sea driven with the
wind and tossed," 1, 6. One of the principal elements
of the perfection spoken of in v. 13, is stability in the
truth ; and, therefore, the state of imperfection as contrasted with it is described as one of instability and
liability to be driven about by every wind of doctrine.

Children are not only unstable but easily deceived.
They are an easy prey to the artful and designing. The
apostle therefore adds : ἐν τῇ κυβείᾳ τῶν ἀνθρώπων,
through (ἐν being instrumental) *the artifice of men.*
Κυβεία from κύβος (*cube, die*) means *dice-playing;* in
which there are many arts of deception, and therefore
the word is used for craft or deceit. It is explained by
the following phrase, ἐν πανουργίᾳ πρὸς τὴν μεθοδείαν
τῆς πλάνης, which, according to Luther's version, means
Tauscherei damit sie uns erschleichen zu verfuhren, *the
cunning with which they track us to mislead.* The artifice (κυβεία) is that craft which is used by seducers or
errorists. The preposition πρὸς may mean *according
to.* 'Cunning according to the craft which error uses ;
or which is characteristic of error.' Or it may agreeably to its commom force indicate direction or ten-
dency. 'The cunning which is directed to the craft of
error, i. e. that craft which is designed to seduce.' The
sense is the same. The word μεθοδεία occurs only here
and in 6, 11—where in the plural form it is rendered
wiles; "the wiles of the devil." It is derived from
μεθοδεύω (μετὰ ὁδός), *to follow any one, to track him,* as
a wild animal its prey. Hence the substantive means

the cunning or craft used by those who wish to entrap or capture.

There are two things in this connection which can hardly escape notice. The one is the high estimate the apostle places on truth; and the other is the evil of error. Holiness without the knowledge and belief of the truth, is impossible; perfect holiness implies, as v. 13 teaches, perfect knowledge. Error, therefore, is evil. Religious error springs from moral evil and produces it. "False teachers" are in Scripture always spoken of as bad, as selfish, malignant, or deceitful. This principle furnishes incidentally one of the surest of the criteria of truth. Those doctrines which the good hold, which are dear to the spiritual, to the humble and the holy, are true. This is the only real authority which belongs to tradition. In this passage the apostle attributes departure from the truth to the cunning and deceit which are characteristic of error, or of false teachers. In Rom. 16, 17. 18; 2 Cor. 2, 17; 11, 13; Gal. 2, 4; Col. 2, 8. 18, the same character is given of those who seduce men from the faith. Error, therefore, can never be harmless, nor false teachers innocent. Two considerations however should secure moderation and meekness in applying these principles. The one is, that though error implies sin, orthodoxy does not always imply holiness. It is possible "to hold the truth in unrighteousness;" to have speculative faith without love. The character most offensive to God and man is that of a malignant zealot for the truth. The other consideration is, that men are often much better than their creed.

That is, the doctrines on which they live are much nearer the truth, than those which they profess. They deceive themselves by attaching wrong meaning to words, and seem to reject truth when in fact they only reject their own misconceptions. It is a common remark that men's prayers are more orthodox than their creeds.

V. 15. These remarks are not foreign to the subject; for the apostle, while condemning all instability with regard to faith, and while denouncing the craft of false teachers, immediately adds the injunction to adhere to the truth in love. It is not mere stability in sound doctrine, but faith as combined with love that he requires. The only saving, salutary faith is such as works by love and purifies the heart.

'Αληθεύοντες δὲ ἐν ἀγάπῃ our version renders "but speaking the truth in love." But this does not suit the context. This clause stands opposed to what is said in verse 14. We are not to be children driven about by every wind of doctrine, but we are to be steadfast in professing and believing the truth. This interpretation which is demanded by the connection is justified by the usage of the word ἀληθεύειν, which means not only *to speak the truth*, but also to be ἀληθής in the sense of being open, upright, truthful, adhering to the truth. And the truth here contemplated is the truth of God, the truth of the Gospel, which we are to profess and abide by. The words ἐν ἀγάπῃ are commonly and properly connected with ἀληθεύοντες, "professing the truth in love." They may however be connected with the

following word, so as to give the sense, "let us increase
in love." But this leaves the participle too naked, and
is not indicated by the position of the words. Besides,
in the next verse, which is part of the same sentence,
we have αὔξησιν ποιεῖται εἰς οἰκοδομὴν, εν ἀγάπῃ, which
would be a needless repetition of the same idea.

We are "to grow up into (rather *unto*) him," εἰς
αὐτόν. This is to be explained by a reference to the
expressions εἰς ἄνδρα τέλειον, εἰς μέτρον ἡλικίας κτλ. in
v. 13. These are different forms of expressing the idea
that conformity to Christ is the end to be attained.
We are to grow so as to be conformed to him, τὰ πάντα,
as to all things. Him, "who is the head, viz. Christ."
We are to be conformed to our head—because he is
our head, i. e. because of the intimate union between
him and us. The slight confusion in the metaphor
which presents Christ as the model to which we are to
be conformed, and the head with whose life we are to
be pervaded, is no serious objection to this interpretation, which is demanded by the context.

V. 16. *From whom the whole body fitly joined together, and compacted by that which every joint supplieth, according to the effectual working in the measure
of every part, maketh increase of the body to the edifying of itself in love.* The church is Christ's body; he
is the head. The body grows. Concerning this growth
the apostle says—1. It is from him, (ἐξ οὗ). He is the
causal source, from whom all life and power are derived. 2. It depends on the intimate union of all the
parts of the body with the head by means of appro-

priate bonds. 3. It is symmetrical. 4. It is a growth in love. Such is the general meaning of this passage; though there is much diversity of opinion as to the meaning of some of the terms employed, and as to the relation of the several clauses.

First as to the meaning of the words : Συναρμο-λογέω (ἁρμός and λέγω) *to bind together the several parts of any thing.* It is used of a building 2, 21, and of the human body. In both cases there is a union of parts fitted to each other. It is peculiarly appropriate here, as the church is compared to the body composed of many members intimately connected. Συμβιβάζω, *to bring together, to convene, to join;* figuratively, *to combine mentally.* It is properly used of bringing persons together, so as to reconcile them, or to unite them in friendship. It therefore serves to explain the preceding term. The church is figuratively a body composed of many joints or members; and literally, it is a company of believers intimately united with each other. Hence the apostle uses both terms in reference to it. Ἁφή (ἁπτώ) properly means *touch, the sense of touch.* Hence metonymically *feeling.* Therefore διὰ πάσης ἁφῆς ἐπιχορηγίας may mean, 'by every feeling, or experience of aid.' The word however is sometimes used in the sense of *band* or *joint.* The parallel passage in Col. 2, 19, διὰ τῶν ἁφῶν καὶ συνδέσμων, *by joints and bands,* seems to be decisive for that sense here. The word ἐπιχορηγία (χορηγέω, χορός, ἄγω), *supply, aid,* has no difficulty in itself. The only question is what aid or contribution is meant, and what is the force of the genitive. The word

may refer to the mutual assistance furnished each other
by the constituent members of the body. Thus Luther,
who paraphrases the clause in question,—durch alle
Gelenke, dadurch eins dem andern Handreichung thut
—*by every joint whereby one member aids another.* Or
it may refer to the supplies of vital influence received
from Christ the head. "Through every joint of supply," then means, *through every joint or band which is
the means of supply.* The parallel passage in Col. 2,
19, is in favour of the latter view. There it is said: τὸ
σῶμα διὰ τῶν ἁφῶν ἐπιχορηγούμενον, *the body receiving
nourishment or supplies through the joints or bands.*
The nourishing and sustaining influence, the ἐπιχορηγία,
is certainly in this case that which flows from Christ,
and therefore the same interpretation should be given
to the passage before us. As to the force of the case,
it is by some taken as the genitive of apposition.
"Joint or band of supply," would then mean, *the band
which is a supply.* The divine influence furnished by
Christ is the bond by which the members of his body
are united. This is true, but in Col. 2, 19, which, being
the plainer passage, must be our guide in interpreting
this, the supply is said to be διὰ τῶν ἁφῶν, *through the
joints.* Here, therefore, the parallel phrase, διὰ πάσης
ἁφῆς τῆς ἐπιχορηγίας, must mean, 'through every joint
for supply;' that is, which is the means or channel of
the divine influence. There is an obvious distinction
between "the bands" and "the aid" here spoken of.
The latter is the divine life or Holy Spirit communicated to all parts of the church; the former (the ἁφαί)

are the various spiritual gifts and offices which are made the channels or means of this divine communication.

The second point to be considered is the relation of the several clauses in this passage. The clause διὰ πάσης ἁφῆς, κτλ. may be connected with the last clause of the verse, αὔξησιν ποιεῖται. The sense would then be, 'The body by means of every joint of supply makes increase of itself.' This sense is correct and suited to the context. This however is not the most natural construction. The relative position of the members of the sentence is in favour of referring this clause to the preceding participles. 'The body joined together and united by means of every joint of supply.' The parallel passage in Colossians determines this to be the apostle's meaning. He there refers the union of the body, and not its growth, to the bands (ἁφαί) of which he speaks. He describes the body as συμβιβαζόμενον διὰ τῶν ἁφῶν, and therefore here συμβιβ. διὰ πάσης ἁφῆς, which are in juxtaposition, should go together.

The clause, "*according to the effectual working in the measure of every part*," admits of three constructions. It may be connected with the preceding participles—"joined together by every joint of supply according to the working, &c., συμβιβ. διὰ—κατὰ. Or it may be connected with the preceding words, ἐπιχορηγίας κατ' ἐνέργειαν,—'the supply is according to the working of each particular part.' Or thirdly, it may be connected with αὔξησιν ποιεῖται ; the increase is according to the working, &c. It is hard to decide between these two latter methods. In favour of the second is the position of the words—and also the congruity of the figure. It is more natural to say that the divine influence is according to the working of every part, i. e. according to its capacity and function; than to say, "the growth is according to the working, &c." The increase of the body is due to the living influence which pervades it, and not to the efficiency of the several members. In either case, however, the idea of symmetrical development is included.

The body—maketh increase of the body, i. e. of itself. The substantive is repeated on account of the length of the sentence. This increase is an edification in love, i. e. connected with love. That is the element in which the progress of the church to its consummation is effected.

As then the human body, bound together by the vital influence derived from the head through appropriate channels and distributed to every member and organ according to its function, constantly advances to maturity; so the church, united as one body by the divine influence flowing from Christ its head through appropriate channels, and distributed to every member according to his peculiar capacity and function, continually advances towards perfection. And as in the human body no one member, whether hand or foot, can live and grow unless in union with the body; so union with the mystical body of Christ is the indispensable condition of growth in every individual believer. Fallitur ergo siquis seorsum crescere appetit.—CALVIN.

And further, as in the human body there are certain channels through which the vital influence flows from the head to the members, and which are necessary to its communication; so also there are certain divinely appointed means for the distribution of the Holy Spirit from Christ to the several members of his body. What these channels of divine influence are, by which the church is sustained and carried forward, is clearly stated in v. 11, where the apostle says, " Christ gave some, apostles; and some, prophets; and some evangelists; and some, pastors and teachers, for the perfecting of the saints." It is, therefore, through the ministry of the word that the divine influence flows from Christ the head to all the members of his body, so that where that ministry fails the divine influence fails. This does not mean that the ministry as men or as officers are the channels of the Spirit to the members of the church, so that without their ministerial intervention no man is made a partaker of the Holy Ghost. But it means that the ministry as dispensers of the truth are thus the channels of divine communication. By the gifts of revelation and inspiration, Christ constituted some apostles and some prophets for the communication and record of his truth; and by the inward call of his Spirit he makes some evangelists and some pastors for its constant proclamation and inculcation. And it is only (so far as adults are concerned) in connection with the truth, as thus revealed and preached, that the Holy Ghost is communicated. The ministry, therefore, apostles, prophets, evangelists and teachers, were given for the edification of the church, by the communication of that truth in connection with which alone the Holy Ghost is given.

All this Rome perverts. She says that prelates, whom she calls apostles, are the channels of the Holy Spirit, first to the priests and then to the people ; and that this communication, is not by the truth, but tactual, by the laying on of hands. No one therefore can be united to Christ except through them, or live except as in communion with them. Thus error is always the caricature of truth.

SECTION II.—Vs. 17–32.—Ch. V. 1–2.

17. This I say therefore, and testify in the Lord, that ye henceforth walk not as other Gentiles walk, in the vanity of their
18. mind, having the understanding darkened, being alienated from
the life of God through the ignorance that is in them, because
19. of the blindness of their heart : who, being past feeling, have
given themselves over unto lasciviousness, to work all unclean-
20. ness with greediness. But ye have not so learned Christ; if so
21. be that ye have heard him, and have been taught by him, as
22. the truth is in Jesus: that ye put off concerning the former
conversation the old man, which is corrupt according to the de-
23. ceitful lusts; and be renewed in the spirit of your mind; and
24. that ye put on the new man, which after God is created in
25. righteousness and true holiness. Wherefore putting away lying,
speak every man truth with his neighbour : for we are mem-
26. bers one of another. Be ye angry, and sin not : let not the
27. sun go down upon your wrath : neither give place to the devil.
28. Let him that stole, steal no more : but rather let him labour,
working with *his* hands the thing which is good, that he may
29. have to give to him that needeth. Let no corrupt communica-

tion proceed out of your mouth, but that which is good to the use of edifying, that it may minister grace unto the hearers.

30. And grieve not the Holy Spirit of God, whereby ye are sealed

31. unto the day of redemption. Let all bitterness, and wrath, and anger, and clamour, and evil-speaking, be put away from you,

32. with all malice: and be ye kind one to another, tender-hearted, forgiving one another, even as God for Christ's sake hath forgiven you.

Ch. V. 1. Be ye therefore followers of God as dear children; and

2. walk in love, as Christ also hath loved us, and hath given himself for us an offering and a sacrifice to God for a sweet-smelling savour.

ANALYSIS.

This Section contains first a general exhortation to holiness, vs. 17–24; and secondly, injunctions in respect to specific duties, vs. 25–ch. V. 2. The exhortation to holiness is, agreeably to the apostle's manner, first in the negative form not to walk as the heathen do, vs. 17–19, and secondly, positive, to walk as Christ had taught them, vs. 20–24. The heathen walk in the vanity of their mind, i. e. in a state of moral and spiritual fatuity, not knowing what they are about, nor whither they are going, v. 17; because they are in mental darkness, and are alienated from the life of God through the ignorance that is in them, and through the hardness of their hearts, v. 18; as is evinced by their giving themselves up to uncleanness and avarice, v. 19. The Christian walk is the opposite of this—because believers have been taught. Instead of ignorance, truth dwells in them, enlightening and purifying. Hence they are led to put off the old man—and to put on the new man,

which is more and more conformed to the image of
God, vs. 20–24.   Therefore, they must avoid lying and
speak the truth, v. 25 ; abstain from anger and guard
against giving Satan any advantage, vs. 26. 27.   Avoid
theft, and be diligent and liberal, v. 28.   Avoid all
corrupting language, but let their conversation be
edifying, so as not to grieve the Holy Spirit, vs. 29. 30.
Instead of malicious feelings, they should exercise and
manifest such as are mild, benevolent, and forgiving,
being in this matter the followers of God, vs. 31—
ch. V. 2.

COMMENTARY.

V. 17. The apostle, having in the preceding section
taught that Christ had destined his church to perfect
conformity to himself, and made provision for that end,
as a natural consequence, solemnly enjoins on those
who profess to be Christians to live in accordance with
this high vocation.   "This *therefore* I say and testify
in the Lord, that he henceforth walk not as the other
Gentiles walk, in the vanity of their mind."   *To testify*,
in this case, is solemnly to enjoin, as a man does who
calls upon God to bear witness to the truth and importance of what he says.   Μαρτυρέω is to act as a witness,
and μαρτύρομαι to invoke as a witness.   The latter is
the word here used.   *In the Lord*, means in communion with the Lord.   Paul speaks as one who had
access to the mind of Christ, knew his will, and could
therefore speak in his name.   The exhortation is, *not*
to walk as the Gentiles do.   *To walk*, in Scripture lan-

guage, includes all the manifestations of life, inward and outward, seen and unseen. It does not express merely the outward, visible deportment. Men are said to walk with God, which refers to the secret fellowship of the soul with its Maker, more than to the outward life. So here the walk, which the apostle enjoins us to avoid, is not only the visible deportment characteristic of the Gentiles, but also the inward life of which the outward deportment is the manifestation.

They walk "in the vanity of their mind." The language of the New Testament being the language of Jews, is more or less modified by Hebrew usage. And the usage of Hebrew words is of course modified by the philosophy and theology of the people who employed them. There are two principles which have had an obvious influence on the meaning of a large class of Hebrew words, and therefore on the meaning of the Greek terms which answer to them. The one is the unity of the soul which forbids any such marked distinction between its cognitive and emotional faculties, i. e. between the understanding and the heart, as is assumed in our philosophy, and therefore is impressed on our language. In Hebrew the same word designates what we commonly distinguish as separate faculties. The Scriptures speak of an "understanding heart," and of " the desires of the understanding," as well as of " the thoughts of the heart." They recognize that there is an element of feeling in our cognitions and an element of intelligence in our feelings. The idea that the heart may be depraved and the intellect unaffected is, according to the anthropology of the Bible, as incongruous, as that one part of the soul should be happy and another miserable, one faculty saved and another lost.

Another principle nearly allied to the former is the moral and spiritual excellence of truth. Truth is not merely speculative, the object of cognition. It has moral beauty. In scriptural language, therefore, knowledge includes love; wisdom includes goodness; folly includes sin; the wise are holy, fools are wicked. Truth and holiness are united as light and heat in the same ray. There cannot be the one without the other. To know God is eternal life; to be without the knowledge of God is to be utterly depraved. Saints are the children of light; the wicked are the children of darkness. To be enlightened is to be renewed; to be blinded is to be reprobated. Such is the constant representation of Scripture. ·

The νοῦς, *mind*, therefore, in the passage before us, does not refer to the intellect to the exclusion of the feelings, nor to the feelings to the exclusion of the intellect. It includes both; the reason, the understanding, the conscience, the affections are all comprehended by the term. Sometimes one and sometimes another of these modes of spiritual activity is specially referred to, but in the present case the whole soul is intended. The word ματαιότης, *vanity*, according to the scriptural usage just referred to, includes moral as well as intellectual worthlessness, or fatuity. It is of all that is comprehended under the word νοῦς, the

understanding and the heart, that this vanity is predicated. Every thing included in the following
verses respecting the blindness and depravity of the
heathen is therefore comprehended in the word
vanity.

V. 18. *Having the understanding darkened, being
alienated from the life of God through the ignorance
that is in them, because of the blindness of their heart.*
This verse at once explains and confirms the preceding
statement. The heathen walk in vanity, i. e. in intellectual and moral darkness, because their understanding is darkened, and because they are alienated from
the life of God.

The word διάνοια, *understanding*, in the first clause,
means *a thinking through ; the mind* (quatenus intelli-
git, appetit et sentit) as opposed to the body ; *an act
of the mind*, a thought, purpose, or disposition ; *the
intelligence* as opposed to the feelings. We are required to love God, ἐν ὅλῃ τῇ διανοίᾳ, *with the whole
mind ;* men are said to be enemies, τῇ διανοίᾳ, Col. 1,
21, *as to their state of mind*, and proud τῇ διανοίᾳ τῆς
καρδίας αὐτῶν. The apostle Peter exhorts us " to gird
up the loins *of the mind ;*" and speaks of our " pure
mind." And the apostle John says : " God has given
us διανοίαν that we may know." The word is opposed
to σάρξ in Eph. 2, 3, and to καρδία in Matt. 22, 37,
Heb. 8, 10 and elsewhere. It depends therefore on the
connection whether the word is to be understood of the
whole soul, or of the intelligence, or of the disposition.
In this case it means *the intelligence ;* because it is dis-

tinguished from νοῦς in the preceding verse, and from καρδία in the last clause of this one.

"Alienated from the life of God," means strangers to that life. "The life of God," means the life of which God is the author. It is spiritual life. That is, the life of which the indwelling Spirit is the principle or source. "Vitam Dei," says Beza, "appellat vitam illam, qua Deus vivit in suis." Comp. 3, 16, 17, and the remarks on that passage.

In the last clause of the verse πώρωσις is rendered *blindness*, it more properly means *hardness*. It does not come from πωρός, *blind*, but from πῶρος a peculiar kind of stone, and then any thing hard or callous. The verb πωρόω is rendered *to harden*, Mark 6, 52; 8, 17; John 12, 40, and in all these passages it is used of the heart. So in Rom. 11, 7, "the rest were hardened." The noun is rendered "hardness" in Mark 3, 5, and "blindness" in Rom. 11, 25. This is easily accounted for, as the verb is often used in reference to the eyes when covered with an opaque hardened film, and hence πεπώρωται is the same at times with τετύφλωται. The phrase, therefore, πώρωσις τῆς καρδίας, may be rendered either *blindness* or *hardness of the heart*. The latter is the proper meaning, unless the other be required by the context, which is not the case in the present instance.

The principal difficulty in this verse concerns the relation of its several clauses. First, the participle ὄντες may be connected with the second, clause, so as to read, "Dark as to the understanding, being (ὄντες) alienated from the life of God." This is the view taken by our translators, which supposes that the first clause merely expresses a characteristic of the heathen, for which the second assigns the reason. 'They are dark ened, because alienated.' But this is not consistent with the relation of this verse to the preceding. 'The heathen walk in vanity because darkened,' &c. Besides, according to the apostle, the heathen are not in darkness because alienated from the life of God, but they are alienated from that life because of their ignorance. Secondly, the four clauses included in the verse may be considered as so related that the first is connected with the third, and the second with the fourth. The passage would then read, 'Having the understanding darkened on account of the ignorance that is in them; alienated from the life of God on account of the hardness of their hearts.' But this unnaturally dissociates the clauses, contrary to one of the most marked peculiarities of the apostle's style; whose sentences are like the links of a chain, one depending on another in regular succession. This mode of construction also makes ignorance the cause of the darkness, whereas it is the effect. A man's being enveloped in darkness is the cause of his not seeing, but his not seeing is not the cause of the darkness. Idiocy is the cause of ignorance and not the reverse. The apostle conceives of the heathen as men whose minds are impaired or darkened, and therefore they are ignorant. Thirdly, the clauses may be taken as they stand, ὄντες being connected with the first clause. 'The heathen walk in vanity, being (i. e. because they are) darkened as to the understanding, alienated from the life of God through the ignorance that is in them, through the hardness óf their heart.' Darkness of mind is thè cause of ignorance, ignorance and consequent obduracy of heart are the cause of alienation from God. This is both the logical and theological order of sequence. The soul in its natural state cannot discern the things of God—therefore it does not know them, therefore the heart is hard and therefore it is destitute of holiness. This is what the apostle teaches in 1 Cor..2, 14–16. The blind cannot see; therefore they are ignorant of the beauty of creation, therefore they are destitute of delight in its glories. You cannot heal them by light. The eye must first be opened. Then comes vision, and then joy and love. This view of the passage is in accordance with the analogy of Scripture; which constantly represents regeneration as necessary to spiritual discernment, and spiritual discernment as necessary to holy affections. Therefore the apostle says of the heathen that their understanding is darkened, a film is over their eyes, and they are alienated from God because of the ignorance consequent on their mental blindness.

V. 19. *Who*, not the simple relative, but οἵτινες, *such as who.* The practical proof of their being in the state described is to be found in the fact that being without feeling they give themselves over to the sins mentioned. Ἀπηλγηκότες, *no longer susceptible of pain.* Conscience ceases to upbraid or to restrain them. They, therefore, give themselves up *to excess*, to practise all kinds of uncleanness, ἐν πλεονεξίᾳ, *with greediness*, i. e. insatiably. The parallel passage, 2 Pet. 2, 14, "Having eyes full of adultery, and that cannot cease from sin," would favour this interpretation so far as the idea is concerned. But the word πλεονεξία always elsewhere means, *covetousness; a desire to have more*. And as this gives a good sense it is not right to depart from the established meaning. Ἐν πλεονεξίᾳ, therefore, means *with*, i. e. together with, covetousness. The heathen give themselves up to uncleanness and covetousness. These two vices are elsewhere thus associated, as in ch. 5, 3. 5, "Let not uncleanness or covetousness be named among you." "No unclean person, nor covetous man, &c." See also Col. 3, 5. Rom. 1, 29. 1 Cor. 5, 10. Here as in Rom. 1, 24, immorality is connected with impiety as its inevitable consequence. Men in their folly think that morality may be preserved without religion, and even that morality is religion; but reason, experience and Scripture all prove that if men do not love and fear God they give themselves up to vice in some form, and commonly either to uncleanness or avarice. There is a two-fold reason for this; one is the nature of the soul which has no independent source of goodness in itself, so that if it turns from God it sinks into pollution, and the other is the punitive justice of God. He abandons those who abandon him. In Rom. 1; 24 and elsewhere, it is said 'God gives the impious up to uncleanness;' here it is said, they give themselves up. These are only different forms of the same truth. Men are restrained from evil by the hand of God, if he relaxes his hold they rush spontaneously to destruction. All systems of education, all projects of reform in social or political life, not founded in religion, are, according to the doctrine of this passage and of all Scripture, sure to lead to destruction.

V. 20. *But ye have not so learned Christ.* That is, your knowledge of Christ has not led you to live as the heathen. As we are said to learn a thing, but never *to learn* a person, the expression μανθάνειν τὸν Χριστόν, is without example. But as the Scriptures speak of preaching Christ, which does not mean merely to preach his doctrines, but to preach Christ himself, to set him forth as the object of supreme love and confidence, so "to learn Christ" does not mean merely, to learn his doctrines, but to attain the knowledge of Christ as the Son of God, God in our nature, the Holy one of God, the Saviour from sin, whom to know is holiness and life. Any one who has thus learned Christ cannot live in darkness and sin. Such knowledge is in its very nature light. Where it enters, the mind is irradiated, refined, and purified. Nihil ergo de Christo didicit qui nihil vita ab infidelibus differt; neque enim a mortificatione carnis separari potest Christi cognitio. —Calvin.

V. 21. *If so be ye have heard him.* "To hear him" does not mean to hear about him. This the apostle in writing to Christians could not express in a hypothetical form. He knew that the Ephesian Christians had heard about Christ. To hear, in this connection, implies intelligence and obedience, as in the frequently occurring phrase, "He that hath ears to hear, let him hear;" and "To-day if ye will hear his voice, &c.," and in a multitude of other cases. To hear the voice of God or of Christ, therefore, is not merely to perceive with the outward ear but to receive with the understanding and the heart. The particle εἴγε, *if indeed*, does not express doubt; but 'if, as I take for granted.' The apostle assumes that they were obedient to the truth. 'Ye have not so learned Christ as to allow of your living as do the Gentiles, if, as I take for granted, you have really heard his voice and have been taught *by him.*' Ἐν αὐτῷ, however, does not properly mean *by* him, but 'in communion with him.' 'Ye have been taught in him, inasmuch as truth is in Jesus, to put off the old man.' The knowledge of Christ, hearing him, union with him, his inward teaching, are necessarily connected with the mortification of sin.

The clause καθώς ἐστιν ἀλήθεια ἐν τῷ Ἰησοῦ, rendered in our version *as the truth is in Jesus*, is variously explained. The interpretation intimated above supposes καθώς to have its frequent causal sense; *since, inasmuch as;* and *truth* to mean moral truth, or excellence. This sense it very often has. It frequently means true religion, and is used antithetically to unrighteousness, as in Rom. 2, 8. The principle here involved is, that knowledge of God is inconsistent with a life of sin, because knowledge implies love, and God is holy. To know him, therefore, is to love holiness. The apostle's argument is : 'If you know Christ you will forsake sin, because he is holy—truth, i. e. moral excellence is in him. If you have been taught any thing in virtue of your communion with him, you have been taught to put off the old man.'

Another interpretation supposes καθώς to mean *as*, expressing the manner. 'If ye have been taught as the truth is in Jesus,' i. e. correctly taught. But this requires the article even in English—*the* truth, meaning the definite system of truth which Jesus taught. In the Greek, however, the article necessary to give colour to this interpretation is wanting. Besides, the expression "the truth is in Jesus" is obscure and un-scriptural, if truth be taken to mean true doctrine. And more than this, this interpretation supposes there may be a true and false teaching *by*, or in communion with, Christ. This cannot be. The apostle's hypothesis is, not whether Christ has taught them correctly, but whether he has taught them at all.

A third interpretation makes the following infinitive the subject of the sentence ; 'Truth in Jesus is, to put off the old man.' The meaning of the whole passage would then be, 'If you know Christ ye cannot live as the heathen, for truth in Jesus is to put away sin,' i. e. true fellowship with Christ is to put off, &c. But this violates the natural construction of the passage, according to which the infinitive ἀποθέσθαι depends on ἐδι-δάχθητε, 'Ye have been taught to put off, &c.' And the expression, 'It is truth in Jesus to put away sin' is in itself awkward and obscure. The first mentioned interpretation, therefore, is on the whole to be preferred.

V. 22. Sanctification includes dying to sin, or mortification of the flesh, and living to righteousness; or as it is here expressed, putting off the old man and putting on the new man. The obvious allusion is to a change of clothing. To put off, is to renounce, to remove from us, as garments which are laid aside. To put on, is to adopt, to make our own. We are called upon to put off the works of darkness, Rom. 13, 12, to put away lying, Eph. 4, 25; to put off anger, wrath, malice, &c., Col. 3, 8; to lay aside all filthiness, James 1, 21. On the other hand, we are called upon to put on the Lord Jesus Christ, Rom. 13, 14, Gal. 3, 27; the armour of light, Rom. 13, 12; bowels of mercy, Col. 3, 12; and men are said to be clothed with power from on high, Luke 24, 49; with immortality or incorruption, &c., 1 Cor. 15, 53. As a man's clothes are what strike the eye—so these expressions are used in reference to the whole phenomenal life—all those acts and attributes by which the interior life of the soul is manifested;—and not only that, but also the inherent principle itself whence these acts flow. For here we are said to put off *the old man*, that is, our corrupt nature, which is old or original as opposed to the new man or principle of spiritual life. Comp. Col. 3, 9, " Lie not one to another, seeing you have put off the old man with his deeds." Rom. 6, 6, " Knowing this, that our old man is crucified with him." What is here called "the old man" Paul elsewhere calls himself, as in Rom.

7, 14, " I am carnal," " In me there dwelleth no good
thing," v. 18 ; or, "law in the members," v. 23 ; or
" the flesh " as opposed to the spirit, as in Gal. 5, 16. 17.
This evil principle or nature is called old because it
precedes what is new, and because it is corrupt. And
it is called " man," because it is ourselves. We are to
be changed—and not merely our acts. We are to
crucify ourselves. This original principle of evil is not
destroyed in regeneration, but is to be daily mortified,
in the conflicts of a whole life.

The connection, as intimated above, is with the
former clause of v. 21, ἐδιδάχθητε—ἀποθέσθαι ὑμᾶς.
When the subject of the infinitive in such construction
is the same with that of the governing verb, it is
usually not expressed. The presence of ὑμᾶς therefore
in the text is urged as a fatal objection to this construction. A reference, however, to Luke 20, 20, Rom. 2,
19, Phil. 3, 13, will show that this rule has its exceptions.

The intervening clause, κατὰ τὴν προτέραν ἀνα-
στροφήν, concerning the former conversation, belongs to
the verb and not to the following noun. The meaning
is not, ' the old man as to the former conversation,'
(which would require τὸν κατὰ τὴν προτ. κτλ.); but,
' put away as concerns the former conversation the old
man.' It is not the old nature as to its former manifestations only that is to be put away, but the old principle entirely. And as that was formerly dominant,
the apostle says, as to your former manner of life, put
off the old man.

"Which is corrupt," φθειρόμενον; "which tends to
destruction." This latter rendering is to be preferred,
because the epithet *old* includes the idea of corruption.
It would be, therefore, tautological to say, 'the corrupt
man which is corrupt.' It is the old man or corrupt
nature which tends to perdition (qui tendit ad exitium.
—GROTIUS), which is to be laid aside, or continually
mortified.

It tends to destruction, κατὰ τὰς ἐπιθυμίας τῆς ἀπάτης,
according to the deceitful lusts, or as ἀπάτης has the
article and therefore is not so properly a mere qualifying genitive—*the lusts which deceit has*. The apostle
says, Rom. 7, 11, *sin deceived him*, and Heb. 3, 11,
speaks of "the deceitfulness of sin." It is indwelling
sin itself which deceives by means of those desires
which tend to destruction.

V. 23. In this and the following verse we have the
positive part of sanctification which is expressed by
"renewing" and "putting on the new man." The
verb ἀνανεοῦσθαι, *to be made new*, is passive. This renewal is always represented as the work of God. "We
are his workmanship created in Christ Jesus unto good
works," ch. 2, 10. It is therefore called "a renewing
of the Holy Ghost." Titus 3, 5. Both these phrases
"to be renewed" and "to put on the new man" may
express either the instantaneous act of regeneration, or
the gradual work of sanctification. Thus in Rom. 12,
2, we are exhorted "not to be conformed to the world,
but to be transformed by the renewing of the mind."
So in this place, and in the parallel passage in Col. 3,

9. 10, these terms express the whole process by which the soul is restored to the image of God. It is a process of renewal from the beginning to the end. The apostle says, "his inner man is renewed day by day." 2 Cor. 4, 16.

The distinction between νέος, *young*, *new* as to origin; and καινός, *fresh*, *bright*, *unused*, new as to nature or character, is generally preserved in the New Testament. Thus in Matt 9, 17, οἶνον νέον εἰς ἀσκοὺς καινούς, recent, or newly made wine into fresh bottles. Μνημεῖον καινόν, *new sepulchre*, i. e. one which had not been used, however long it may have been prepared. Hence καινός, is an epithet of excellence. In the passage " Until I drink it new with you in the kingdom of God," Mark 14, 25, the word is καινόν, not νέον. The same idea is implied in all the expressions, *new creature*, *new heavens*, *new commandment*, *new name*, *new Jerusalem*, &c., &c. In all these cases the word is καινός. The same distinction properly belongs to the derivatives of these words; ἀνανεόω is to make νέος, and ἀνακαινίζω, ἀνακαινόω, is to make καινός. Hence when reference is had to the renewal of the soul, which is a change for the better, the words used are always the derivatives of καινός, except in this passage. See Rom. 12, 2; 2 Cor. 4, 16; Col. 3, 10; Tit. 3, 5. Still as what is νέος is also καινός ; as freshness, vigour and beauty are the attributes of youth, the same thing may be designated by either term. The soul as renewed is, therefore, called in this passage καινὸς ἄνθρωπος and νέος ἄνθρωπος in Col. 3, 10 ; and the spiritual change which in Col. 3, 10, is expressed by ἀνακαινόω, and in Rom. 12, 2, and Tit. 3, 5, by ἀνακαίνωσις, is here expressed by ἀνανεόω.

The subject of this renewal, that as to which men are to be made new, is expressed in the clause τῷ πνεύματι τοῦ νοὸς ὑμῶν, i. e. *as to the spirit of your mind.* This combination is unexampled. Grotius says : Spiritus mentis est ipsa mens ; as Augustin before him had said : Spiritum mentis dicere voluit eum spiritum, quae mens vocatur. But here spirit and mind are distinguished. The spirit of a man is not that spirit which is a man ; but which man has. Others take the word spirit here to be temper, disposition. " Renewed as to the temper of your mind." This is a very unusual, if not doubtful meaning of the word in the New Testament. Others, again, say that the word spirit means the Holy Spirit, and that the passage should be rendered, " by the Spirit which is in your mind." But this is impossible. The " spirit of the mind " is here as plainly distinguished from the Spirit of God as in Rom. 8, 16, where the Spirit of God is said to bear witness with our spirit.

It may be remarked in reference to this phrase :—
1. That although the passage in Rom. 12, 2, " renewal of your mind," obviously expresses the same general idea as is here expressed by saying, " renewed as to the spirit of the mind," it does not follow that " mind " and " spirit of the mind," mean exactly the same thing. The one expression is general, the other precise and definite. 2. The words πνεῦμα, νοῦς, καρδία, ψυχή,

spirit, mind, heart, soul, are used in Scripture both for the whole immaterial and immortal element of our nature, that in which our personality resides; and also for that element under some one of its modes of manifestation, sometimes for one mode and sometimes for another; as νοῦς sometimes designates the soul as intelligent and sometimes the soul as feeling. 3. Though this is true, yet predominantly one of these terms designates one, and another a different mode of manifestation; as νοῦς the understanding, καρδία the feelings, ψυχή the seat of sensation. 4. Of these terms πνεῦμα is the highest. It means breath, wind, invisible power, life. The idea of power cannot be separated from the term; τὸ πνεῦμά ἐστι τὸ ζωοποιοῦν. John 6, 63. It is, therefore, applied to God, to the Holy Ghost, to angels, to Satan, to demons, to the soul of man. The "spirit of the world," 1 Cor. 2, 12, is the controlling, animating principle of the world, that which makes it what it is. The spirit of the mind therefore is its interior life; that of which the νοῦς, καρδία, ψυχή are the modes of manifestation. That, therefore, which needs to be renewed, is not merely outward habits or modes of life; not merely transient tempers or dispositions, but the interior principle of life which lies back of all that is outward, phenomenal, or transient.

V. 24. Καὶ ἐνδύσασθαι τὸν καινὸν ἄνθρωπον, *and that ye put on the new man.* As we are called to put off our corrupt nature as a ragged and filthy garment, so we are required to put on our new nature as a garment of light. And as the former was personified as an old man, decrepit, deformed, and tending to corruption, so the latter is personified as a new man, fresh, beautiful, and vigorous, like God, for it is τὸν κατὰ Θεὸν κτισθέντα, κτλ., *after God created in righteousness and holiness of the truth.* In the parallel passage it is said to be renewed " after the image of God," Col. 3, 10. " After God," therefore, means after his image. That in which this image consists is said to be righteousness and holiness. The former of these words, δικαιοσύνη, when it stands alone often includes all the forms of moral excellence; but when associated with ὁσιότης, the one means rectitude, the being or doing right; and the other, holiness. The one renders us just to our neighbours; the other, pious towards God. The two substantives are united in Luke 1, 75; the adjectives, just and holy, in Tit. 1, 8; and the adverbs, holily and justly, in 1 Thess. 2, 10. The Greeks made the same distinction, πρὸς Θεοὺς ὅσιον καὶ πρὸς ἀνθρώπους δίκαιόν ἐστι. In our version this clause is rendered, " in righteousness and true holiness;" but the word ἀληθείας stands in the same relation to both nouns, and if taken as a mere qualifying genitive the translation should be, " in true righteousness and holiness." Most modern commentators, however, consider " *the truth* " here as opposed to " *the deceit* " spoken of in verse 22. " Righteousness and holiness of the truth " would then mean that righteousness and holiness which the truth has, or which the truth produces. If the principle of indwelling sin is there personified as ἀπάτη, *deceit,* producing and exercising those lusts

which lead to destruction; the principle of spiritual
life is here personified as ἀλήθεια, *truth*, which produces righteousness and holiness. Truth is spiritual
knowledge, that knowledge which is eternal life, which
not only illuminates the understanding but sanctifies
the heart. The Holy Ghost is called the Spirit of truth
as the author of this divine illumination which irra-
diates the whole soul. This truth came by Jesus Christ,
John 1, 17. He is the truth and the life, John 14, 6.
We are made free by the truth, and sanctified by the
truth. The Gospel is called the word of truth, as the
objective revelation of that divine knowledge which
subjectively is the principle of spiritual life. Taking
the word in this sense, the passage is brought into
nearer coincidence with the parallel passage in Col. 3,
10. Here the image of God is said to consist in righteousness and holiness of the truth; there it is said to
consist in knowledge. "The new man is renewed unto
knowledge after the image of him that created him."
These passages differ only in that the one is more con-
cise than the other. Knowledge (the ἐπίγνωσις τοῦ
Θεοῦ) includes righteousness, holiness, and truth. Nothing, therefore, can be more contrary to Scripture
than to undervalue divine truth, and to regard doctrines as matters pertaining merely to the speculative
understanding. Righteousness and holiness, morality
and religion, are the products of the truth, without which
they cannot exist.

This passage is of special doctrinal importance, as
teaching us the true nature of the image of God in

which man was originally created. That image did not consist merely in man's rational nature, nor in his immortality, nor in his dominion, but specially in that righteousness and holiness, that rectitude in all his principles, and that susceptibility of devout affections which are inseparable from the possession of the truth, or true knowledge of God. This is the scriptural view of the original state of man, or of original righteousness, as opposed, on the one hand, to the Pelagian theory that man was created without moral character; and on the other, to the Romish doctrine, that original righteousness was a supernatural endowment not belonging to man's nature. Knowledge, and consequently righteousness and holiness, were immanent or concreated in the first man, in the same sense as were his sense of beauty and susceptibility of impression from the external world. He opened his eyes and saw what was visible, and perceived its beauty; he turned his mind on God, perceived his glory, and was filled with all holy affections.

V. 25. Having enforced the general duty of holiness, or of being conformed to the image of God, the apostle insists on specific duties. It will be observed that in almost every case there is first a negative, then a positive statement of the duty, and then a motive. Thus here: lie not, but speak truth, for ye are members one of another. *Wherefore*, i. e. on the ground of the general obligation to be conformed to the divine image, *putting away lying*, as one part of the filthy garments belonging to the old man; *speak every man truth with his neighbour.* A neighbour, ὁ πλησίον, the Scripture teaches us, is any one near to us, a fellow man of any creed or nation; and to all such we are bound to speak the truth. But the context shows that Paul is here speaking to Christians, and the motive by which the duty is enforced shows that by neighbour he here means a fellow-Christian, as in Rom. 15, 2. The motive in question is the intimate relation in which believers stand to each other. They are all members of the same body intimately united, as he taught in verse 16, with each other and with Christ their common head. As it would be unnatural and absurd for the hand to deceive the foot, or the eye the ear, so there is a violation of the very law of their union for one Christian to deceive another. It is characteristic of the apostle and of the Scriptures generally, to enforce moral duties by religious considerations. This method, while it presents the higher and peculiar ground of obligation, is not intended to exclude other grounds. The obligation of veracity rests on the intrinsic excellence of truth, on the command of God, and on the rights of our fellow men. They have the same right that we should not deceive them as that we should not defraud them. But all this does not hinder that the duty should be enforced by a reference to the peculiar relation of believers as united by the indwelling of the Holy Spirit into the mystical body of Christ.

Vs. 26. 27. His next exhortation has reference to anger; with regard to which he teaches—1. Not to allow anger to be an occasion of sin. 2. Not to cherish it. 3. Not to give Satan any advantage over us when we are angry.

The words ὀργίζεσθε καὶ μὴ ἁμαρτάνετε, *be ye angry and sin not*, are borrowed from the Septuagint version of Ps. 4, 5, and admit of different interpretations. 1. As the original text in Ps. 4, 5, admits of being rendered *Rage and sin not*, i. e. do not sin by raging*— so the words of the apostle may mean, do not commit the sin of being angry. To this it is objected, that it makes the negative qualify both verbs, while it belongs really only to the latter. It is not necessary to assume that the apostle uses these words in the precise sense of the original text; for the New Testament writers often give the sense of an Old Testament passage with a modification of the words, or they use the same words with a modification of the sense. This is not properly a quotation; it is not cited as something the Psalmist said, but the words are used to express Paul's own idea. In Rom. 10, 18, "Their sound is gone into all the earth," we have the language of the 19th Ps. but not an expression of the sense of the Psalmist. 2. Others make the first imperative in this clause permissive and the second commanding, 'Be angry and (but) do not sin.' 3. Or the first is conditional, 'if angry, sin not.' That is, sin not in anger; let not your anger be an occasion of sin. Repress it and bring it under control that it may not hurry you into the commission of sin. The meaning is the same as would be expressed

---

* See Dr. J. A. Alexander's Commentary on the Psalms.

by saying, ὀργιζόμενοι μὴ ἁμαρτάνετε, *being angry sin
not.* This is perhaps the most satisfactory view of the
passage. It is indeed objected that the apostle is here
speaking of sins, and that in v. 31, he forbids all anger,
and therefore any interpretation which assumes that
anger is not itself a sin is inadmissible. But it is certain that all anger is not sinful. Christ himself, it is
said, regarded the perverse Jews "with anger." Mark
3, 5. The same generic feeling, if mingled with holy
affections, or in a holy mind, is virtuous; if mingled
with malice it is sinful. Both feelings, or both combi-
nations of feeling, are expressed in Scripture by the
term anger. Nothing in itself sinful can be attributed
to God, but anger is attributed to him. Verse 31 is
not inconsistent with this interpretation, for there the
context shows the apostle speaks of malicious anger—
just as "all hatred" means all malice, and not the
hatred of evil.

Let not the sun go down upon your wrath. The
word is here παροργισμός, *paroxysm* or *excitement.* Anger even when justifiable is not to be cherished. The
wise man says: "Anger resteth in the bosom of
fools." Eccl. 7, 9.

Neither give place to the devil.—" *To give place to* "
is to get out of the way of, to allow free scope to; and
therefore to give an occasion or advantage to any one.
We are neither to cherish anger, nor are we to allow
Satan to take advantage of our being angry. Anger
when cherished gives the Tempter great power over us,
as it furnishes a motive to yield to his evil suggestions.

The word διάβολος is rendered by Luther, *Lästerer*, *slanderer*. It is used as an adjective in that sense in 1 Tim. 3, 11 ; 2 Tim. 3, 3, and Tit. 2, 3, but with the article (ὁ διάβολος) it always means Satan—the great accuser—the prince of the demons or fallen angels, who is the great opposer of God and seducer of men— against whose wiles we are commanded to be constantly on our guard.

V. 28. The next exhortation relates to theft—we are not to steal—but to labour, that we may not only honestly support ourselves, but be able also to give to those who need.

The word ὁ κλέπτων does not mean one who stole, but one who steals, the thief. But how, it is asked, could the apostle assume that there were thieves in the Ephesian church, especially as he is addressing those who had been renewed, and whom he is exhorting to live agreeably to their new nature ? To get over this difficulty Calvin says, Paul does not refer merely to such thefts as the civil law punishes, but to all unjust acquisition. And Jerome says, Ephesios monet, ne sub occasione emolumenti furti crimen incurrant, furtum nominans, omne quod alterius damno quaeritur. This enlargement of the idea of theft, though it transcends the limits assigned the offence in human laws, does not go beyond the law of God. As the command, " Thou shalt do no murder," includes the prohibition of malice; so the command, "Thou shalt not steal," forbids every thing that doth or may unjustly hinder our neighbour's wealth or outward estate. It is very certain that many things tolerated by the customs of men; many modes of getting the property of others into our own possession practised even by those professing to be Christians, are in the light of the divine law only different forms of theft, and will be revealed as such in the judgment of the last day. The spirit of the apostle's command no doubt includes all the forms of dishonesty. Still it may be questioned if this principle gives the true explanation of the passage. Others say, that as in the Corinthian church fornication and even incest was tolerated, See 1 Cor. 6, 1–6,—it is not incredible that theft should be disregarded in the church of Ephesus, or at least not visited with discipline. It is however probable that our version, which agrees with the Vulgate and with Luther's translation, expresses the true sense. Not that ὁ κλέπτων means the same with ὁ κλέψας, but as "murderer" means one guilty of murder, however penitent, so "thief" may mean one guilty of theft. Certain inmates of the prisons are called thieves because of their past, and not because of their present conduct.

The positive part of the apostle's injunction is, instead of sustaining himself unjustly on the labour of others, *let him labour, working with his hands the thing that is good.* As he used his hands to steal, let him use them in doing what is right—i. e. in honest labour. Paul elsewhere lays down the general principle, "if any would not work neither should he eat." 2 Thess. 3, 10. No one is entitled to be supported by others, who is able to support himself. This is one great principle of scriptural economics. Another, however, no less important is, that those who cannot work are entitled to aid—and therefore the apostle adds as a motive why the strong should labour—that they *may have to contribute to him that hath need.* No man liveth for himself; and no man should labour for himself alone, but with the definite object to be able to assist others. Christian principles, if fairly carried out, would speedily banish pauperism and other cognate evils from our modern civilization.

Vs. 29, 30—Forbid corrupt communication—enjoin profitable discourse, assign as a motive the good of others and reverence for the Holy Spirit.

Let no corrupt communication proceed out of your mouth. Πᾶς λόγος σαπρός, *any foul word.* The word σαπρός means literally *putrid,* and then figuratively offensive and injurious. *But that which is good to the use of edifying,* ἀγαθὸς πρὸς οἰκοδομήν, *adapted to edification.* The words οἰκοδομὴν τῆς χρείας, *edification of the necessity,* means the edification the necessity calls for—or which is suited to the occasion. This is the common and satisfactory interpretation. Our version "*to the use of edifying*"—transposes the words. *That it may give grace to the hearers.* The phrase χάριν διδόναι, *to give grace,* is one of frequent occurrence, and always means—to confer a favour—i. e. to give pleasure or profit. There is no necessity for departing from this sense here. The meaning is, 'that it may benefit the hearers.' *And grieve not the Holy Spirit of God,* i. e. by such corrupt language. Under the head of πᾶς λόγος σαπρος the apostle includes, as appears from Col. 3, 8, all irreligious, malicious and impure language, which not only injures others, but grieves the Holy Spirit. As a temple is sacred, and every thing that profanes it is an offence to God, so the indwelling of the Holy Ghost in the people of God is made the reason why we should treat them with reverence, as this apostle teaches when he says, "Know ye not that ye are the temple of God, and that the Spirit of God dwelleth in you? If any man defile the temple of God, him will God destroy; for the temple of God is holy, which temple ye are." 1 Cor. 3, 16. 17. To pollute, therefore, the souls of believers by suggesting irreligious or impure thoughts to them, is a profanation of the temple of God and an offence to the Holy Ghost. This is one phase of the truth here presented. Another, and the one more immediately intended in this clause is, that the blessed Spirit who condescends to dwell in our own hearts is grieved and offended whenever we thus sin. Thus in 1 Cor. 6, 19, Paul says, "What! know ye not that your body is the temple of the Holy Ghost, which is in you, which ye have of God, and ye are not your own?" Reverence, therefore, for the Holy Spirit who dwells in others, and for that same Spirit as dwelling in ourselves, should prevent our ever giving utterance to a corrupting thought. The Spirit, says the apostle, *is grieved.* Not only is his holiness offended, but his love is wounded. If any thing can add to the guilt of such conduct, it is its ingratitude, for it is by him, as the apostle adds, *We are sealed unto the day of redemption.* His indwelling certifies that we are the children of God, and secures our final salvation. See 1, 13. To grieve Him, therefore, is to wound him on whom our salvation depends. Though he will not finally withdraw from those in whom he dwells, yet when grieved he withholds the manifestations of his presence. And a disregard for those manifestations is proof that we have not the Spirit of Christ and are none of his.

The apostle next exhorts his readers to put away all malicious and revengeful feelings, to be kind and forgiving. This exhortation is enforced by the consideration of the mercy of God, and the great love of Christ, vs. 31—ch. V. 2.

V. 31. *Let all bitterness, and wrath, and anger, and clamor, and evil speaking, be put away from you.* These are intimately related evils. *Bitterness,* a word transferred from the sphere of sensations to that of the mind. The adjective πικρός means sharp, as an arrow, then pungent to the taste, disagreeable, and then venomous. The poisonous water given to the woman suspected of adultery, Numbers 5, 18, is called the "bitter water." The word bitterness, therefore, in its figurative sense means what is corroding, as grief, or any thing which acts on the mind as poison does on the body, or on the minds of others as venom does on their bodies. The venom of the serpent lies harmless in his fang; but all evil feelings are poison to the subject of them as well as venom to their object. The command, therefore, to lay aside all bitterness, is a com mand to lay aside every thing which corrodes our own minds or wounds the feelings of others. Under this head are the particulars which follow, viz. *wrath;* θυμός, (from θύω, to burn,) means the mind itself as the seat of passions and desires—then the mind in the commotion of passion. 'Οργή, *anger*, is the passion itself, i. e. the manifestation of θυμός, as clamor and evil speaking are the outward expression of anger. The context shows that βλασφημία is neither blasphemy as directed against God, nor merely slander as directed against men; but any form of speech springing from anger, and adapted either to wound or to injure others. *With all malice.* Κακία is a general term for *badness* or *depravity* of any kind. Here the context shows that it means *malevolence*, the desire to injure. We are to lay aside not only wrath and anger but all other forms of malevolent feeling.

V. 32. Exhortation to the opposite virtues. We are required to be χρηστοί. The word properly means *useful;* then disposed to do good. Thus God is said to be χρηστός, *kind* or *benignant*, to the unthankful and the evil, Luke 6, 35. *Tender-hearted*, εὔσπλαγχνοι, which in the parallel passage, Col. 3, 12, is expressed by "bowels of compassion." That is, pity, compassion towards the suffering. *Forgiving one another*, χαρι-ζόμενοι ἑαυτοῖς. The verb means to give as a matter of favour, then to forgive, to pardon freely. *Even as*, i. e. because *God in Christ hath freely forgiven you.* This is the motive which should constrain us to forgive others. God's forgiveness towards us is free; it precedes even our repentance and is the cause of it. It is exercised notwithstanding the number, the enormity and the long continuance of our transgressions. He forgives us far more than we can ever be called upon to forgive others. God forgives us *in Christ*. Out of Christ he is, in virtue of his holiness and justice, a consuming fire; but in him, he is long-suffering, abundant in mercy, and ready to forgive.

Vs. 1. 2. As God has placed us under so great obligation, " be ye, therefore, imitators of God." The exhortation is enlarged. We are not only to imitate God in being forgiving, but also as becomes *dear children, by walking in love*. As God is love, and as we by regeneration and adoption are his children, we are bound to exercise love habitually. Our whole walk should be characterized by it. *As Christ also hath loved us*. This is the reason why we should love one another. We should be like Christ, which is being like God, for Christ is God. The apostle makes no distinction between our being the objects of God's love and our being the objects of the love of Christ. We are to be imitators of God in love, for Christ hath loved us. *And given himself for us*. Here as elsewhere the great evidence of divine love is the death of Christ. See ver. 25. ch. 3, 19. John 15, 13. " Greater love hath no man than this, that a man lay down his life for his friends." Gal. 2, 20, " Who loved me and gave himself for me." 1 John 3, 16, " Hereby perceive we the love *of God*, because he laid down his life for us, and we ought to lay down our lives for the

brethren." Christ's death was *for us* as a sacrifice,
and therefore, from the nature of the transaction, in our
place. Whether the idea of substitution be expressed
by ὑπὲρ ἡμῶν depends on the context rather than on
the force of the preposition. To die for any one, may
mean either for his benefit or in his stead, as the connection demands. Christ gave himself, *as an offering
and a sacrifice*, προσφορὰν καὶ θυσίαν ; the latter term
explains the former. Any thing presented to God was
a προσφορά, but θυσία was something slain. The addition of that term, therefore, determines the nature of
the offering. This is elsewhere determined by the
nature of the thing offered, as in Heb. 10, 10, " the
offering of the body of Christ ; " or, " himself," Heb.
9, 14. 25 ; by the effects ascribed to it, viz. expiation
of guilt and the propitiation of God, which are the appropriate effects of a sin-offering ; see Heb. 2, 17 ; 10,
10. 14 ; Rom. 3, 25 ; 5, 9. 10 : by explanatory expressions, " the one offering of Christ " is declared to be
μίαν ὑπὲρ ἁμαρτιῶν θυσίαν, Heb. 10, 12 ; " a sacrifice
for sin," and προσφορὰ περὶ ἁμαρτίας, Heb. 10, 18 ;
ἀντίλυτρον, and λύτρον ἀντὶ πολλῶν, as in 1 Tim. 2, 6.
Matt. 20, 28 ; it is called a propitiation, Rom. 3, 25, as
well as a ransom. Christ himself, therefore, is called
the Lamb of God who bore our sins ; his blood is the
object of faith or ground of confidence, by which, as
the blood of a sacrifice, we are redeemed, 1 Pet. 1, 18.
19. He saves us as a priest does, i. e. by a sacrifice.
Every victim ever slain on Pagan altars was a declaration of the necessity for such a sacrifice ; all the blood

shed on Jewish altars was a prophecy and promise of propitiation by the blood of Christ; and the whole New Testament is the record of the Son of God offering himself up as a sacrifice for the sins of the world. This, according to the faith of the church universal, is the sum of the Gospel—the incarnation and death of the eternal Son of God as a propitiation for sin. There can, therefore, be no doubt as to the sense in which the apostle here declares Christ to be an offering and a sacrifice.

There is some doubt as to the construction of the words, " to God." They may be connected with what precedes, " He gave himself as a sacrifice to God;" or with the following clause, " For a sweet savour to God," i. e. acceptable to him. The sense of the whole would then be, ' He gave himself, $\pi\alpha\rho\acute{\epsilon}\delta\omega\kappa\epsilon\nu$ $\acute{\epsilon}\alpha\nu\tau\acute{o}\nu$, (unto death, $\epsilon\grave{\iota}\varsigma$ $\vartheta\acute{\alpha}\nu\alpha\tau o\nu$,) an offering and sacrifice well pleasing to God.' The reasons in favour of this construction are—1. That $\pi\alpha\rho\alpha\delta\iota\delta\acute{o}\nu\alpha\iota$ means properly to deliver up to the power of any one, and is not the suitable or common term to express the idea of presenting as a sacrifice. The word almost always used in such cases is $\pi\rho o\sigma\phi\acute{\epsilon}\rho\epsilon\iota\nu$, to bring near to, to offer. 2. With Paul the favourite construction of $\pi\alpha\rho\alpha\delta\iota\delta\acute{o}\nu\alpha\iota$ is with $\epsilon\grave{\iota}\varsigma$ and not with the dative. 3. In Hebrew, from which the phrase $\epsilon\grave{\iota}\varsigma$ $\acute{o}\sigma\mu\grave{\eta}\nu$ $\epsilon\grave{\upsilon}\omega\delta\acute{\iota}\alpha\varsigma$ here used is borrowed, the expression is רֵיחַ־נִיחֹחַ לַיהֹוָה (a sweet smelling savour to Jehovah), which the Septuagint render, $\acute{o}\sigma\mu\grave{\eta}$ $\epsilon\grave{\upsilon}\omega\delta\acute{\iota}\alpha\varsigma$ $\tau\tilde{\omega}$ $K\upsilon\rho\acute{\iota}\omega$. It is not probable in using so familiar a scriptural phrase Paul would depart from the common

construction. The Hebrew phrase properly means a
savour of rest; that is, one which composes, pacifies,
or pleases. The last is what the Greek expresses, and
therefore the equivalent expression is εὐάρεστος τῷ
Θεῷ, *well pleasing to God.* Rom. 12, 1. Phil. 4, 18.
It was in the exercise of the highest conceivable love,
which ought to influence all our conduct, that Christ
delivered himself unto death, an offering and sacrifice
well pleasing unto God.

CHAPTER V

SECTION I.—Vs. 3–20.

3. But fornication, and all uncleanness, or covetousness, let it
4. not be once named among you, as becometh saints; neither
   filthiness, nor foolish talking, nor jesting, which are not con-
5. venient: but rather giving of thanks. For this ye know, that
   no whoremonger, nor unclean person, nor covetous man, who
   is an idolater, hath any inheritance in the kingdom of Christ
6. and of God. Let no man deceive you with vain words: for
   because of these things cometh the wrath of God upon the
7. children of disobedience. Be not ye therefore partakers with
8. them. For ye were sometime darkness, but now *are ye* light
9. in the Lord: walk as children of light; (for the fruit of the
10. Spirit *is* in all goodness, and righteousness, and truth;) prov-
11. ing what is acceptable unto the Lord. And have no fellow-
    ship with the unfruitful works of darkness, but rather reprove
12. *them.* For it is a shame even to speak of those things which
13. are done of them in secret. But all things that are reproved,
    are made manifest by the light: for whatsoever doth make
14. manifest is light. Wherefore he saith, Awake, thou that sleep-
    est, and arise from the dead, and Christ shall give thee light.

15. See that ye walk circumspectly; not as fools, but as wise, re-
16. deeming the time, because the days are evil. Wherefore be ye
17. not unwise, but understanding what the will of the Lord *is*.
18. And be not drunk with wine, wherein is excess; but be filled
19. with the Spirit; speaking to yourselves in psalms, and hymns,
     and spiritual songs, singing and making melody in your heart
20. to the Lord; giving thanks always for all things unto God and
     the Father in the name of our Lord Jesus Christ.

ANALYSIS.

It becomes saints to avoid not only the sins of uncleanness and covetousness, but also all impropriety of
conduct and frivolity of language, vs. 3–4. Because
uncleanness and covetousness not only exclude from
heaven, but, whatever errorists may say, bring down
the wrath of God, vs. 5–6. Christians, therefore, should
not participate in those sins, seeing they have been
divinely enlightened and made the recipients of that
light whose fruits are goodness, righteousness and truth.
They are bound to exemplify this in their conduct,
avoiding and reproving the deeds of darkness, vs. 7–10.
Those deeds are too shameful to be named; still they
may be corrected by the power of that light which it
is the prerogative of believers to disseminate. Therefore the Scriptures speak of the light which flows from
Christ as reaching even to the dead, vs. 12–14. Christians therefore should be wise, making the most of
every occasion for good, in the midst of the evils by
which they are surrounded, vs. 13–16. They should
seek exhilaration not from wine, but from the Holy

Spirit, and give expression to their gladness in psalms and hymns, praising and thanking God through Jesus Christ, vs. 17–20.

COMMENTARY.

V. 3. *But fornication and all uncleanness, or covetousness, let it not be once named among you, as becometh saints.*

In the preceding section the apostle had spoken of sins against our neighbour; here from v. 3 to v. 20 he dwells principally on sins against ourselves. Not only fornication, but every thing of the same nature, or that leads to it, is to be avoided—and not only avoided, but not even named among believers. The inconsistency of all such sins with the character of Christians, as *saints,* men selected from the world and consecrated to God, is such as should forbid the very mention of them in a Christian society. With the sins of uncleanness the apostle here, as in the preceding chapter, v. 19, connects πλεονεξία, *covetousness.* The word is to be taken in its ordinary sense, as there is nothing in the context to justify any departure from it. The assumption that sins of sensuality are alone mentioned in this and the following verse, leads to very forced interpretations of several of the terms employed.

V. 4. *Neither filthiness.* The word αἰσχρότης, is not simply *obscenity,* but whatever is morally hateful. The adjective αἰσχρός means *deformed, revolting,* what excites disgust, physical or moral. It is the opposite of καλός, which means both beautiful and good; and

hence τὸ καλόν καὶ τὸ αἰσχρόν, means *virtue and vice.*
The substantive is equally comprehensive, and includes
whatever is vile or disgusting in speech or conduct.
Lesser evils are expressed by the words μωρολογία and
εὐτραπελία, *foolish talking* and *jesting.* The former
means such talk as is characteristic of fools, i. e. frivo-
lous and senseless. The latter, according to its etymology and early usage, means *urbanity, politeness.*
Naturally enough however the word came to have a
bad sense, as the adjective εὐτράπελος, *what turns
easily,* as the wind, when applied to language or speech,
means not only adroit, skilful, agreeable, witty, but
also flippant, satirical, scurrilous. Hence the substantive is used for *jesting* and *scurrility.* The former
sense is best suited to this passage, because it is connected with foolish talking, and because the apostle
says of both simply that they *are not convenient,* not
becoming or suitable. This is too mild a form of expression to be used either of αἰσχρότης (filthiness) or of
εὐτραπελία in the worse sense of those terms. Paul
says, these things (foolish talking and jesting) do not
become Christians; οὐκ ἀνήκοντα, *what does not pertain to any one,* or, *to his office.* Foolish talking and
jesting are not the ways in which Christian cheerfulness should express itself, but rather *giving of thanks.*
Religion is the source of joy and gladness, but its joy
is expressed in a religious way, in thanksgiving and
praise.

V. 5. The apostle reverts to what he said in v. 3,
and enforces the exhortation there given. "For this ye

know, that no whoremonger, nor unclean person, nor
covetous man, who is an idolater, hath any inheritance
in the kingdom of Christ and of God." The form of
expression is peculiar, ἴστε* γινώσκοντες, *ye know knowing.* Many refer this to the familiar Hebrew idiom, in
which the infinitive and finite tense of a verb are thus
joined, which in Greek and English is imitated by
uniting the participle and verb; as " dying thou shalt
die," " multiplying I will multiply," " blessing I will
bless," &c. But in all these cases the infinitive and
finite tense are different forms of the same verb. Here
we have different words. The preferable interpretation
is to refer ἴστε to what precedes in v. 3, and γινώσκοντες
to what follows: ' This ye know, viz., that such vices
should not be named among you, knowing that no one
who indulges in them, &c.'

Covetous man who is an idolater. The words ὅς
ἐστιν εἰδωλολάτρης are by many referred to all the preceding nouns, so that the fornicator, the unclean person,
and the covetous man, are all alike declared to be idol-
aters. This is possible so far as the grammatical construction is concerned; but it is not natural, and not
consistent with the parallel passage in Col. 3, 5, where
the apostle singles out covetousness from a list of sins,
and says, ' It is idolatry.' This too has its foundation
both in nature and in Scripture. The analogy between
this supreme love of riches, this service of Mammon

---

* The common text has ἐστε, but the evidence in favour of ἴστε is so
strong that it is adopted by all recent editors.

and idolatry, is more obvious and more distinctly recognized in Scripture than between idolatry and any
other of the sins mentioned. It is well that this should
be understood, that men should know, that the most
common of all sins, is the most heinous in the sight of
God. For idolatry, which consists in putting the creature in the place of God, is every where in his word
denounced as the greatest of all sins in his sight.
The fact that it is compatible with outward decorum
and with the respect of men, does not alter its nature.
It is the permanent and controlling principle of an
irreligious heart and life, turning the soul away from
God. There is no cure for this destructive love of
money, but using it for other than selfish purposes.
Riches, therefore, must ruin their possessor, unless he
employs them for the good of others and for the glory
of God.

It is of the covetous man no less than of the fornicator, the apostle says, he has no inheritance in the
kingdom of Christ. That is, in that kingdom which
Christ came to establish—which consists of all the redeemed, washed in his blood, sanctified by his Spirit,
and made perfectly blessed in the full enjoyment of
God to all eternity. This kingdom is sometimes called
the kingdom of Christ, and sometimes the kingdom of
God; for where Christ reigns, God reigns. Here it is
designated the βασιλεία τοῦ Χριστοῦ καὶ Θεοῦ, that is,
of him who is at once Χριστός and Θεός; Christ and
God. This is certainly the most natural interpretation.
As every one admits that τῷ Θεῷ καὶ πατρί means " to

him who is at once God and Father." There is no
reason why the same rule should not be applied in this
case. Compare Titus 2, 13. This view of the passage,
which makes it a direct assertion of the divinity of our
Lord, is strenuously insisted upon by some of the most
eminent of modern interpreters, as Harless and Rückert,
the one orthodox and the other rationalistic. Others,
however, say that *Christ* here designates the Redeemer,
and *God*, the divine Being; and that the kingdom is
called not only the kingdom of Christ, but also the kingdom of God. This is the view more commonly adopted,
though in violation of a general rule of grammar, the
article being omitted before $\Theta\epsilon o\hat{v}$. If, in Titus 2, 13,
$\dot{\epsilon}\pi\iota\phi\acute{a}\nu\epsilon\iota a$ $\tau\hat{\eta}s$ $\delta\acute{o}\xi\eta s$ $\tau o\hat{v}$ $\mu\epsilon\gamma\acute{a}\lambda o\upsilon$ $\Theta\epsilon o\hat{v}$ $\kappa a\grave{\iota}$ $\sigma\omega\tau\hat{\eta}\rho os$ $\dot{\eta}\mu\hat{\omega}\nu$
$\dot{I}\eta\sigma o\hat{v}$ $X\rho\iota\sigma\tau o\hat{v}$, means that Jesus Christ is at once the
great God and our Saviour, and Winer admits (Gram.
p. 148) that it is for doctrinal reasons only he dissents
from that interpretation; then there can be no reasonable doubt in the present case, where the form of expression is so similar, the writer being the same, that
the idea is the same. If it were a rare or uncertain
thing for Paul to recognize Christ as God, it would be
wrong to press rules of grammar to make him teach
that doctrine. But since every page almost of his
epistles teems with evidence that Christ was his God,
it is wrong to depart from those rules in order to prevent his teaching it.

V. 6. It is not only among the heathen, but among
the mass of men in all ages and nations, a common
thing to extenuate the particular sins to which the

apostle here refers. It is urged that they have their origin in the very consitution of our nature; that they are not malignant; that they may co-exist with amiable tempers; and that they are not hurtful to others, that no one is the worse for them if no one knows them, &c. Paul, therefore, cautions his readers in every age of the church, not to be deceived by such vain words; assuring them that for these things (for fornication and covetousness), the wrath of God cometh on the children of disobedience. *With vain words*, κενοῖς λόγοις. Κενός means *empty*. Κενοὶ λόγοι, therefore, are empty words; words which contain no truth, and are therefore both false and fallacious, as those will find who trust to them. *The wrath of God.* This expression is a fearful one, because the wrath of man is the disposition to inflict evil, limited by man's feebleness; whereas the wrath of God is the determination to punish in a being without limit either as to his presence or power. This wrath, the apostle says, *cometh* on the children of disobedience. The present is either for the certain future, 'will assuredly come;' or it has its proper force. The wrath of God against these sins is now manifested in his dealings with those who commit them. He withdraws from them his Spirit, and finally gives them up to a reprobate mind. On the phrase " children of disobedience," see ch. 2, 2.

V. 7. Such being the determination of God to punish the unclean and the covetous, the apostle says, " Be ye not therefore partakers with them." That is, be not their associates in these sins, which of necessity would expose you to the penalty threatened against them.

V. 8. This is enforced by a reference to their conversion from a previous state of sin and misery to one of holiness and blessedness. *For ye were sometime darkness.* As *light* stands for knowledge, and as knowledge, in the scriptural sense of the word, produces holiness, and holiness happiness; so *darkness* stands for ignorance, such ignorance as inevitably produces sin, and sin misery. Therefore, the expression, " ye were darkness," means, ye were ignorant, polluted, and wretched. *But now ye are light in the Lord,* i. e. in virtue of union with the Lord, ye are enlightened, sanctified, and blessed. *Walk as children of the light,* i. e. as the children of holiness and truth. " Children of light," means *enlightened;* as ' children of famine,' means the ' famished;' see ch. 2, 2. The exhortation is that they should walk in a way consistent with their character as men illuminated and sanctified by their union with the Lord Jesus.

V. 9. *For the fruit of light,** i. e. the fruit or effect of divine illumination is in all, i. e. consists in all the forms of goodness, righteousness, and truth. *Goodness,* ἀγαθωσύνη, is that which makes a man ἀγαθός, *good;* and *righteousness,* δικαιοσύνη, is that which makes a man δίκαιος, *righteous.* These Greek words differ very

---

* The common text has here πνεύματος instead of φωτός. The latter reading is now universally adopted as the correct one on the authority not only of the MSS. but of the context.

much as the corresponding English terms do. Goodness is benevolence and beneficence; righteousness is adherence to the rule of right. Yet both are used for moral excellence in general. The evil and the good, included all .classes of the vicious and the virtuous. *Good works* are works of any kind which are morally excellent. When however the words are contrasted as in Rom. 5, 7, or distinguished as in Rom. 7, 12, *good* means benevolent or beneficent; and *righteous*, just or upright. Goodness is that quality which adapts a thing to the end for which it was designed, and renders it serviceable. Hence we speak of a good tree, of good soil, as well as of a good man. *Righteousness* can properly be predicated only of persons or of what is susceptible of moral character; as it means conformity to law; or if predicated of the law itself, it means conformity to the nature of God, the ultimate standard of rectitude. *Truth*, here means religious or moral truth, or religion itself. The fruits of light, therefore, are all the forms of piety and virtue.

V. 10. Verse 9 is a parenthesis, as the 10th verse is grammatically connected with the 8th. " Walk as children of the light, proving, &c.," περιπατεῖτε—δοκιμάζοντες. Δοκιμάζειν is to try, to put to the test, to examine; then to judge or estimate; and then to approve. Thus it is said, " The fire shall try every man's work ; " God is said " To try the heart ; " we are said " To be renewed so as to prove the will of God," Rom. 12, 2, that is, to examine and determine what the will of God is. And so in this passage believers are required to walk as children of light, examining and determining what is acceptable to the Lord. They are to regulate their conduct by a regard to what is well pleasing to Him. That is the ultimate standard of judging whether any thing is right or wrong, worthy or unworthy of those who have been enlightened from above.

The word LORD is in the New Testament so predominantly used to designate the Lord Jesus Christ, that it is always to be referred to him unless the context forbids it. Here the context so far from forbidding, requires such reference. For in the former part of the sentence *Lord* evidently designates Christ. " Ye are light in the Lord, therefore, walk as children of the light, proving what is acceptable to the Lord." This, therefore, is one of the numerous passages in the New Testament, in which Christ is recognized as the Lord of the conscience, whose will is to us the ultimate standard of right and wrong, and to whom we are responsible for all our inward and outward acts. It is thus that the sacred writers show that Christ was their God, in whose presence they constantly lived, whose favour they constantly sought, and on whom all their religious affections terminated. He was not merely the God of their theology, but of their religion.

V. 11. The apostle having in the previous verse insisted on the duty of Christians of so walking as to show by their works that they were the subjects of divine illumination, adds here a statement of their duty in reference to the sins of those still in darkness. Those

sins he calls " the unfruitful works of darkness." By
unfruitful is meant not merely *barren* or *worthless*, but
positively evil. For in a moral subject the negation
of good is evil. *Works of darkness* are those works
which spring from darkness, i. e. from ignorance of
God; as " works of light " are those works which
light or divine knowledge produces.

The duty of Christians in reference to the works of
darkness is twofold ; first, to have no communion with
them ; and secondly, to reprove them. The former is
expressed by the words μὴ συγκοινωνεῖτε, *have not fellowship* with them. Those who have things in common ; who are congenial ; who have the same views,
feelings, and interests ; and who therefore delight in
each other's society, are said to be in fellowship. In
this sense believers have fellowship with God and with
each other. So we are said to have fellowship in any
thing which we delight in and partake of. To have
fellowship with the works of darkness, therefore, is to
delight in them and to participate in them. All such
association is forbidden as inconsistent with the character of the children of light. Our second duty is *to
reprove them*. Ἐλέγχειν is not simply to reprove in
the sense of admonishing or rebuking. It means to
convince by evidence. It expresses the effect of illumination by which the true nature of any thing is
revealed. When the Spirit is said to reprove men of
sin, it means that he sheds such light upon their sins
as to reveal their true character, and to produce the
consequent consciousness of guilt and pollution. In

1 Cor. 14, 24, Paul says the effect of intelligible preach
ing of the Gospel is conviction—which is explained by
saying "the secrets of the heart are revealed." The
duty, therefore, here enjoined is to shed light on these
works of darkness; to exhibit them in their true nature
as vile and destructive. By this method they are corrected; as is more fully taught in the following verses.
The ethics as well as the theology of the Bible are
founded on the principle, that knowledge and holiness,
ignorance and sin, are inseparable. If you impart
knowledge you secure holiness; and if you render
ignorant you deprave. This of course is not true of
secular knowledge—i. e. of the knowledge of other
than religious subjects ; nor is it true of mere speculative knowledge of religious truth. It is true only of
that knowledge which the Scriptures call spiritual discernment. Of that knowledge, however, intellectual
cognition is an essential element. And so far as human
agency in the production of the conviction of sin is
concerned, it is limited to holding forth the word of
life ; or letting the light of divine truth shine into the
darkened minds of men, and upon their evil deeds.

V. 12. These works of darkness should be thus reproved, "for it is a shame even to speak of those things
which are done of them in secret." There are two
reasons why sins are called works of darkness. The
first and principal one is, as before remarked, because
they spring from darkness or ignorance of God; and
the second is, because they are committed in darkness.
They shun the light. The exceeding turpitude of these

sins the apostle gives as the reason why they should be reproved.

V. 13. Vile however as those sins are, they are capable of being corrected. They are not beyond cure. Reprove them. Let in the light of divine truth upon them, and they will be corrected or healed. For the truth is divinely efficacious. It is the organon of God; that through which he exerts his power in the sanctification and salvation of men. Such seems to be the general meaning of this difficult verse.

It is connected with the preceding verse, and is designed to enforce the command, ἐλέγχετε, *reprove.* 'Reprove the things done in secret by the wicked—for though they are too bad to be even named, yet being reproved, they are made manifest by the light, and thereby corrected, for every thing made manifest, i. e. revealed in its true nature by divine light, becomes light; that is, is reformed.' This interpretation gives a simple and consistent sense, assumes no unusual signification of the terms employed, nor any forced construction, and is suited to the context. It supposes—
1. That τὰ πάντα ἐλεγχόμενα refers to τὰ κρυφῇ γινόμενα of v. 12. The things done in secret are the *all things,* which being reproved, are manifested. 2. The words ὑπὸ τοῦ φωτός are not to be connected with ἐλεγχόμενα, as though the sense were, 'being reproved by the light;' but with φανεροῦται, so that the sense is, 'are made manifest by the light.' This construction is required by the following clause. 3. φανερούμενον is passive, and not middle with an active sense. The

meaning is, 'Whatever is manifested;' not 'whatever makes manifest.' As the word φανεροῦται just before is passive, it is unnatural to make φανερούμενον active. Besides, the apostle is not speaking of the nature of spiritual light, but of its effects. It illuminates or turns into light all it touches, or wherever it penetrates.

If φανερούμενον be taken as active, as is done by Calvin and many others, and by our translators, the sense would be, 'Reprove these things; it is your office to do so, for you are light, and light is that which makes manifest.' This however is not what Paul says. He does not say 'Reprove evil, for you are light,' but, 'Reprove evil, for evil when reproved by light is manifest, and when manifest, it is light,' that is, it is changed into light, or corrected. In v. 8, he had said, "Ye are light;" so here he says, what is illuminated by the truth becomes light. The sense is the same in both cases. The penetration of spiritual light, or divine truth, carries with it such power, that it illuminates and sanctifies all in whom it dwells. Hence the apostle elsewhere prays that the word of God may dwell in the hearts of believers in all wisdom and spiritual understanding. According to the apostle, the relation between truth and holiness is analogous to that between light and vision. Light cannot create the eye, or give to a blind eye the power of vision. But it is essential to its exercise. Wherever it penetrates, it dissipates darkness and brings every thing into view—and causes it to produce its appropriate effect. So truth cannot regenerate, or impart the principle of spiritual life.

But it is essential to all holy exercises. And wherevei
the truth penetrates, it dissipates the clouds of error,
and brings every thing to view, so that when spiritually
discerned it produces its proper effect on the soul.
Truth being thus essential, it is the duty of Christians to
bring it to bear upon all those who are ignorant and on
all the works of darkness.

V. 14. As light is thus efficacious, and as it is accessible, or may be obtained, therefore the Scriptures
call even upon the sleeping and the dead to arise and
meet its life-giving beams. $Διὸ λέγει$, scil. $ἡ γραφή$.
As this formula of quotation is never used in the New
Testament except when citations are made from the
Old Testament, it cannot properly be assumed that the
apostle here quotes some Christian hymn with which
the believers in Ephesus were familiar; or some apocry-
phal book; or some inspired book no longer extant.
We must understand him either as referring to many
exhortations of the Old Testament Scriptures, the substance of which he condenses in the few words here
used; or as giving the spirit of some one passage,
though not its words. Both these methods of explanation may be sustained by appeal to similar passages.
The apostles in quoting the Old Testament sometimes
combined several passages in the same quotation—and
sometimes give as the teaching of the prophets what is
nowhere taught or asserted in express terms, but is
abundantly or clearly implied in what they say. At
other times again, the reference is obviously to some
one passage, and yet neither the Hebrew nor Septua-

gint is accurately followed, but the general idea is reproduced. We without the authority and divine guidance of the apostles deal in the same way with the word of God, of which almost every sermon would furnish examples. It is generally assumed that Paul here refers to Is. 60, 1, "Arise, shine; for thy light is come, and the glory of the Lord is risen upon thee." Or, as De Wette renders it; "Auf, werde licht, denn es kommt dein Licht, und die Herrlichkeit Jehovah's gehet über dir auf." *Up, become light; for thy light comes, and the glory of Jehovah riseth over thee.* The analogy between this passage and the quotation of the apostle is plain. There are in both—1. The call to those who are asleep or dead to rise. 2. To receive the light. 3. The promise that Jehovah, Lord, or Christ, equivalent terms in the mind of the apostle, would give them light. There can, therefore, be little doubt that it was the language of Isaiah Paul intended in substance to quote. Beza thinks that Is. 26, 19, "Awake and sing, ye that dwell in the dust," &c., is to be included in the reference; and others join Is. 9, 2, "The people that walked in darkness have seen a great light; they that dwell in the land of the shadow of death, upon them hath the light shined." It is true that in these, as well as in other passages, the power of light, i. e. of divine truth, its advent in the person of Christ, and the call to those who are in darkness to accept it, are included. But the probability is that Is. 60, 1, was the passage most distinctly in the apostle's mind.

Those asleep and the dead are in darkness, and
therefore those involved in spiritual darkness are addressed as sleeping. The light which comes from
Christ has power to reach even the dead—as our Lord,
in the use of another figure, says, "The hour is coming,
and now is, that the dead shall hear the voice of the
Son of God, and they that hear shall live," John 5, 25.
This does not mean that the dead must be revived before they hear the voice of the Son of God, but his
voice causes them to hear and live. So the passage
before us does not mean that those asleep must arise
from the dead and come to Christ for light; but that
the light which Christ sheds around him, has power to
awake the sleeping dead. Thus the passage is a confirmation of what is said in the preceding verse, viz.,
that every thing made manifest by the light, is light.

V. 15. If this verse be considered as connected in-
ferentially by οὖν with the preceding, then the association of ideas is: ' If believers are bound to dispel the
darkness from the hearts and lives of others, how careful should they be not to be dark themselves, i. e. they
should walk as wise men.' This however seems forced.
The exhortation contained in this and the following
verse is most naturally connected with that contained
in verses 10 and 11. Believers as children of light are
required to have no fellowship with the works of darkness, but rather to reprove them; *see therefore*, i. e.
take heed therefore, πῶς ἀκριβῶς περιπατεῖτε, *that ye
walk circumspectly*. Πῶς, however, does not mean
that, though often used where ὅτι or ἵνα might be

employed. It here as elsewhere means *how*, *in what manner.* " See in what manner ye render your deportment accurate." Ἀκριβῶς περιπατεῖν is to walk strictly by rule, so as not to deviate by a hair's breadth. *Not as unwise, but as wise.* Paul often uses the word σοφία for divine truth. The σοφοί are those who possess this truth, which he had before called light, and the ἄσοφοι are those who have it not. So that *wise* and *unwise* are here equivalent to the *enlightened* and *those in darkness.* His exhortation, therefore, is that believers should carefully deport themselves not as the heathen and unrenewed, who have not the divine light of which he had been speaking, but as those who are enlightened from above and are therefore wise.

V. 16. Ἐξαγοραζόμενοι τὸν καιρόν, *redeeming the time.* This is one manifestation of wisdom, one method in which their Christian character as the children of light should be exhibited. The words have been variously explained :—1. Making use of, availing yourselves of the occasion for doing good, not allowing it to pass unimproved. 2. Buying back the time, redeeming it, as it were, from Satan or from the world. 3. Making the most of time, i. e. using it to the best advantage. 4. Adapting yourselves to the occasion, &c. The decision between these different views depends partly on the sense to be given to ἐξαγοραζόμενοι, and partly on the question whether καιρός is to be taken in its proper sense, *opportunity, appropriate time ;* or in the general sense of χρόνος, *time..* The words ἀγοράζειν and ἐξαγοράζειν, have in common the idea of acquiring by purchase. The latter in virtue of the force of the ἐκ properly means to purchase back, or to make free by purchase. But it is also used in the sense of the simple verb, as in Daniel 2, 8, whence the expression in the text is probably derived. There, according to the Septuagint, the king said to the Chaldeans, who declined to interpret his dream until they knew what it was, οἶδα ἐγὼ ὅτι καιρὸν ὑμεῖς ἐξαγοράζετε, " I know you wish to gain time." This sense of the verb suits the passage before us. Then if καιρός means here what it does in almost every other passage, where it occurs in the New Testament, the most natural interpretation of the clause is, " availing yourselves of the occasion," i. e. improving every opportunity for good. If καιρός be taken for χρόνος, which is barely admissible, the sense would be, " making the most of time," i. e. rescuing it from waste or abuse. Both of these interpretations are good and suited to the following clause, *because the days are evil.* Πονηρός, *evil,* may be taken either in a physical or moral sense. The patriarch said, " Few and evil have the days of the years of my life been ; " Gen. 47, 9. The moral sense of the word, however, is better suited to the context. *Evil days,* mean days in which sin abounds. It is parallel to the expressions, " evil generation," Matt. 12, 39 ; and " evil world," Gal. 1, 4. Because sin abounds is a good reason why Christians should seize upon every opportunity to do good ; and also why they should make the most of time. So that this clause suits either of the interpretations of the first part of the verse. That καιρός properly and commonly means *opportunity*, or *suitable time*, is a strong reason for preferring the former of the two interpretations mentioned. The same exhortation and in the same connection is found in Col. 4, 5. Here the apostle says, " See that ye walk as wise men, redeeming the time ; " there, " Walk in wisdom, redeeming the time." So that this right use of time, or this seizing on every opportunity for doing good, is in both places represented as the evidence and effect of wisdom, i. e. of divine truth, which is the wisdom of God, which he has revealed, 1 Cor. 2, 6–13.

V. 17. *Therefore*, i. e. either because the days are evil ; or, because ye are bound to walk as wise men. The latter mode of connection is to be preferred, because the reference is to the main idea of the preceding verses 15 and 16, and not to a subordinate clause. *Be ye not*, ἄφρονες, *senseless, unthinking, trifling*. Comp. Luke 11, 40, " Ye fools (ye unthinking ones), did not he that made that which is without, make that which is within also ; " also Luke 12, 20 ; 1 Cor. 15, 36 ; 2 Cor. 11, 16, &c. In all these cases ἄφρων means one who does not make a right use of his understanding ; who does not see things in their true light, or estimate them according to their relative importance. It is here opposed to συνιέντες. 'Be ye not senseless, undiscriminating between what is true and false, right and wrong, important and unimportant, but understanding, i. e. discerning what the will of the Lord is.' That is, seeing things as he sees them, and making his will or judgment the standard of yours, and the rule of your conduct. The will of the Lord is the will of Christ. That Lord here means Christ, is plain not only from the general usage of the New Testament, so often referred to, but also from the constant use of the word in this chapter as a designation of the Redeemer. Here again, therefore, the divinity of Christ is seen to be a practical doctrine entering into the daily religious life of the believer. His will is the rule of truth and duty.

V. 18. *And* (especially) *be not drunk with wine.* This is an ἀφρόσυνη, a want of sense, especially inconsistent with the intelligence of the true believer. The man who has a right discernment will not seek refreshment or excitement from wine, but from the Holy Spirit. Therefore the apostle adds, *but be filled with the Spirit.* In drunkenness, he says, there is ἀσωτία, *revelry, debauchery, riot,* whatever tends to destruction; for the word is derived from ἄσωτος, which means, *what cannot be saved,* one given up to a destructive course of life. Comp. Tit. 1, 6. 1 Pet. 4, 4. Men are said to be filled with wine when completely under its influence; so they are said to be filled with the Spirit, when he controls all their thoughts, feelings, words, and actions. The expression is a common one in Scripture. Of our Lord himself it was said, " He was full of the Holy Ghost," Luke 4, 1; so of Stephen that " he was full of faith and of the Holy Ghost," Acts 6, 5; and of Barnabas, Acts 11, 24, &c. To the Christian, therefore, the source of strength and joy is not

wine, but the blessed Spirit of God. And as drunkenness produces rioting and debauchery, so the Holy
Spirit produces a joy which expresses itself in psalms,
and hymns, and spiritual songs. Quid gignit ebrie-
tas? dissolutam proterviam, ut quasi excusso freno
indecenter homines exultent. Quid spiritualis laetitia,
quum ea perfusi sumus? hymnos, psalmos, laudes Dei,
gratiarum actiones. Hi sunt vere jucundi fructus et
delectabiles. CALVIN.

V. 19. Λαλοῦντες ἑαυτοῖς (i. e. ἀλλήλοις, as in 4, 32,
and elsewhere), *speaking to each other*, not *to yourselves*.
Compare Col. 3, 16, where it is, διδάσκοντες καὶ νουθε-
τοῦντες ἑαυτούς, *teaching and admonishing one another*.
"Speaking to each other," signifies the interchange
of thoughts and feelings expressed in the psalms and
hymns employed. This is supposed to refer to responsive singing, in the private assemblies and public
worship of Christians, to which the well-known passage
of Pliny: *Carmen Christo quasi Deo dicunt secum in-
vicem*, seems also to refer. Whether the passage refers
to the responsive method of singing or not, which is
somewhat doubtful from the parallel passage in Colossians (where Paul speaks of their teaching one another),
it at least proves that singing was from the beginning
a part of Christian worship, and that not only psalms
but hymns also were employed.

The early usage of the words ψαλμός, ὕμνος, ᾠδή,
appears to have been as loose as that of the corresponding English terms, *psalm, hymn, song*, is with us. A
psalm was a hymn, and a hymn a song. Still there

was a distinction between them as there is still. A *psalm* was, agreeably to the etymology of the word ψαλμός, a song designed to be sung with the accompaniment of instrumental music. 2. It was one of the sacred poems contained in the book of Psalms, as in Acts 13, 33, ἐν τῷ ψαλμῷ τῷ δευτέρῳ, *in the second Psalm ;* and Acts 1, 20, ἐν βίβλῳ ψαλμῶν, *in the book of Psalms.* 3. Any sacred poem formed on the model of the Old Testament Psalms, as in 1 Cor. 14, 26, where ψαλμόν appears to mean such a song given by inspiration, and not one of the psalms of David. *A Hymn* was a song of praise to God ; a divine song. ARRIAN, Exped. Alex. 4, ὕμνοι μὲν ἐς. τοὺς θεοὺς ποιοῦνται, ἔπαινοι δὲ ἐς ἀνθρώπους. AMMON. de differ. vocbl. ὁ μὲν γὰρ ὕμνος ἔστι θεῶν, τὸ δὲ ἐγκώμιον τῶν ἀνθρώπων. PHAVOR. ὕμνος· ἡ πρὸς θεὸν ᾠδή. Such being the general meaning of the word, Josephus uses it of those Psalms which were songs of praise to God : ὁ Δαυΐδος ᾠδὰς εἰς τὸν Θεὸν καὶ ὕμνους συνετάξατο, Ant. 7. 12, 3. Psalms and hymns then, as now, were religious songs ; ᾠδαί were religious or secular, and therefore those here intended are described as *spiritual.* This may mean either *inspired,* i. e. derived from the Spirit ; or expressing spiritual thoughts and feelings. This latter is the more probable ; as not only inspired men are said to be filled with the Spirit, but all those who in their ordinary thoughts and feelings are governed by the Holy Ghost.

Singing and making melody in your hearts to the Lord. If this clause be considered as coördinate with the preceding, then it refers to a different kind of singing. The former expressed by λαλοῦντες ἑαυτοῖς is singing audibly, the latter by ᾄδοντες ἐν τῇ καρδίᾳ is the music of the heart, the rhythm of the affections not clothed in words. In favour of this view, which is adopted by several of the best modern commentators, as Harless, Rückert, Olshausen, and Meyer, it is urged that the apostle says, ἐν τῇ καρδίᾳ ὑμῶν and not simply ἐκ καρδίας, *from the heart;* and that the pronoun ὑμῶν, *your,* would be unnecessary, had he meant only that the singing was to be cordial. Besides, the singing here referred to is that of those filled with the Spirit, and therefore the caution that it should not be a mere lip service is out of place. Notwithstanding these reasons, the great majority of commentators make this clause subordinate to the preceding and descriptive of the kind of singing required, " You are to commence with each in Psalms and Hymns, singing in your heart." Comp. Rom. 1, 9, where the apostle says: ᾧ λατρεύω (not ἐκ πνεύματος but) ἐν τῷ πνεύματί μου, *whom I serve in my spirit,* and 1 Cor. 14, 15. There is no sufficient reason for departing from the ordinary view of the passage.

ᾄδοντες καὶ ψάλλοντες, *singing and making melody,* are two forms of expressing the same thing. The latter term is the more comprehensive; as ᾄδειν is to make music with the voice; ψάλλειν, *to make music in any way;* literally, to play on a stringed instrument; then, to sing in concert with such an instrument; then, to sing or chant. See 1 Cor. 14, 15; James 5, 13; Rom. 15, 9.

To the Lord, i. e. to Christ.   In the parallel passage,
Col. 3, 16, it is *to God.*   In either form the idea is the
same.   In worshipping Christ we worship God.   God
in Christ, however, is the definite, special object of
Christian worship, to whom the heart when filled with
the Spirit instinctively turns.   This special worship of
Christ is neither inconsistent with the worship of the
Father, nor is it ever dissociated from it.   The one runs
into the other.   And

V. 20.   Therefore the apostle connects the two;
"Be ye filled with the Spirit, singing hymns to Christ,
and giving thanks to God even the Father."   The Spirit
dictates the one as naturally as the other.   We are to
give thanks *always.*   It is not a duty to be performed
once for all, nor merely when new mercies are received; but always, because we are under obligation
for blessings temporal and spiritual already received,
which calls for perpetual acknowledgment.   We are to
give thanks *for all things;* afflictions as well as for our
joys, say the ancient commentators.   This is not in the
text, though Paul, as we learn from other passages,
gloried in his afflictions.   Here the words are limited
by the context, *for all our mercies.   In the name of the
Lord Jesus.*   The apostles preached in the name of the
Lord Jesus; they wrought miracles in his name; believers are commanded to pray in his name; to give
thanks in his name, and to do all things in his name.
In all these cases the general idea is that expressed by
Bengel : ut perinde sit, ac si Christus faciat.   What we
do in the name of Christ we do by his authority, and

relying on him for success. Christ gives us access to the Father; we come to God through him; he gives the right to come, and it is on him we depend for acceptance when we come. Τῷ Θεῷ καὶ πατρί, *God even the Father*, i. e. to God the Father of our Lord Jesus Christ. This is the covenant title of God under the new dispensation, and presents the only ground on which he can be approached as our Father.

SECTION II.—Vs. 17–33.

21. Submitting yourselves one to another in the fear of God.
22. Wives, submit yourselves unto your own husbands, as unto the
23. Lord. For the husband is the head of the wife, even as Christ is the head of the church : and he is the Saviour of the body.
24. Therefore as the church is subject unto Christ, so *let* the wives
25. *be* to their own husbands in every thing. Husbands, love your wives, even as Christ also loved the church, and gave himself
26. for it; that he might sanctify and cleanse it with the washing
27. of water by the word: that he might present it to himself a glorious church, not having spot or wrinkle, or any such thing;
28. but that it should be holy and without blemish. So ought men to love their wives, as their own bodies. He that loveth his
29. wife loveth himself. For no man ever yet hated his own flesh; but nourisheth and cherisheth it, even as the Lord the church:
30. for we are members of his body, of his flesh, and of his bones.
31. For this cause shall a man leave his father and mother, and shall be joined unto his wife, and they two shall be one flesh.
32. This is a great mystery : but I speak concerning Christ and the
33. church. Nevertheless, let every one of you in particular so love his wife even as himself: and the wife *see* that she reverence *her* husband.

ANALYSIS.

The apostle enjoins mutual obedience as a Christian duty, v. 21. Under this head he treats of the relative duties of husbands and wives, parents and children, masters and servants. The remainder of this chapter is devoted to the duties of husbands and wives. As the conjugal relation is analogous to that which Christ sustains to the church, the one serves to illustrate the others. The apostle, therefore, combines the two subjects throughout the paragraph.

Wives should be subject to their husbands as the church is to Christ. 1. The motive to this subject is a regard to the Lord, v. 22. 2. The ground of it is, that the husband is the head of the wife, as Christ is the head of the church, v. 23. 3. This subjection is not confined to any one sphere, but extends to all, v. 24.

Husbands should love their wives. 1. The measure of this love is Christ's love for the church for whose redemption he died, vs. 25–27. 2. The ground of love is in both cases the same—the wife is flesh of her husband's flesh, and bone of his bone. So the church is flesh of Christ's flesh and bone of his bone. Husband and wife are one flesh; so are Christ and the church. What is true of the one is true of the other, vs, 29–31. 3. The union between Christ and his church is indeed of a higher order than that between husband and wife—nevertheless the analogy between the two cases is such as to render it obligatory on the husband to love his wife as being himself, and on the wife to reverence her husband, vs. 32–33.

V. 21. That a new paragraph begins with this verse is generally conceded. First, because the preceding exhortations are evidently brought to a close in v. 20— with the words *to God even the Father.* And secondly, because the command to be obedient one to another, amplified through this chapter and part of the next, does not naturally cohere with what precedes. This being the case, the participle ὑποτασσόμενοι *being obedient,* with which this verse begins, cannot be explained by referring it to the verb πληροῦσθε in v. 18. The sense would then be, 'Be filled with the Spirit—submitting yourselves one to another.' This construction of the passage for the reasons just stated is rejected by most commentators. Others take the participle for the imperative and render the words, 'Be subject one to another.' But this is contrary to the usage of the language. The most common explanation is to connect this verse with the following, 'Being subject one to another (as ye are bound to be), ye wives be subject to your husbands.' From the general obligation to obedience follows the special obligation of wives, children, and servants, as explained in what follows.

This command to submit one to another is found in other passages of the New Testament, as in 1 Pet. 5, 5, " All of you be subject one to another, and be clothed with humility." Rom. 12, 10. Phil. 2. 3. The scriptural doctrine on this subject is that men are not isolated individuals, each one independent of all others. No man liveth for himself and no man dieth for himself. The essential equality of men and their mutual dependence lay the foundation for the obligation of mutual subjection. The apostle however is here speaking of the duties of Christians. It is, therefore, the Christian duty of mutual submission of which this passage treats. It not only forbids pride and all assumption of superiority, but enjoins mutual subjection, the subjection of a part to the whole, and of each one to those of his fellow believers with whom he is specially connected. Every Christian is responsible for his faith and conduct to his brethren in the Lord, because he constitutes with them one body having a common faith and a common life. The independency of one Christian of all others, or of one Christian society of all similar societies, is inconsistent with the relation in which believers stand to each other, and with the express commands of Scripture.

We are to be thus subject one to another ἐν φοβῷ Χριστοῦ.* This may mean either that the fear of Christ, at whose bar we are to stand in judgment, should constrain us to this mutual subjection; or that the duty should be religiously performed. The motive should be reverence for Christ, a regard for his will and for

* The common text reads Θεοῦ, but the authority of the MSS. and versions is so decidedly in favour of Χριστοῦ that it is now universally adopted.

his glory. It is in this way all social duties, even the most humiliating, are raised into the sphere of religion, and rendered consistent with the highest elevation and liberty. This idea is specially insisted upon by the apostle when he comes to speak of the duty of servants to their masters. It ought not to escape the reader's notice that the relation in which this and similar passages suppose us to stand to Christ, is such as we can sustain to no other than to a divine person. He to whom we are responsible for all our conduct, and reverence for whom is the great motive to the performance of duty, is God.

V. 22. *Wives, submit yourselves to your own husbands, as unto the Lord.* The general duty of mutual submission includes the specific duty of wives to be subject to their husbands, and this leads the apostle to speak of the relative duties of husbands and wives. And as the marriage relation is analogous to the relation between Christ and his church, he is thus led to illustrate the one by the other. As the relation is the same, the duties flowing from it are the same; obedience on the part of the wife, and love on the part of the husband. The apostle teaches the nature, the ground, and the extent of the obedience due from the wife to the husband.

As to the nature of it, it is religious. It is ὡς τῷ Κυρίῳ, *as to the Lord.* The ὡς, *as,* does not express similarity, as though the obedience of the wife to her husband was to be as devout and as unconditional as that which she is bound to render to the Lord. But her obedience to her husband is to be regarded as part of her obedience to the Lord. See 6, 5. 6. It terminates on him, and therefore is religious, because determined by religious motives and directed towards the object of the religious affections. This makes the burden light and the yoke easy. For every service which the believer renders to Christ, is rendered with alacrity and joy.

V. 23. But although the obedience of the wife to the husband is of the nature of a religious duty because determined by religious motives, it has in common with all other commands of God, a foundation in nature. The apostle, therefore, says, wives are to be obedient to their husbands, *because the husband is the head of the wife, even as Christ is the head of the church.* The ground of the obligation, therefore, as it exists in nature, is the eminency of the husband; his superiority in those attributes which enable and entitle him to command. He is larger, stronger, bolder; has more of those mental and moral qualities which are required in a leader. This is just as plain from history as that iron is heavier than water. The man, therefore, in this aspect, as qualified and entitled to command, is said to be the image and glory of God, 1 Cor. 11, 7; for, as the apostle adds in that connection, the man was not made out of the woman, but the woman out of the man; neither was the man created for the woman, but the woman for the man. This superiority of the man, in the respects mentioned, thus taught in Scripture, founded in nature, and proved by all experience, cannot be denied or disregarded without destroying society and degrading both men and women; making the one effeminate and the other masculine. The superiority of the man, however, is not only consistent with the mutual dependence of the sexes, and their essential equality of nature, and in the kingdom of God, but also with the inferiority of men to women in other qualities than those which entitle to authority. The scriptural doctrine, while it lays the foundation for order in requiring wives to obey their husbands, at the same time exalts the wife to be the companion and ministering angel to the husband. The man, therefore, so far as this particular point is concerned, stands in the same relation to his wife, that Christ does to the church. There is however a relation which Christ bears to his church, which finds no analogy in that of the husband to the wife. Christ is not only the head of the church, but he is its Saviour, καὶ αὐτός ἐστι σωτὴρ τοῦ σώματος. Why the apostle added these words is not easy to determine. Perhaps it was to mark the distinction between the cases otherwise so analogous. Perhaps it was, as many suppose, to suggest to husbands their obligation to provide for the safety and happiness of their wives. Because Christ is the head of the church, he is its Saviour; therefore as the husband is the head of the wife, he should not only rule, but protect and bless.*

---

* Sicuti Christus ecclesiae suae praeest in ejus salutem, ita nihil esse mulieri utilius nec magis salubre, quam ut marito subsit. Perire igitur affectant quae renuunt subjectionem, sub qua salvae esse poterant.—CALVIN.

The most probable explanation is, that as the apostle's design is not merely to teach the nature of the relation between husband and wife, but also that between Christ and the church, the clause in question is added for that purpose, without any bearing on the conjugal relation. This clause is not in apposition with the preceding, but is an independent proposition. Christ is the head of the church ; and he is the Saviour of his body.

V. 24. *But*, ἀλλά, i. e. notwithstanding there is this peculiarity in the relation of Christ to the church which has no parallel in the relation of the wife to the husband, 'nevertheless, as the husband is the head of the wife, let the wife be subject to her husband *in every thing*, even as the church is subject to Christ her head.' Our translators give ἀλλά here a syllogistic force and render it, *therefore*, as though it introduced the conclusion from the preceding argument. But this is contrary to the common use of the particle and is unnecessary, as its ordinary meaning gives a good sense.

As verse 22 teaches the nature of the subjection of the wife to her husband, and verse 23 its ground, this verse teaches its extent. She is to be subject ἐν παντί, *in every thing*. That is, the subjection is not limited to any one sphere or department of the social life, but extends to all. The wife is not subject as to some things, and independent as to others, but she is subject as to all. This of course does not mean that the authority of the husband is unlimited. It teaches its extent, not its degree. It extends over all depart-ments, but is limited in all; first, by the nature of the relation; and secondly, by the higher authority of God. No superior, whether master, parent, husband or magistrate, can make it obligatory on us either to do what God forbids, or not to do what God commands. So long as our allegiance to God is preserved, and obedience to man is made part of our obedience to him, we retain our liberty and our integrity.

V. 25. As the peculiar duty of the wife is submission, the special duty of the husband is love. With regard to this the apostle teaches its measure and its ground. As to its measure it should be analogous to the love which Christ bears to his church. Its ground is the intimate and mysterious union which subsists between a man and his wife.

Husbands, love your wives, even as Christ also loved the church and gave himself for it. Husbands should love their wives, καθώς, *even as,* i. e. both *because* and *as.* As their relation to their wives is analogous to that of Christ to his church, it imposes the obligation to love them as he loves the church. But Christ so loved the church as to die for it. Husbands, therefore, should be willing to die for their wives. This seems to be the natural import of the passage, and is the interpretation commonly given to it. It has also its foundation in nature. Christ's love is held up as an example and a rule. His love is indeed elsewhere declared to be infinite. We cannot love as he loved, in any other sense than that in which we can be merciful as our Father in heaven is merciful. Nevertheless, it cannot be doubted that true conjugal love will ever lead the husband to sacrifice himself for his wife.*

Vs. 26. 27. As the apostle unites with his design of teaching the duties arising from the conjugal relation, the purpose to illustrate the nature of the union between Christ and his church, these verses relate to the latter point and not to the former. They set forth the design of Christ's death. Its remote design was to gain the church for himself as an object of delight. Its proximate design was to prepare it for that high destiny. These ideas are presented figuratively. The church is regarded as the bride of Christ. This is designed to teach—1. That it is an object of a peculiar and exclusive love. As the love which a bridegroom has for his bride is such as he has for no one else; so the love which Christ has for his church is such as he has for no other order of creatures in the universe, however exalted. 2. As the bride belongs exclusively to her husband, so the church belongs exclusively to Christ. It sustains a relation to him which it sustains to no other being, and in which no other being participates. 3. This relation is not only peculiar and exclusive, but the union between Christ and his church is

---

* The idea that all love, and therefore all holiness, is benevolence, and is proportioned to the capacity of its object, is one of those absurdities into which men inevitably fall when they give themselves up to the guidance of the speculative understanding, and disregard the teachings of the heart and of the conscience. A mother loves her infant, in every true sense of the word love, a hundred fold more than she loves a stranger, though he may be the greatest man who ever lived.

more intimate than any which subsists between him and any other order of creatures. We are flesh of his flesh, and bone of his bones. 4. The church is the special object of delight to Christ. It is said of Zion, " As the bridegroom rejoices over the bride, so shall thy God rejoice over thee," Is. 62, 5. He is to present it to himself as his own peculiar joy. Such being the high destiny of the church, the proximate end of Christ's death was to purify, adorn, and render it glorious, that it might be prepared to sit with him on his throne. She is to be as a bride adorned for her husband. These are not imaginations, nor exaggerations, nor empty figures; but simple, scriptural, sanctifying, and saving truths. And what is true of the church collectively, is true of its members severally. Each is the object of Christ's peculiar love. Each sustains to him this peculiar, exclusive, and intimate relation. Each is the object in which he thus delights, and each is to be made perfectly holy, without spot, and glorious.

Though the general sense of this passage is thus plain, there is no little difficulty attending the interpretation of its details. Christ, it is said, gave himself for the church, ἵνα αὐτὴν ἁγιάσῃ, which Calvin renders, Ut segregaret eam sibi, *that he might separate it for himself;* which, he says, is done by the remission of sin, and the renewing of the Holy Ghost. Though the verb ἁγιάζειν has this sense, yet as in Paul's writings it is commonly used to express cleansing from pollution, and as this sense best suits the context, it is generally preferred. The design of Christ's death was to make his people holy. It accomplishes this end by reconciling them to God, and by securing for them the gift of the Holy Ghost. Thus in Gal. 3, 13. 14, it is said, " Christ has redeemed us from the curse of the law, that we might receive the promise of the Spirit."

With regard to the next clause, καθαρίσας τῷ λουτρῷ τοῦ ὕδατος, *having cleansed* (or *cleansing*) *it with the washing of water*, we must inquire—1. What is intended by λουτρὸν τοῦ ὕδατος. 2. What is meant by καθαρίσας ; and 3. In what relation this clause stands to the preceding. Does " the washing of water" here mean baptism, or a washing which is analogous to a washing with water ? The latter interpretation is admissible. The apostle may mean nothing more than a spiritual lustration. In Ez. 16, 9, speaking of Israel, God said, " Then washed I thee with water ; yea, I thoroughly washed away thy blood from thee, and I anointed thee with oil." And in 36, 25, " Then will I sprinkle clean water upon you, and ye shall be clean." Also in Heb. 10, 22, it is said, " Let us draw near with a true heart, in full assurance of faith, having our hearts sprinkled from an evil conscience, and our bodies washed with pure water." In all these cases washing with water is a figurative expression for spiritual purification. Commentators, however, almost without exception understand the expression in the text to refer to baptism. The great majority of them, with Calvin and other of the Reformers, do not even discuss the question, or seem to admit any other

interpretation to be possible.   The same view is taken
by all the modern exegetical writers.   This unanimity
of opinion is itself almost decisive.   Nothing short of
a stringent necessity can justify any one in setting
forth an interpretation opposed to this common consent
of Christians.   No such necessity here exists.   Baptism
is a washing with water.   It was *the* washing with
water with which Paul's readers as Christians were
familiar, and which could not fail to occur to them as
the washing intended.   Besides, nothing more is here
attributed to baptism than is attributed to it in many
other passages of the word of God.   Compare particularly Acts 22, 16, " Arise, be baptized, and wash away
thy sins, ἀπόλουσαι τὰς ἁμαρτίας σου."   There can be
little doubt, therefore, that by " the washing with
water," the apostle meant baptism.

   As to the meaning of the participle καθαρίσας there
is more doubt.   The verb signifies to cleanse either
literally, ceremonially, or figuratively.   As the Scriptures speak of a twofold purification from sin, one from
guilt by expiation, the other from pollution by the
Spirit, and as καθαρίζειν is used in reference to both,
the question is, which is here intended.   Does the
apostle speak of pardon, or of sanctification as effected
by this washing with water?   The word expresses
sacrificial purification.   Heb. 9, 22. 23.   1 John 1, 7,
" The blood of Jesus Christ his Son cleanses us from
all sin."   Heb. 9, 14 ; comp. Heb. 1, 3, " Having by
himself made purification of our sin."   In favour of
taking it in this sense here, is the fact that baptism is

elsewhere connected with the remission of sin ; as in
Acts 22, 16, and Acts 2, 38, "Repent and be baptized
every one of you in the name of Jesus Christ, for the
remission of sins." The meaning of the word, however, depends upon its relation to the preceding clause.
Καθαρίσας may be connected with ἁγιάσῃ, and taken
in the same tense with it. It then expresses the mode
in which Christ cleanses his church. 'He gave himself for it that he might cleanse it, purifying it by the
washing of water.' In this case, if ἁγιάσῃ expresses
moral purification or sanctification, so must καθαρίσας.
But if this participle be taken in the past tense, according to its form, then it must express something
which precedes sanctification. The meaning would
then be, 'Christ gave himself for the church, that he
might sanctify it, *having purified* it by the washing
with water.' * In this case καθαρίσας must refer to
expiation or sacrificial purification, i. e. to washing
away of guilt. The context is in favour of this view,
and so is the analogy of Scripture. The Bible always
represents remission of sin or the removal of guilt as
preceding sanctification. We are pardoned and reconciled to God, in order that we may be made holy.
Christ, therefore, having by his blood cleansed his
church from guilt, sanctifies or renders it holy. In

* Participium Graecum καθαρίσας est praeteriti temporis, ac si dicas :
Postquam mundarit. Verum quia apud Latinos nullum est tale participium activum, malui tempus negligere, quam vertendo Mundatum per-
vertere quod erat longe majoris momenti, nempe ut soli Deo relinquatur
mundandi officium.

either view we are said to be cleansed (whether from guilt or from pollution) by baptism. What does this mean? How does baptism in either of these senses wash away sin? The Protestant and scriptural answer to this question is, that baptism cleanses from sin just as the word does. We are said to be saved by the truth, to be begotten by the truth, to be sanctified by the truth. This does not mean—1. That there is any inherent, much less magic, power in the word of God as heard or read to produce these effects. 2. Nor that the word always and every where, when rightly presented, thus sanctifies and saves, so that all who hear are partakers of these benefits. 3. Nor does it mean that the Spirit of God is so tied to the word as never to operate savingly on the heart except in connection with it. For infants may be subjects of regeneration, though incapable of receiving the truth. In like manner when the Scriptures speak of baptism as washing away sin, Acts 22, 16; or as uniting us to Christ, Gal. 3, 27; or as making Christ's death our death, Rom. 6, 4; Col. 2, 12; or as saving us, 1 Pet. 3, 21; they do not teach—1. That there is any inherent virtue in baptism, or in the administrator, to produce these effects; nor 2. That these effects always attend its right administration; nor 3. That the Spirit is so connected with baptism that it is the only channel through which he communicates the benefits of redemption, so that all the unbaptized perish. These three propositions, all of which Romanism and Ritualism affirm, are contrary to the express declarations of Scripture and to universal experience. Multitudes of the baptized are unholy; many of the unbaptized are sanctified and saved.

How then is it true that baptism washes away sin, unites us to Christ, and secures salvation? The answer again is, that this is true of baptism in the same sense that it is true of the word. God is pleased to connect the benefits of redemption with the believing reception of the truth. And he is pleased to connect these same benefits with the believing reception of baptism. That is, as the Spirit works with and by the truth, so he works with and by baptism, in communicating the blessings of the covenant of grace. Therefore, as we are said to be saved by the word, with equal propriety we are said to be saved by baptism; though baptism without faith is as of little effect as is the word of God to unbelievers. The scriptural doctrine concerning baptism, according to the Reformed churches is—1. That it is a divine institution. 2. That it is one of the conditions of salvation. "Whosoever believes and is baptized shall be saved," Mark 16, 16. It has, however, the necessity of precept, not the necessity of a means *sine qua non.* It is in this respect analogous to confession. "With the heart man believeth unto righteousness, and with the mouth confession is made unto salvation," Rom. 10, 10. And also to circumcision. God said, "The uncircumcised male child—should be cut off from his people," Gen. 17, 14. Yet children dying before the eighth day were surely not cut off from heaven. And the apostle teaches that if an uncircumcised man kept the law,

" his uncircumcision was counted to him for circumcision," Rom. 3, 26.   3. Baptism is a means of grace, that is, a channel through which the Spirit confers grace ; not always, not upon all recipients, nor is it the only channel, nor is it designed as the ordinary means of regeneration. Faith and repentance are the gifts of the Spirit and fruits of regeneration, and yet they are required as conditions of baptism. Consequently the Scriptures contemplate regeneration as preceding baptism. But if faith, to which all the benefits of redemption are promised, precedes baptism, how can those benefits be said to be conferred; in any case, through baptism ?   Just as a father may give an estate to his son, and afterwards convey it to him formally by a deed. Besides, the benefits of redemption, the remission of sin, the gift of the Spirit, and the merits of the Redeemer, are not conveyed to the soul once for all. They are reconveyed and appropriated on every new act of faith, and on every new believing reception of the sacraments. The sinner coming to baptism in the exercise of repentance and faith, takes God the Father to be his Father ; God the Son, to be his Saviour ; and God the Holy Ghost to be his Sanctifier, and his word to be the rule of his faith and practice. The administrator then, in the name and by the authority of God, washes him with water as a sign of the cleansing from sin by the blood of Christ, and of sanctification by the Holy Spirit; and as a seal to God's promise to grant him those blessings on the condition of the repentance and faith thus publicly avowed.

Whatever he may have experienced or enjoyed before, this is the public conveyance to him of the benefits of the covenant, and his inauguration into the number of the redeemed. If he is sincere in his part of the service, baptism really applies to him the blessings of which it is the symbol. 4. Infants are baptized on the faith of their parents. And their baptism secures to them all the benefits of the covenant of grace, provided they ratify that covenant by faith; just as circumcision secured the benefits of the theocracy, provided those circumcised in infancy kept the law. The doctrine of baptismal regeneration, that is, the doctrine that inward spiritual renovation always attends baptism rightly administered to the unresisting, and that regeneration is never effected without it, is contrary to Scripture, subversive of evangelical religion, and opposed to universal experience. It is, moreover, utterly irreconcilable with the doctrine of the Reformed churches. For that doctrine teaches that all the regenerated are saved. "Whom God calls them he also glorifies," Rom. 8, 30. It is, however, plain from Scripture, and in accordance with the faith of the universal church, that multitudes of the baptized perish. The baptized, therefore, as such, are not the regenerated.

The foregoing remarks are intended to show in what sense the Reformed understand this and similar declarations of Scripture. Christ purifies his church by baptism. That is the initiatory rite; which signifies, seals, and applies to believers all the benefits of the Redeemer's death. The apostle is speaking of the church, the body and bride of Christ, and of the effect of baptism on those who constitute that church, not of its effect on those who are not included in the covenant and are aliens from the commonwealth of Israel.*

* Quod Baptismo nos ablui docet Paulus, ideo est, quod illic nobis ablutionem nostram testatur Deus, et simul efficit quod figurat. Nisi enim conjuncta esset rei veritas, aut exhibitio, quod idem est, impropria haec loqutio esset. Baptismus est lavacrum animae. Interea cavendum, ne quod unius Dei est, vel ad signum, vel ad ministrum transferatur; hoc est, ut minister censetur ablutionis auctor, ut aqua putetur animae sordes purgare; quod nonnisi Christi sanguini convenit. Denique cavendum, ne ulla fiduciae nostrae portio vel in elemento, vel in homine haereat. Quando hic demum verus ac rectus sacramenti usus est, recta nos ad Christum manu ducere, et in ipso sistere. Quod autem aliqui in hoc baptismi elogio magis extenuando sudant, ne signo nimium tribuatur, si vocetur animae lavacrum; perperam faciunt. Nam primum apostolus non docet signum esse, quod mundet sed asserit solius Dei esse opus. Est ergo Deus qui mundat; nec transferri hoc honoris ad signum fas est, aut signo communicari. Verum signo Deum tanquam organo uti, non est absurdum; non quia virtus Dei inclusa sit in signo, sed quia nobis eam pro imbecilitatis nostrae captu tali adminiculo distribuat. Id quosdam male habet, quia putant Spiritui sancto auferri, quod est ejus proprium et quod illi scriptura passim vindicat. Sed falluntur; nam ita Deus per signum agit, ut tota signi efficacia nihilominus a Spiritu suo pendeat. Ita nihil· plus signo tribuitur, quam ut sit inferius organum, et quidem a seipso inutile, nisi quatenus aliunde vim suam mutuatur. Quod praeterea verentur ne libertas Dei sit alligatur, frivolum est. Neque enim affixa est signis Dei gratia, quin citra adminiculum signi libere eam distribuat, si velit, deinde multi signum recipiunt, qui tamen gratiae non fiunt participes, quia signum omnibus est commune, hoc est, bonis indifferenter ac malis; Spiritus autem nonnisi electis confertur; acqui signum, ut diximus, absque Spiritu est inefficax. CALVIN.

There is one other remark suggested by this passage. The turning point in the discussion between Baptists and Paedobaptists, so far as the mode of baptism is concerned, is, whether it is in its essential nature an immersion, or a washing. If the former, then there is but one mode in which it can be administered. If the latter, it may be administered in any mode by which washing can be effected, either by sprinkling, affusion, or immersion. In the passage before us, it is said to be a "*washing* with water."

The principal exegetical difficulty in this verse is the explanation of the words ἐν ῥήματι, *by the word.* 'Ρῆμα is used not only for any particular dictum, whether command, promise, or prophecy, but also for the word of God collectively, and that either with or without the article; Rom. 10, 8. 17. Eph. 6, 17. These words may be connected, as is commonly done, with the preceding clause, 'washing of water.' The idea then is that this washing with water is connected with the word. It is not an ordinary ablution, but one connected with the word of God. This is considered a description of baptism, which is by that connection distinguished from all other washings. By the *word* may then be understood either, the formula of baptism, or the promise of remission of sins and regeneration of which baptism is the sign and seal, and which is the special object of faith to the recipient of the sacrament. Luther's translation is, "Durch das Wasserbad im Wort;" according to the saying of Augustine, which he often quotes, *accedit verbum ad elementum et fit sacramentum.* To this interpretation it is objected, first, that if ῥῆμα be made to mean any thing more than the word of God in general, whether the command to baptize, or the promise, or the formula of baptism, it must have the article. It should be, with *the* word. But the article is wanting in the Greek. Secondly, the obscurity of the expression, "washing of water with the word," or, "baptism with the word." Thirdly, that in order to justify the connection in question, the passage should read, τῷ λουτρῷ τοῦ ὕδατος τῷ, or, τοῦ ἐν ῥήματι. Had Paul thus written there would, indeed, be no question as to the connection intended, but the exceptions to the rule requiring the connecting article in such cases, are very numerous in Paul's writings. Still its absence is certainly in favour of seeking another construction, if such can be found. Others connect the words ἐν ῥήματι with καθαρίσας, and make them explanatory of the preceding clause, 'Having purified it by the washing of water, i. e. having purified it by the word.' But this is certainly unnatural, first because καθαρίσας has in τῷ λουτρῷ, κτλ., its limitation; and secondly, because the phrase "washing with water," needs no explanation. The third method of explanation is to connect the words with ἁγιάσῃ, 'Christ cleansed his church, by the word, having purified it with the washing of water.' The sense is thus good. In John 17, 17, our Lord prays, "Sanctify them by thy truth;" and every where in Scripture the word of God is represented as the great means of sanctification. This interpretation is adopted by many of the best expositors, as Rückert, Meyer, and Winer. The position of the words, however, is so decidedly in favour of the first mentioned explanation, that it has commanded the assent of the great body of interpreters.

V. 27. The ultimate end for which Christ gave himself for the church, and for which he sanctifies it, is to present it to himself, i. e. to gain it for himself as his peculiar possession. There are two questions raised by commentators as to this verse. The first concerns the nature of the metaphor here employed; and the second, the time contemplated in which Christ is thus to present the church to himself. Some, although very few, argue from the character of the epithets, *without spot and blameless*, here applied to the church, that the figure is derived from law of sacrifices. Christ is to present the church to himself as an offering without defect. But 1. This is entirely out of keeping with the whole context, which has reference to the conjugal relation, and is intended to illustrate the union between Christ and the church, by a reference to that between the bridegroom and the bride. 2. The comparison of the church to an offering is not only out of keeping with the context, but with the whole current of scriptural representation. Whereas the comparison of it to a bride is appropriate and familiar. 3. The epithets in question, though often used in reference to sacrifices, are not only appropriate, but are actually employed to express personal or corporeal beauty, which is here the symbol of inward purity.

A larger number of commentators take the ground that the end contemplated in this verse is accomplished in the present life. In other words, that the state of the church here described is one attained in this world. Of those who take this view, some, as the ancient Pelagians, interpret the passage as teaching that perfect holiness is not only attainable, but is actually attained by believers before death. Others do not understand the passage as speaking of holiness, but of propitiation, which is effected once for all. In this view it is parallel to Heb. 10, 10, where we are said to be "sanctified by the offering of the body of Christ once for all;" and ver. 14, where it is said, "By the one offering up of himself he hath for ever perfected them that are sanctified." Both of these passages in Hebrews evidently refer to the perfection of Christ's sacrifice, and they undoubtedly prove, what no one questions, that the words ἁγιάζειν and καθαρίζειν, here used, may express sacrificial purification or expiation. But this is far from proving that these words, and especially the former, are to be so taken here. To sanctify is commonly, in Scripture language, to make spiritually holy, and this sense is far better suited to the context than any other meaning of the word. But if the design of Christ's death as here expressed is to render his church perfectly holy, then there can be no debate as to the time when this end is to be accomplished. For even should it be granted, that here and there one among the multitude of believers does attain perfection in this life, of which neither Scripture nor experience affords any example, still this cannot be affirmed of the whole body of believers. The great majority of commentators, therefore, from Augustin down to the present time, understand the apostle as stating what is to take place when Christ comes the second time to be admired in all them that believe. It is then, when the dead are raised in the likeness of the Son of God, and when those who shall be alive shall be changed—when this corruption shall have put on incorruption, and this mortal shall have put on immortality—it is then that the church shall be " as a bride prepared for her husband," Rev. 21, 2, and 19, 7–9.

῞Ινα παραστήσῃ depends upon what immediately precedes: "having purified it *that he might present it,*" i. e. cause it to stand before or near him as a bride. So the apostle writing to the Corinthians says, he had " espoused them to one husband, παρθενὸν ἁγνὴν παραστῆσαι τῷ Χριστῷ, *to present you as a chaste virgin unto Christ.*" Here the figure is somewhat different. Christ presents the church to himself, αὐτὸς ἑαυτῷ,* *he* and no other, *to himself.* He does it. He gave himself for it. He sanctifies it. He, before the assembled universe, places by his side the bride purchased with his blood. He presents it to himself *a glorious church.* That is glorious which excites admiration. The church is to be an object of admiration to all intelligent beings, because of its freedom from all defect, and because of its

---

* The common Text reads αὐτὴν instead of αὐτός. The latter reading on the authority of the MSS. ABDFG, has, since Griesbach, been almost universally adopted.

absolute perfection. It is to be conformed to the glorified humanity of the Son of God, in the presence of which the disciples on the mount became as dead men, and from the clear manifestation of which, when Christ comes the second time, the heavens and the earth are to flee away. God has predestined his people to be conformed to the image of his Son. And when he shall appear, we shall be like him, for we shall see him as he is, 1 John 3, 2. The figure is preserved in the description here given of the glory of the consummated church. It is to be as a faultless bride; perfect in beauty and splendidly adorned. She is to be without *spot or wrinkle or any such thing*, i. e. without any thing to mar her beauty, free from every indication of age, faultless and immortal. What is thus expressed figuratively is expressed literally in the last clause of the verse, *that it should be holy and without blame*, ἁγία καὶ ἄμωμος. Compare 1, 4, where it is said God hath chosen us, εἶναι ἁγίους καὶ ἀμώμους. It is, therefore, the original purpose of election formed before the foundation of the world, that is to be fulfilled in this consummation of the church.

V. 28. *So ought men to love their wives, as their own bodies.* This does not mean that men ought to love their wives *so as* they love their own bodies; as though the particles *so* and *as*, οὕτως and ὡς, stood related to each other. Οὕτως, *so*, at the beginning of the verse, refers to the preceding representation. As Christ loves the church and gave himself for it, and as the church is his body, *so*, in like manner and agreeably to the analogous relation between them, husbands should love their wives *as*, i. e. as being, or because they are, their own bodies. Christ loves his church because it is his body. Husbands should love their wives because they are their bodies. 'Ωs, *as*, before the latter member of the sentence is not comparative, but argumentative. It does not indicate the measure of the husband's love, as though the meaning were, he should love his wife as much as he loves his own body. But it indicates the nature of the relation which is the ground of his love. He should love his wife, because she is his body.

How is this to be understood? In what sense does the apostle say that the wife is the body of the husband, or, in the following verse, that they are one flesh? It is plain—1. That this does not refer to any material identification. When Adam said of Eve, "This is bone of my bones, and flesh of my flesh," Gen. 2, 23, reference was no doubt had to her being formed out of his substance. But as these terms are used to express the relation of all wives to their husbands, they must have some other meaning than sameness of substance. 2. It is also plain that these terms are not to be understood in any sense inconsistent with the separate subsistence of husband and wife as distinct persons. The consciousness of the one is not the consciousness of the other. 3. It is further plain that the marriage relation is not essential to the completeness or perfection of our nature, in all states of its existence. It is to cease at the resurrection. In the future state men are to be, in this respect, like the angels of God, neither marrying nor given in marriage. 4. On the other hand the marriage union is not merely one of interests and feeling. Husbands and wives are in such a sense one, that the husband is the complement of the wife and the wife of the husband. The marriage relation is necessary to the completeness of our nature and to its full development in the present state. Some indeed, as Paul, may attain a higher degree of perfection in celibacy than in marriage. But this arises from some peculiarity of character or circumstances. There are faculties and virtues, excellencies and feelings, which are latent until developed in the conjugal relation. The Romish doctrine, therefore, which degrades marriage as a state less holy than celibacy, is contrary to nature and the word of God. 5. Besides this oneness between husband and wife arising from the original constitution of their nature, rendering the one necessary as the completion of the other, there is doubtless a oneness of life involved in our Lord's declaration, "They are no more twain, but one flesh," which no one can understand.

Such being the nature of marriage, it follows :— 1. That it is a union for life between one man and one woman ; and consequently that bigamy, polygamy, and voluntary divorce are all inconsistent with its nature. 2. That it must be entered into freely and cordially by the parties, i. e. with the conviction that the one is suited to the other, so that they may complement each other, and become one in the scriptural sense of those words. All coercion on the part of parents, therefore, is contrary to the nature of the relation ; and all marriages of mere convenience are opposed to the design of the institution. 3. The State can neither make nor dissolve the marriage tie. It may enact laws regulating the mode in which it shall be solemnized and authenticated, and determining its civil effects. It may shield a wife from ill-usage from her husband, as it may remove a child from the custody of an incompetent or cruel parent. When the union is in fact dissolved by the operation of the divine law, the State may ascertain and declare the fact, and free the parties from the civil obligation of the contract. But it is impossible that the State should have authority to dissolve a union constituted by God, the duties and continuance of which are determined by his law. 4. According to the Scriptures, as interpreted by Protestant churches, nothing but the death of one of the parties, or adultery, or wilful desertion, can dissolve the marriage contract. When either of the last mentioned causes of dissolution is judicially ascertained and declared, the injured party is free to contract a new marriage.

It is of vital importance to the best interests of society that the true doctrine of marriage, as taught in this passage and in other portions of God's word, should be known and regarded. The highest social duty of a husband is to love his wife ; and a duty which he cannot neglect without entailing great injury on his own soul as well as misery on his household. The greatest social crime, next to murder, which any one can commit, is to seduce the affections of a wife from her husband, or of a husband from his wife. And one of the greatest evils which civil authorities can inflict on society, is the dissolution of the marriage contract (so far as it is a civil contract, for further the civil authority cannot go), on other than scriptural grounds. The same remark may be made in reference to all laws which tend to make those two whom God has pronounced one, by giving to the wife the right to carry on business, contract debts, hold property, sue and be sued, in her own name. This is attempting to correct one class of evils at the cost of incurring others a hundred-fold greater. The word of God is the only sure guide of legislative action as well as of individual conduct.

If, as the Scriptures teach, husband and wife are one, *he that loveth his wife loveth himself*, for she is himself. This is the language of God, originally recorded in Gen. 2, 24, and repeated by our Lord, Matt. 19, 4–6, who after citing the passage in Genesis, adds, " Wherefore they are no more twain, but one flesh." Calvin, in his comment on the passage in Matthew, says, Hoc autem axioma sumit Christus, Ab initio Deus marem adjunxit feminae, ut duo efficerent integrum hominem. Ergo qui uxorem repudiat, quasi dimidiam sui partem a seipso avellit. Hoc autem minime patitur natura, ut corpus suum quispiam discerpat. Neither God by the mouth of Moses, nor our Lord says simply that husband and wife ought to be, but that they are one. It is not a duty, but a fact which they announce. So also it is a fact which the apostle declares when he says, "He that loves his wife loves himself."

V. 29. Conjugal love, therefore, is as much a dictate of nature as self-love; and it is just as unnatural for a man to hate his wife, as it would be for him to hate himself, or his own body. A man may have a body which does not altogether suit him. He may wish it were handsomer, healthier, stronger, or more active. Still it is *his* body, it is himself; and he nourisheth it and cherishes it as tenderly as though it were the best and loveliest man ever had. So a man may have a wife whom he could wish to be better, or more beautiful, or more agreeable; still she is his wife, and by the constitution of nature and ordinance of God, a part of himself. In neglecting or ill-using her he violates the laws of nature as well as the law of God. It is thus Paul presents the matter. If the husband and wife are one flesh, the husband must love his wife, "*for* no man ever yet hated his own flesh, but nourisheth and cherisheth it." Ἐκτρέφειν is properly *to nourish up*, to train up by nurture, as a parent a child; comp. 6, 4. Θάλπειν is, *to warm*, to cherish as a mother does an infant in her bosom. Both terms express tenderness and solicitude, and therefore both are suited to express the care with which every man provides for the wants and comfort of his own body.

Καθὼς καί, *even as also*, Χριστὸς τὴν ἐκκλησίαν, *Christ the church*, i. e. Christ also nourishes and cherishes the church as a man does his own body. The relation between a man and his wife is analogous to that between a man and his own body. And the relation between Christ and his church is analogous to that between a husband and his wife; therefore Christ nourishes and cherishes the church as man does his own body.

V. 30. This verse assigns the reason of the preceding declaration. Christ acts towards his church as a man does towards his body, *for we are members of his body.* This might mean simply that we stand to him in the same intimate and vital union, that a man's body sustains to the man himself. But the meaning is rendered more definite by the words which follow, ἐκ τῆς σαρκὸς αὐτοῦ καὶ ἐκ τῶν ὀστέων αὐτοῦ ; * not members of, but derived from, and partakers of, *his flesh and his bones.* This is the signification of the words, whatever their meaning may be. Ἐκ expresses derivation and participation. This is one of the most difficult passages in the Bible. The doctrine which it teaches is declared by the apostle, in a following verse, to be a great mystery. Any explanation, therefore, which dispels that mystery, and makes the doctrine taught perfectly intelligible, must be false. All that can properly be

---

* These words are omitted in MSS. A B 17, and in the Coptic and Ethiopic versions, and are left out of the text by Lachmann and Tischendorf. The other Uncial MSS., the Syriac version, the Fathers, are in their favour. They are required by the context, and their omission is easily accounted for. Even Mill and Griesbach retain them, as do all other editors, and the commentators almost without exception.

attempted is to guard against false interpretations, and leave the matter just where the apostle leaves it, as something to be believed and reverenced but not understood.

The lowest explanation of the passage before us is that which departs entirely from the signification of the words, and supposes that the apostle intended to teach nothing at all as to the nature of our union with Christ, but simply to affirm the fact. Husbands and wives are intimately united, and so are Christ and his church. This is no explanation at all. It is simply saying that the apostle meant nothing, or nothing specific, by what he says. The Scriptures teach in general terms that Christ and his people are one. When our Lord says they are one as the vine and its branches are one, he teaches something more than the mere fact of union between himself and his people. So, too, when the apostle says the union in question is analogous to that between Adam and his posterity, he teaches not only the fact but also one aspect of its nature. In like manner, when he illustrates it by a reference to the conjugal relation, and says that the point of analogy is that as Eve was formed out of the flesh and bone of Adam, so we are partakers of the flesh and bones of Christ, it is impossible that nothing more should be meant than that we are united to him.

A second interpretation takes the words figuratively, and supposes the apostle meant that as Eve derived her physical existence from Adam, so we derive our spiritual existence from Christ. This interpretation

has many advocates from Chrysostom downwards, but
it is liable to the same objection as the preceding.   It
refuses to admit what the apostle asserts.   He says not
merely that we derive our life from Christ, which is
true; but also that we derive our life from his flesh,
and are partakers of it.   This must mean something
more specific than simply that Christ is the author of
our life, and that he lives in us.*

A third view of the passage assumes that the reference is to the incarnation.   We are partakers of the
flesh of Christ because we have the same human nature
which he assumed.   In Heb. 2, 10, it is said, " Both
he that sanctifieth and they who are sanctified *are* all
of one," i. e. of one nature; and in ver. 14, " Foras-
much then as the children were partakers of flesh and
blood, he also himself likewise took part of the same."
These and similar passages do indeed prove that one
of the essential elements of the union with Christ is this
community of nature.   And it is also true that the
more specific union indicated in the text presupposes
and rests upon the fact of the incarnation.   But the
incarnation cannot be what Paul here refers to.   The
incarnation consists in the eternal Son of God taking

---

* Diese Form des Ausdrucks ist Reminiscenz von Gen. 2, 23, wo Adam
die Entstehung der Eva aus seinem Gebeinen und aus seinem Fleische
ausspricht, welcher Entstehung das genetische Verhältniss der Christen zu
Christo analog ist, naturlich nicht physisch, sondern im geistlichen, *mystischen* Sinne, *in so fern die christliche Dasein und Wesen der Christen,
aus Christo originirt, in Christo sein Principium essendi hat, wie physicher
Weise Eva aus Adam herrührte.* MEYER.

to himself a true body and a reasonable soul; but the union here spoken of arises from *our* participation of Christ's body; that is, of his flesh and of his bones. It is not his taking our flesh and blood, but our partaking of his, after he had assumed them, that is here asserted. Besides, so far as the mere assumption of human nature is concerned, it is a bond of union between Christ and the whole human race; whereas the apostle is here speaking of a union with Christ peculiar to his people.

Fourth; Romanists, Lutherans, and the elder Calvinists, as Calvin himself and Beza, seek a solution of this passage in the Lord's Supper. As in that ordinance we are said to partake of the body and blood of Christ, it is assumed that the union here spoken of is that which is thereby effected. We are "one flesh" with him, because we partake of his flesh. This of course is differently understood according to the different views entertained of that sacrament. Romanists, believing that by the act of consecration the whole substance of the bread is transmuted into the substance of Christ's body, which is received by the communicant, of course believe that in the most literal sense of the words, we are flesh of his flesh. Lutherans, although they believe that the bread remains bread in the Eucharist after consecration, yet as they hold that the true body of Christ is locally present in, with and under the bread, and is received by the mouth, come to the same conclusion as to the nature of the union thereby effected. Partaking literally of Christ's flesh, Christians are literally of one flesh with him. Calvin did not hold that Christ's body was locally present in the Lord's Supper, nor that it was received by the mouth, nor that it was received in any sense by unbelievers. He did hold, however, that the substance of Christ's glorified body, as enthroned in heaven, was in some miraculous way communicated to believers together with the bread in that ordinance. He, therefore, understands the apostle as here referring to that fact, and asserting that we are members of Christ's body because the substance of his body is in the Eucharist communicated to us.* There are two objections to these interpretations :—1. That, according to the com-

---

* Dicit *nos esse ejus membra, ex carne et ossibus.* Primum non est hyperbolica loquutio, sed simplex ; deinde non tantum significat Christum esse naturae nostrae participem, sed altius quiddam exprimere voluit, καὶ ἐμφα- τικώτερον. Refert enim Mosis verba, Gen. 2, 24. Quis ergo exit sensus ? quemadmodum Heva ex Adae mariti sui substantia formata est, ut esset quasi pars illius ; ita nos ut simus vera Christi membra, substantiae ejus communicatione nos coalescere in unum corpus. Denique eam nostri, cum Christo unionem hic Paulus describit, cujus in sacra coena symbolum et pignus nobis datur ... Paulus nos ex membris et ossibus Christi esse testatur. Miramur ergo si corpus suum in coena fruendum nobis exhibet, ut sit nobis vitae aeternae alimentum ? ita ostendimus nullam nos in coena repraesentationem docere, nisi cujus effectus et veritas hic a Paulo praedicatur. CALVIN.

On the following verse, he says, Totum autem ex eo pendet quod uxor ex carne et ex ossibus viri formata est. Eadem ergo unionis ratio inter nos et Christum, quod se quodammodo in nos transfundit. Neque enim ossa sumus ex ossibus ejus, et caro ex carne, quia ipse nobiscum est homo ; sed quia Spiritus sui virtute nos in corpus suum inserit, ut vitam ex eo hauriamus.

mon belief of the Reformed churches, the Bible teaches
no such doctrine concerning the Lord's Supper, as
either of these several views of the passage supposes.
2. That there is not only no allusion to the Lord's Supper in the whole context, but the terms here employed
are never used in Scripture when treating of that
ordinance. " Body and blood" are the sacramental
words always used, and never " flesh and bones."
The reference is to the creation of woman and to the
marriage relation, and not to the Eucharist.

Fifth ; The advocates of that philosophical form of
theology of which Schleiermacher was the founder,
understand the passage before us to teach that we are
partakers of the theanthropic life of Christ. The leading idea of that system, so far as the person of Christ
is concerned, is the denial of all dualism. He has but
one life. That life is not human, and not divine, but
divine and human, or human made divine. Neither
is there any dualism as to soul and body. These are
the same life under different manifestations. To partake of Christ, is to partake of his life. To partake
of his life, is to partake of his theanthropic nature.
To partake of his theanthropic nature, is to partake
of his human, as well as of his divine nature ; and to
partake of his human nature is to partake of his body
as well as of his soul and divinity. We partake of the
theanthropic nature of Christ, as we partake of the
corrupt human nature of Adam. The life of Adam is
the general life of his race, manifested in the individuals composing that race. The theanthropic life

of Christ is the general life of the church, manifested in its members. The church is the development of Christ, as the human race is the development of Adam; or as the oak or forest is the development of an acorn. As, therefore, we are said to be flesh of Adam's flesh and bone of his bones, in the same sense and with the same propriety, are we said to be flesh of Christ's flesh and bone of his bones.* The correctness of this explanation depends on the correctness of the system on which it is founded. As a theology, that system is a revival of the Sabellian and Eutychian heresies; and as a philosophy, it is in the last resort pantheistic. It makes the life of God and the life of man identical. God lives only in his creatures.

Sixth; We must content ourselves with briefly stating what the apostle affirms, guarding against a perversion of his language, and making some approximation to its meaning without pretending to dissipate the mystery which he teaches us rests upon the subject.

---

* OLSHAUSEN, in his comment on this verse, says: Nicht die *geistige* Geburt ist es zunächst, von der hier die Rede ist, die *leibliche* Seite wird hier und v. 31, zu ausdrücklich hervorgehoben; es ist die Selbstmittheilung seines göttlich-menschlichen Wesens, wodurch Christus uns zu seinem Fleisch und Bein macht, er giebt den Seinigen sein Fleisch zu essen, sein Blut zu trinken. On the following verse he remarks: Wie wir zu v. 30, sahen, dass die Gläubigen von Christi Fleisch und Bein sind, weil sie seiner verklärten Leiblichkeit theilhaftig wurden; so ist hier auch die σάρξ μία mit Beziehung auf die Mittheilung des Fleisches und Blutes Christi an seine Glänbiger zu verstehen. Dies sein göttlich-menschliches Wesen theilt der Erlöser zwar auch im Glauben mit (John 6, 45) aber die intensiveste, concentrirteste Mittheilung desselben erfolgt im heiligen Abendmahl.

The text asserts—1. That we are members of Christ s body.   2. That we are partakers of his flesh and of his bones, in such a sense that our relation to Christ is analogous to Eve's relation to Adam.

The three general interpretations of the passage are, First, That as Eve derived her physical life from Adam, so we derive our spiritual life from Christ.   This says too little, as it leaves out of view the specific affirmation of the text.   Second, That as Eve was formed out of the substance of Adam's body, so we are partakers of the substance of Christ's body.   This is Calvin's interpretation, which includes the views given by Romanists, by Lutherans, and Transcendentalists.   This goes beyond the declaration of the text, and imposes a meaning upon it inconsistent with the analogy of Scripture.   The third interpretation takes a middle ground, and understands the apostle to teach, that as Eve derived her life from *the body* of Adam, so we derive our life from *the body* of Christ, and as she was partaker of Adam's life, so we are partakers of the life of Christ. The doctrine taught, therefore, is not community of substance between Christ and his people, but community of life, and that the source of life to his people is Christ's flesh.

In support of this interpretation it may be urged: 1. That it leaves the passage in its integrity.   It neither explains it away, nor does it make it assert more than the words necessarily imply.   The doctrine taught remains a great mystery, as the apostle declares it to be.   2. It takes the terms employed in their ordinary

and natural sense. To partake of one's flesh and blood.
does not, in ordinary life nor according to scriptural
usage, mean to partake of his substance, but it does
mean to partake of his life. The substance of which
the body of any adult is composed is derived exclusively from his food and from the atmosphere. A few
years after the formation of Eve not a particle of
Adam's body entered into the composition of her
frame; and yet she was then as truly as at the beginning, bone of his bone and flesh of his flesh, because
derived from him and partaker of his life. For the
same reasons and in the same sense we are said to be
flesh of Adam's flesh and bone of his bones, although
in no sense partakers of the substance of his body. In
like manner nothing is more common than to speak
of the blood of a father flowing in the veins of his
descendants, and of their being his flesh. This means,
and can only mean, that they are partakers of his life.
There is no community of substance possible in the
case. What life is no man knows. But we know that
it is not matter; and, therefore, there may be community of life, where there is no community of substance. There is a form of life peculiar to nations,
tribes, families, and individuals; and this peculiar type
is transmitted from generation to generation, modify-
ing the personal appearance, the physical constitution,
and the character of those who inherit it. When we
speak of the blood of the Hapsburghs, or of the Bour-
bons, it is this family type that is intended and nothing
material. The present Emperor of Austria derives his

peculiar type of physical life from the head of his race, but not one particle of the substance of his body. Husband and wife are in Scripture declared to be one flesh. But here again it is not identity of substance, but community of life that is intended. As, therefore, participation of one's flesh does not in other connections, mean participation of his substance, it cannot be fairly understood in that sense when spoken of our relation to Christ. And as in all analogous cases it does express derivation or community of life, it must be so understood here.

3. It is clearly taught in Scripture that the union with Christ here described is essential to salvation. It is also clearly taught in the word of God, and held by all Protestants, though not by Romanists, that believers under the Old Dispensation were fully saved. Whatever, therefore, is the nature of the union with Christ here taught, it must be such as is common to believers who lived before and to those who live after the advent of Christ. It is possible that the saints under the Old Dispensation should have derived their life from the body of Christ, as he was the Lamb slain from the foundation of the world, but it is not possible that they could be partakers of the substance of his body, or of his glorified humanity. The passage before us, therefore, cannot teach any such community of substance.

4. The community of life with Christ and derivation of life from his flesh, which is the doctrine this interpretation supposes the passage before us to teach,

is a doctrine elsewhere taught in Scripture. We are not only said to be saved by his body, Rom. 7, 4; by his blood, Eph. 2, 13; by his flesh, 2, 15; by the body of his flesh, Col. 1, 22; but his flesh is said to be our life, and participation of it is said to be the source of eternal life. "Except ye eat the flesh of the Son of Man, and drink his blood, ye have no life in you. Whoso eateth my flesh and drinketh my blood, hath eternal life." John 6, 53. 54.

The union, therefore, between Christ and his people is mysterious. It may be illustrated, but cannot be fully explained. It is analogous to the union between husband and wife, who are declared to be one flesh to express their community of life; and especially to the union between Adam and Eve because she derived her life from his flesh. As the relations are thus analogous, what is said of the one may be said of the other. To prove this, and to justify the use of the language which he had employed, the apostle cites the language of God in Gen. 2, 24. Ver. 31. *For this cause shall a man leave his father and mother, and shall be joined unto his wife, and they two shall be one flesh.* That is, because the relation between husband and wife is more intimate than any other, even than that between parents and children; therefore a man shall consider all other relations subordinate to that which he sustains to his wife, with whom he is connected in the bonds of a common life. As the Scripture speaks in such terms of the conjugal relation, the apostle was justified in using the same terms of the union between

Christ and his people. They also are one flesh because
they have a common life, and because his people derive their life from his flesh as Eve derived hers from
the flesh of Adam.

The principal difficulty hére relates to the connection. The passage stands thus : ' We are members
of Christ's body, of his flesh, and of his bones. For
this cause a man shall leave his father and mother,
and be joined to his wife, and they two shall be one
flesh.' There is an apparent incongruity between the
premises and the conclusion. How does our being
members of Christ's body, prove that a man should
leave his father and mother and be joined to his wife?
There are three methods of getting over this difficulty.
First, some assume that there is no connection between
the two verses, but that the 31st refers back to the 28th.
The sense would then be, ' A man should love his wife,
because she is his body. *For this cause*, a man should
leave his father and cleave to his wife,' &c. This
method of solution is inconsistent both with what precedes and with what follows. It does not agree with
what precedes, because the words, *of his flesh*, &c., in
ver. 30, referring to Christ, form part of the passage in
Genesis, the continuation of which is given in ver. 31.
If the one refers to Christ, the other must. It contra-
dicts what follows; for in ver. 32, the main idea contained in ver. 31 (*they shall be one flesh*), is expressly
said to be affirmed in reference to Christ and the
church.

The second method of explanation assumes an immediate connection between the two verses 30 and 31, and understands the whole of the latter to refer to the relation between Christ and his church. It then may be explained either in reference to the present, or the future. If to the present, the sense would be, 'We are members of Christ's body, and, *therefore*, he left his Father and all dear to him in heaven that he might be united to his people.' But how is it possible that the words, "a man shall leave his father and mother," can mean Christ left God and heaven? If the passage be understood in reference to the future, the meaning will be, 'We are members of Christ's body, and *therefore* hereafter when he comes the second time, he will leave his Father's throne, and take his church as his bride.'* But this view not only does the same violence to the meaning of the words, but is in direct contradiction to the whole context. Paul does not say that hereafter the church shall be united to Christ as his bride, but that his people are now members of his body, flesh of his flesh, and bone of his bones.

The third explanation assumes that the first part of the verse has no reference to Christ and the church, and that the passage is quoted from Genesis solely for

* *Deshalb*, weil wir Glieder Christi, von seinem Fleisch und von seinem Beinen sind, *wird verlassen ein Mensch* (d. i. Christus, bei der Parusie) *seinen Vater und seine Mutter* (d. i. nach der mystischen Deutung Pauli: er wird seinen Sitz zur Rechten Gottes verlassen) *und vereiniget werden mit seinem Weibe* (mit der Gemeinde), *und* (und dann) *werden die Zwei* (der Mann und die Frau, d. i. der herabgestiegene Christus und die Gemeinde) *zu Einem Fleische sein* (Eine ethische Person ausmachen). MEYER.

the sake of the last words, *they shall be one flesh.* The meaning and the connection then are, ' As Eve was formed out of the body of Adam, and therefore, it is said, a man shall leave his father and mother, and be joined to his wife, and they two shall be one flesh. So, since we are members of Christ's body, *therefore,* Christ and his church are one flesh.' This view is, 1. In entire accordance with the context. 2. It avoids the forced and unnatural interpretations which are unavoidable if the former part of the 31st verse be understood in reference to Christ. 3. It satisfies the demands of the 32d verse, which asserts that the words *one flesh* do refer to Christ and the church. And 4. It is in accordance with the usage of the apostles in quoting the language of the Old Testament. They often recite a passage of Scripture as it stands in the Old Testament, for the sake of some one clause or expression in it, without intending to apply to the case before them, any other portion of the passage quoted. In Heb. 2, 13, the whole stress and argument rest on the single word *children ;* see also Gal. 3, 16. Very frequently the particles indicating the grammatical or logical connection of the passage in its position in the Old Testament, are included in the quotation, although entirely unsuited to the connection in which the passage is introduced. This is so frequently done as to be almost the rule. It is, therefore, not an arbitrary proceeding to make the last words of this verse refer to Christ, while the former part of it is made to refer to the context of the passage as it stands in Genesis.

V. 32. *Τὸ μυστήριον τοῦτο μέγα ἐστίν, this mystery is great.* The word mystery does not refer to the passage in Gen. 2, 24, as though the apostle intended to say that that passage had a mystical sense which he had just unfolded by applying it to the relation between Christ and his church. It is the union between Christ and his people, the fact that they are *one flesh,* he declares to be a great mystery. The word *μυστήριον* is used here, as it is every where else, for something hidden, something beyond the reach of human knowledge. Whether its being thus hidden arises from its lying in the future, or because of being imperfectly revealed, or because it is in its own nature incomprehensible, must be determined by the connection. In this place the last is probably the idea intended. The thing itself is beyond our comprehension. The Vulgate renders this passage, *sacramentum hoc magnum est.* The Latin word *sacramentum,* besides its usual classical sense, ' a sacred deposit,' was often used to signify any thing sacred, or which had a hidden import. In this latter sense it agrees in meaning with the word *μυστήριον,* which also is used to designate something the meaning of which is hidden. Hence in the Vulgate it is often translated as it is here. In the Latin church the word *sacramentum,* however, gradually changed its meaning. Instead of being applied to every thing having a sacred or secret meaning, it was confined to those rites or acts which were assumed to have the power of conferring grace. This is the Romish idea of a sacrament. The Papal theologians taking the word in this sense here, and understanding the apostle to refer to marriage, quote this passage in proof that matrimony is a sacrament. The answer to this argument is obvious. In the first place, it is not marriage, but the union between Christ and his church, that Paul declares to be a μυστήριον, and the Vulgate a *sacramentum*. And in the second place, neither the Greek nor Latin term means *a sacrament* in the Romish sense of the word. The Vulgate translates 1 Tim. 3, 16, *magnum est pietatis sacramentum*, which no Romanist understands as teaching that the manifestation of God in the flesh is a sacrament in the ecclesiastical meaning of the term.

V. 33. The relation of this verse to what precedes, as indicated by πλήν, admits of two explanations. That particle is used at the beginning of a clause, after an interruption, to introduce the resumption of the main subject. It may be so here. The principal object of the whole paragraph from v. 21, is to unfold the true nature of the conjugal relation and its duties. With this was connected an exposition of the analogous relation between Christ and the church. This latter point in verses 30. 31, is the only one brought into view. Here the apostle reverts to the main subject. *But,* to resume my subject, *let every one of you in particular so love his wife even as himself.* This explanation is the one commonly adopted. Πλήν, however, may mean, *nevertheless,* as it is rendered in our version, and this verse be connected with the 32d. ' The relation between Christ and the church is a great

mystery; *nevertheless*, do you also love your wives.'
That is, although there is something in the relation
between Christ and the church which infinitely transcends the conjugal relation, nevertheless there is sufficient analogy between the cases, to render it obligatory
on husbands to love their wives as Christ loves his
church. This view of the connection is to be preferred,
especially because of the words καὶ ὑμεῖς, *you also*,
which evidently suppose the reference is to what
immediately precedes.

Ὑμεῖς οἱ καθ᾽ ἕνα, *you severally*, ἕκαστος τὴν ἑαυ
τοῦ γυναῖκα οὕτως ἀγαπάτω ὡς ἑαυτόν, *let each one so
love his wife as himself*. The construction varies; the
verb ἀγαπάτω being made to agree with ἕκαστος, instead of ὑμεῖς the real subject. The meaning is the
same as in ver. 28. The husband is to love his wife
as being himself. In the next clause (ἡ δὲ γυνὴ ἵνα
φοβῆται τὸν ἄνδρα), ἡ δὲ γυνή is the nominative absolute, and ἵνα depends on a verb understood. *But as to
the woman*, let her see, *that she reverence her husband*.
The word φοβέω may express the emotion of fear in
all its modifications and in all its degrees from simple
respect, through reverence, up to adoration, according
to its object. It is, however, in all its degrees an
acknowledgment of superiority. The sentiments, therefore, which lie at the foundation of the marriage relation, which arise out of the constitution of nature,
which are required by the command of God, and are
essential to the happiness and well-being of the par-

ties, are, on the part of the husband, that form of love which leads him to cherish and protect his wife as being himself, and on the part of the woman, that sense of his superiority out of which trust and obedience involuntarily flow.

CHAPTER VI

SECTION I.—Vs. 1–9.

1. Children, obey your parents in the Lord: for this is right.
2. Honour thy father and mother, (which is the first command-
3. ment with promise,) that it may be well with thee, and thou
4. mayest live long on the earth.   And, ye fathers, provoke not your children to wrath: but bring them up in the nurture and
5. admonition of the Lord.   Servants, be obedient to them that are *your* masters according to the flesh, with fear and trembling,
6. in singleness of your heart, as unto Christ; not with eye-service, as men-pleasers; but as the servants of Christ, doing the
7. will of God from the heart; with good will doing service, as
8. to the Lord, and not to men: knowing that whatsoever good thing any man doeth, the same shall he receive of the Lord,
9. whether *he be* bond or free.   And, ye masters, do the same things unto them, forbearing threatening: knowing that your Master also is in heaven; neither is there respect of persons with him.

Children should obey their parents. This obedience should be in the Lord, determined and regulated by a regard to Christ, v. 1. The ground of the obligation is—1. It is itself right. 2. It is enforced by an express command in the decalogue, to which a special promise is annexed, vs. 1–3.

Parents should do nothing to cherish evil feelings in the minds of their children, but bring them up in the discipline of Christianity, vs. 4, 5.

Servants should be obedient to their masters. This obedience should be rendered—1. With solicitude. 2. with singleness of mind. 3. As part of their obedience to Christ, v. 5. Therefore, not only when observed by men or from the desire to please men, but as serving Christ and desiring to please him ; rendering their services with readiness as to the Lord and not to men ; because they know that at his bar all men, whether bond or free, shall be treated according to their works, vs. 6–8.

Masters are to act on the same principles of regard to the authority of Christ, and of their responsibility to him in their conduct towards their slaves, avoiding all harshness, because master and slave have a common Master in heaven ; with whom there is no respect of persons, v. 8.

COMMENTARY.

V. 1. *Children, obey your parents.* The nature or character of this obedience, is expressed by the words, *in the Lord.* It should be religious; arising out of the conviction that such obedience is the will of the Lord. This makes it a higher service than if rendered from fear or from mere natural affection. It secures its being prompt, cordial and universal. That Κύριος here refers to Christ is plain from the whole context. In the preceding chapter, v. 21, we have the general exhortation under which this special direction to children is included, and the obedience there required is to be rendered *in the fear of Christ.* In the following verses also Κύριος constantly has this reference, and therefore must have it here. The ground of the obligation to filial obedience is expressed in the words, *for this is right.* It is not because of the personal character of the parent, nor because of his kindness, nor on the ground of expediency, but because it is *right;* an obligation arising out of the nature of the relation between parents and children, and which must exist wherever the relation itself exists.

V. 2. This consideration is enforced by a reference to the express command of God. The duty is so important as to be included in that brief summary of the moral law given by God on Mount Sinai. It was engraven by the finger of God on the tables of stone, *Honour thy father and thy mother.* Any flagrant breach of this command was, according to the Mosaic law, punished with death. *To honour* is to reverence; and, therefore, the command has reference to the inward feeling as well as to the outward conduct. This precept is said to be πρώτη, ἐν ἐπαγγελίᾳ. This may mean, it is the first commandment in the decalogue which has a specific promise attached; for the promise connected with the second commandment does not relate to the observance of that particular precept, but to keeping God's covenant. Or it may mean that it is the first commandment of the second table of the law, and has a promise annexed; or, πρώτη may be taken here as in Mark 12, 28. 30, in the sense of chief, i. e. the first in importance. The sense would then be, 'Honour thy father and mother; this is the prime commandment, the first in importance among those relating to our social duties; and it has the specific promise annexed. It shall be well with thee on the earth.' This view of the passage is on the whole to be preferred. It is not likely that Paul would call this "the first commandment with promise," when it is in fact the only command in the decalogue which has any specific promise annexed to it. And to say that it is the first in order of arrangement in the second table of the law, not only adds nothing to its importance, but supposes the apostle to refer to a distinction between the two tables of the decalogue, not elsewhere recognized in Scripture.

The promise itself has a theocratical form in the Old Testament. That is, it has specific reference to prosperity and length of days in the land which God had given to his people as their inheritance. The apostle generalizes it by leaving out the concluding words, and makes it a promise not confined to one land or people, but to obedient children every where. If it be asked whether obedient children are in fact thus distinguished by long life and prosperity? The answer is, that this, like all other such promises, is a revelation of a general purpose of God, and makes known what will be the usual course of his providence. That some obedient children are unfortunate and short lived, is no more inconsistent with this promise, than that some diligent men are poor, is inconsistent with the declaration, 'The hand of the diligent maketh rich.' Diligence, as a general rule, does secure riches; and obedient children, as a general rule, are prosperous and happy. The general promise is fulfilled to individuals, just so far " as it shall serve for God's glory, and their own good."

V. 4. The duty of parents, who are here represented by the father, is stated in a negative and positive form. *And ye fathers, provoke not your children to wrath.* This is what they are not to do. They are not to excite the bad passions of their children by severity, injustice, partiality, or unreasonable exercise of authority. A parent had better sow tares in a field from which he expects to derive food for himself and family, than by his own ill conduct nurture evil in the heart of his child. The positive part of parental duty is expressed in the comprehensive direction, ἀλλ' ἐκτρέφετε αὐτὰ ἐν παιδείᾳ καὶ νουθεσίᾳ Κυρίου, i. e. educate them, bring them up, developing all their powers *by* (ἐν instrumental) the instruction and admonition of the Lord. Παιδεία is a comprehensive word; it means *the training* or *education of a child*, including the whole process of instruction and discipline. Νουθεσία, from νουθετέω (νοῦς, τίθημι) *to put in mind*, is included under the more general

term, and is correctly rendered *admonition*. It is the
act of reminding one of his faults or duties. Children
are not to be allowed to grow up without care or control. They are to be instructed, disciplined, and ad-
monished, so that they be brought to knowledge, self-
control, and obedience. This whole process of education is to be religious, and not only religious, but
Christian. It is *the nurture and admonition of the
Lord,* which is the appointed and the only effectual
means of attaining the end of education. Where this
means is neglected or any other substituted in its place,
the result must be disastrous failure. The moral and
religious element of our nature is just as essential and
as universal as the intellectual. Religion therefore is
as necessary to the development of the mind as knowledge. And as Christianity is the only true religion,
and God in Christ the only true God, the only possible
means of profitable education is the nurture and admonition of the Lord. That is, the whole process of
instruction and discipline must be that which he pre-
scribes, and which he administers, so that his authority
should be brought into constant and immediate contact
with the mind, heart and conscience of the child. It
will not do for the parent to present himself as the ultimate end, the source of knowledge and possessor of
authority to determine truth and duty. This would be
to give his child a mere human development. Nor
will it do for him to urge and communicate every thing
on the abstract ground of reason; for that would be to
merge his child in nature. It is only by making God,

God in Christ, the teacher and ruler, on whose authority every thing is to be believed and in obedience to whose will every thing is to be done, that the ends of education can possibly be attained. It is infinite folly in men to assume to be wiser than God, or to attempt to accomplish an end by other means than those which he has appointed.

V. 5. The five following verses treat of the relative duties of masters and servants. Δοῦλος and κύριος are here relative terms, although in Greek the antithetical term to δοῦλος is commonly δεσπότης, as in 1 Tim. 6, 1; Titus 2, 9; compare also 1 Pet. 2, 18. Δοῦλος, from δέω, *to bind*, means a bondman, or slave, as distinguished from a hired servant, who was called μίσθιος or μισθωτός. That such is its meaning here is plain not only from the common usage of the word, but also from the antithesis between δοῦλος and ἐλεύθερος, *bond* and *free*, in v. 8. Κύριος means *possessor, owner, master*. It implies the relation which a man may bear both to persons and things. The nature of that relation, or the kind and degree of authority involved in it, however, is not determined by the word, but in each case by the context. It is evident both from the meaning of the terms here used, and from the known historical fact that slavery prevailed throughout the Roman empire during the apostolic age, that this and other passages of the New Testament refer to that institution. It is dealt with precisely as despotism in the State is dealt with. It is neither enjoined nor forbidden. It is simply assumed to be lawful, so that a Christian may consistently be an autocrat in the State, or a master of slaves. In this view the scriptural doctrine on this subject, differs on the one hand, from the doctrine that slave-holding is in itself sinful, on the ground that one man cannot lawfully possess or exercise the rights and authority over his fellow-men, which are involved in the relation of a master to his slaves. This of necessity leads to setting up a rule of faith and practice higher than the Scriptures, and thus tends to destroy their authority. It leads to uncharitable feelings and to unrighteous judgments, as well as to unwarrantable measures for abating the evil. On the other hand, the scriptural doctrine is opposed to the opinion that slavery is in itself a desirable institution, and as such to be cherished and perpetuated. This leads to results no less deplorable than the other error. As slavery is founded on the inferiority of one class of society to another, the opinion that it ought to be cherished naturally leads to the adoption of means to increase or to perpetuate that inferiority, by preventing the improvement of the subject class. It presents also a strong temptation to deny the common brotherhood of men, and to regard the enslaved as belonging to an inferior race. The great mistake of those who adopt the former error, is—1. That they assume the right of property in the master to extend to more than the services of the slave. The only right of property possible in the case is a right to use the slave as a man possessing the same nature with his master, and may, by the law of God and the constitution of things, be properly used.

And 2. The confounding slave-laws with slavery, which is as unreasonable as to confound despotism as a form of civil government, with the laws of any particular despotic state. Those laws may be good or bad. Their being bad, as they too often are, does not prove either in the case of despotism or slavery that the institution itself is contrary to the divine law. The mistake of those who hold the other extreme opinion on this subject, so far as the Bible is concerned, is that what the Scriptures tolerate as lawful under given circumstances, may be cherished and rendered perpetual. This is as unreasonable, as to maintain that children should, if possible, always remain minors.

The Bible method of dealing with this and similar institutions is to enforce, on all concerned, the great principles of moral obligation—assured that those principles, if allowed free scope, will put an end to all evils both in the political and social relations of men. The apostle, therefore, without either denouncing or com mending slavery, simply inculcates on master and slave their appropriate duty. On the slave he enjoins the duty of obedience. In the expression, *masters, according to the flesh,* there is evidently an implied reference to a higher authority. It limits the authority of the master to what is external; the soul being left free. The slave has two masters; the one κατὰ σάρκα, the other κατὰ πνεῦμα. The one, man; the other, Christ. The directions here given relate to their duty to the former. As to the nature of the obedience required, the apostle teaches—1. That it should be rendered μετὰ φόβου καὶ τρόμου, *with fear and trembling*, i. e. with conscientious solicitude. That nothing servile is intended by these terms is plain from the context, and from a comparison with other passages in which the same expression is used. It is not the fear of man, but the reverential fear of God of which the apostle speaks, as what follows clearly proves. In 1 Cor. 2, 3, Paul tells the Corinthians that he came among them "with fear and trembling;" and in 2 Cor. 7, 15, he speaks of their having received Titus, "with fear and trembling;" and in Phil. 2, 12, he exhorts believers to work out their salvation "with fear and trembling." In all of these cases solicitude to do what is right is all the terms imply.

2. This obedience is to be rendered ἐν ἁπλότητι τῆς καρδίας, *with simplicity of heart*, i. e. with singleness of mind—meaning just what we appear to mean. It is opposed to hypocrisy, false pretence, deceit and cunning. Compare Rom. 12, 8 ; 2 Cor. 8, 2 ; 9, 11. The word ἁπλότης signifies *singleness*, from ἁπλόος, *one-fold*, as opposed to διπλόος, *two-fold*, or, *double*. The thing enjoined is, therefore, the opposite of double-mindedness. 3. This obedience is to be rendered ὡς τῷ Χριστῷ, *as to Christ*. Slaves were to regard their obedience to their masters as part of their obedience to Christ. This would give it the character of a religious service, because the motive is regard to divine authority, and its object is a divine person. It thus ceases to be servile, and becomes consistent with the highest mental elevation and spiritual freedom.

V. 6. The apostle explains in the two following verses what he means by *simplicity of heart*, or sincere obedience. It is not *eye-service*. That is, such service as is rendered only when the eye of the master sees what is done ; as though the only object were to please men. Servants are required to act as the δοῦλοι τοῦ Χριστοῦ, *the slaves of Christ*, whose eyes are every where; and, therefore, if their desire is to please him, they must be as faithful in their master's absence as in his presence. Ποιοῦντες τὸ θέλημα τοῦ Θεοῦ, *doing the will of God*. This is descriptive of the servants of Christ, in opposition to men-pleasers. They act from a regard to the will of God, and from a desire to please him,—ἐκ ψυχῆς, *ex animo*, *from the soul*. Sometimes ψυχή means the seat of the desires and affections, and then agrees in sense with καρδία. Sometimes the two are distinguished, as in Mark 12, 30, " with all the heart (καρδία,) and with all the soul (ψυχή)." Here the sense is, that the principle of obedience is nothing external, but is within. It is an obedience which springs from the soul—the whole inner man. These words are commonly and most naturally connected with the preceding clause ; 'doing the will of the Lord from the soul.' By many commentators and editors they are connected with what follows, 'from the soul, with good will, doing service.' This gives δουλεύοντες two nearly equivalent qualifying clauses, and leaves the preceding participle ποιοῦντες without any.

V. 7. The whole character of the obedience of the slave is summed up in this verse, δουλεύοντες, ὡς τῷ Κυρίῳ καὶ οὐκ ἀνθρώποις, *doing service, to the Lord and not to men.* This, as the Scriptures teach, is not peculiar to the obedience of the slave to his master, but applies to all other cases in which obedience is required from one man to another. It applies to children in relation to their parents, wives to husbands, people to magistrates. Those invested with lawful authority are the representatives of God. The powers (i. e. those invested with authority) are ordained by God; and therefore all obedience rendered to them out of regard to his will, is obedience to Him. And as obedience to God is rendered to one infinitely true and good, it is even more elevating than obedience to truth and goodness. Foreign as all this is to the proud and rebellious heart of man, which spurns all superiority and authority, it is daily illustrated by the cheerful and patient submission of the people of God even to the capricious and unreasonable exercise of the authority of those to whom God has placed them in subjection. It is to be remarked that the apostle presents this principle not merely in a religious, but a Christian form. We are required *to do service, as to the Lord, and not to men.* It is to Christ, God manifested in the flesh; to him, who being in the form of God, thought it no robbery to be equal with God, but humbled himself, taking on him the condition of a slave, μορφὴν δούλου λαβών ; it is to this infinitely exalted and infinitely condescending Saviour, who came not to be served, but to serve, that the obedience of every Christian, whether servant, child, wife, or subject, is really and consciously rendered. Thus the most galling yoke is made easy, and the heaviest burden light.

The words μετ᾿ εὐνοίας qualify δουλεύοντες, *with a willing mind doing service.* This stands opposed to the sullenness and inward indignation with which a service extorted by fear of punishment is often rendered. No service rendered to Christ can be of that character. It is rendered with alacrity and cheerfulness.

V. 8. This verse presents for the encouragement of the slave, the elevating truth that all men stand on a level before the bar of Christ. In him and before him, there is neither Jew nor Greek, bond nor free, male nor female, but so far as these external distinctions are concerned, all are alike. The apostle, therefore, says to slaves, render this cheerful obedience, εἰδότες *knowing,* i. e. because ye know, *that whatsoever good thing any man doeth, the same shall he receive of the Lord, whether he be bond or free.* In this world some men are masters and some are slaves. In the next, these distinctions will cease. There the question will be, not, Who is the master? and, Who the slave? but who has done the will of God? In this clause ὅ ἐάν τι is for ὅ,τι ἐάν, as it is in Col. 3, 23, ἐάν being for ἄν. Κομίζομαι is to receive for one self, to receive back as a recompense. 2 Cor. 5, 10. At the bar of Christ and from his hands every man shall receive according to his works, whether bond or free.

V. 9. Having enjoined on slaves their peculiar duties, the apostle turns to masters. Καὶ οἱ κύριοι, *and ye masters.* The force of καὶ here is—'Not slaves only have their duties; you masters have your peculiar obligations.' The duty of masters is expressed by the comprehensive words, τὰ αὐτὰ ποιεῖτε πρὸς αὐτούς, *do the same things towards them.* This does not refer exclusively to μετ᾽ εὐνοίας in the preceding clause, as though the sense were, 'As slaves are to obey with kind feeling, so masters are to rule in the same temper.' The reference is more general. Masters are to act towards their slaves with the same regard to the will of God, with the same recognition of the authority of Christ, with the same sincerity and good feeling which had been enjoined on the slaves themselves. Masters and slaves are men and brethren, the same great principles of moral and religious obligation govern both classes. In the parallel passage, Col. 4, 1, the expression is, οἱ κύριοι, τὸ δίκαιον, καὶ τὴν ἰσότητα τοῖς δούλοις παρέχεσθε, *ye masters, give unto your servants that which is just and equal.* That is, act towards them on the principles of justice and equity. Justice requires that all their rights, as men, as husbands, and as parents should be regarded. And these rights are not to be determined by the civil law, but by the law of God. "As the laws," says Calvin, "gave great license to masters, many assumed that every thing was lawful which the civil statute allowed; and such was their severity that the Roman emperors were obliged to restrain their tyranny. But although no edicts of princes interposed in behalf of the slave, God concedes nothing to the master beyond what the law of love allows." Paul requires for slaves not only what is strictly just, but τὴν ἰσότητα. What is that? Literally, it is *equality*. This is not only its signification, but its meaning. Slaves are to be treated by their masters on the principles of equality. Not that they are to be equal with their masters in authority, or station, or circumstances; but they are to be treated as having, as men, as husbands, and as parents, equal rights with their masters. It is just as great a sin to deprive a slave of the just recompense for his labour, or to keep him in ignorance, or to take from him his wife or child, as it is to act thus towards a free man. This is the equality which the law of God demands, and on this principle the final judgment is to be administered. Christ will punish the master for defrauding the slave as severely as he will punish the slave for robbing his master. The same penalty will be inflicted for the violation of the conjugal or parental rights of the one as of the other. For, as the apostle adds, there is no respect of persons with him. At his bar the question will be, 'What was done?' not 'Who did it?' Paul carries this so far as to apply the principle not only to the acts, but to the temper of masters. They are not only to act towards their slaves on the principles of justice and equity, but are *to avoid threatening*.* This includes all manifestations of contempt and ill-temper, or undue severity. All this is enforced by the consideration that masters

---

* Minarum enim et omnis atrocitatis hoc initium est, quod servos domini, quasi sua tantum causa natos, nihilo pluris faciunt quam pecudes. Ergo sub una specie vetat ne contumeliose et atrociter tractentur.—CALVIN.

have a master in heaven to whom they are responsible for their treatment of their slaves. The common text has here the reading καὶ ὑμῶν αὐτῶν ὁ κύριος—*your master*. Lackman, Rückert, Harless, Meyer and others adopt the reading αὐτῶν καὶ ὑμῶν, *of them and of you*, i. e. *your common master as in heaven*.

It is thus that the Holy Spirit deals with slavery. Slaves are not commanded to refuse to be slaves, to break their bonds and repudiate the authority of their masters. They are required to obey with alacrity and with a sincere desire to do their duty to their masters, as part of their duty to Christ. Masters are not commanded as an immediate and imperative duty to emancipate their slaves, but to treat them according to the principles of justice and equity. It is not to be expected that men of the world will act in conformity with the Gospel in this, any more than in other respects. But believers will. And the result of such obedience if it could become general would be, that first the evils of slavery, and then slavery itself, would pass away as naturally and as healthfully as children cease to be minors.

SECTION II.—Vs. 10–24.

10. Finally, my brethren, be strong in the Lord, and in the power
11. of his might. Put on the whole armour of God, that ye may
12. be able to stand against the wiles of the devil. For we
   wrestle not against flesh and blood, but against principalities,
   against powers, against the rulers of the darkness of this
13. world, against spiritual wickedness in high *places*. Wherefore
   take unto you the whole armour of God, that ye may be able

to withstand in the evil day, and having done all, to stand.

14. Stand therefore, having your loins girt about with truth, and

15. having on the breast-plate of righteousness; and your feet shod

16. with the preparation of the gospel of peace; above all, taking
the shield of faith, wherewith ye shall be able to quench all

17. the fiery darts of the wicked. And take the helmet of salvation, and the sword of the Spirit, which is the word of God:

18. praying always with all prayer and supplication in the Spirit,
and watching thereunto with all perseverance and supplication

19. for all saints; and for me, that utterance may be given unto
me, that I may open my mouth boldly, to make known the

20. mystery of the gospel, for which I am an ambassador in bonds:

21. that therein I may speak boldly, as I ought to speak. But that
ye also may know my affairs, *and* how I do, Tychicus, a beloved brother and faithful minister in the Lord, shall make

22. known to you all things: whom I have sent unto you for the
same purpose, that ye might know our affairs, and *that* he

23. might comfort your hearts. Peace *be* to the brethren, and love
with faith from God the Father and the Lord Jesus Christ.

24. Grace *be* with all them that love our Lord Jesus Christ in sincerity. Amen.

ANALYSIS.

Directions in reference to the spiritual conflict. As such a conflict is inevitable, the believer should— 1. Muster strength for the struggle. 2. He should seek that strength from Christ. 3. Since his enemies are not human but superhuman, Satan and all the powers of darkness, the believer needs not only more than human strength, but also divine armour. He should, therefore, take the panoply of God, that he may be able to stand in the evil day. That panoply consists—

1. In the knowledge and reception of the truth.   2. In the righteousness of Christ.   3. In the alacrity which flows from the peace of the Gospel.   4. In the consciousness of salvation.   5. In faith.   6. In the word of God, which is the sword of the Spirit.

To obtain strength to use this armour aright, and to secure victory for ourselves and for the army of which we are a part, we should pray.   These prayers should be—1. Of all kinds.   2. On every occasion.   3. Importunate and persevering.   4. By the aid of the Holy Spirit.   5. For all saints.

Believing in the efficacy of such prayers, the apostle begs the Ephesian believers to pray for him, that God would enable him to preach the Gospel in a suitable manner.

To relieve their anxiety he had sent Tychicus to inform them of his circumstances and of his health.

He invokes the Father and Son to bestow upon the brethren the blessings of divine peace and love united with faith ; and implores the special favour of God for all who love the Lord Jesus Christ with a love that cannot die.

COMMENTARY.

V. 10. Though the redemption purchased by Christ, as described in this epistle, is so complete and so free, yet between the beginning and the consummation of the work there is a protracted conflict.   This is not a figure of speech.   It is something real and arduous. Salvation, however gratuitous, is not to be obtained without great effort. The Christian conflict is not only real, it is difficult and dangerous. It is one in which true believers are often grievously wounded; and multitudes of reputed believers entirely succumb. It is one also in which great mistakes are often committed and serious loss incurred from ignorance of its nature, and of the appropriate means for carrying it on. Men are apt to regard it as a mere moral conflict between reason and conscience on the one side, and evil passions on the other. They therefore rely on their own strength, and upon the resources of nature for success. Against these mistakes the apostle warns his readers. He teaches that every thing pertaining to it is supernatural. The source of strength is not in nature. The conflict is not between the good and bad principles of our nature. He shows that we belong to a spiritual, as well as to a natural world, and are engaged in a combat in which the higher powers of the universe are involved; and that this conflict, on the issue of which our salvation depends, is not to be carried on with straws picked up by the wayside. As we have superhuman enemies to contend with, we need not only superhuman strength, but divine armour and arms. The weapons of our warfare are not natural, but divine.

Finally, my brethren, be strong in the Lord, τὸ λοιπὸν, ἀδελφοί μου, ἐνδυναμοῦσθε ἐν Κυρίῳ. He concludes his epistle so full of elevated views, and so rich in disclosures of the mysteries of redemption, with directions as to the struggle necessary to secure salvation. His first exhortation is to muster strength for

the inevitable conflict, and to seek that strength from
the right source. We are to *be strong in the Lord.*
As a branch separated from the vine, or as a limb
severed from the body, so is a Christian separated from
Christ. He, therefore, who rushes into this conflict
without thinking of Christ, without putting his trust
in him, and without continually looking to him for
strength and regarding himself as a member of his
body, deriving all life and vigour from him, is de-
mented. He knows not what he is doing. He has
not strength even to reach the field. With him the
whole conflict is a sham. The words καὶ ἐν τῷ κράτει
τῆς ἰσχύος αὐτοῦ mean, *in the vigour derived from his
strength.* The vigour of a man's arm is derived from
the strength of his body. It is only as members of
Christ's body that we have either life or power. It is
not we that live, but Christ that liveth in us; and the
strength which we have is not our own but his. When
we are weak, then are we strong. When most empty
of self, we are most full of God.

V. 11. The second direction has reference to the
arms requisite for the successful conduct of this conflict; ἐνδύσασθε τὴν πανοπλίαν τοῦ Θεοῦ, *put on the
whole armour of God.* Πανοπλία, *panoply,* includes
both the defensive and offensive armour of the soldier.
The believer has not only to defend himself, but also
to attack his spiritual enemies; and the latter is as
necessary to his safety as the former. It will not do
for him to act only on the defensive, he must endeavour to subdue as well as to resist. How this is to be

done, the following portion of the chapter teaches. *The armour of God,* means that armour which God has provided and which he gives. We are thus taught from the outset, that as the strength which we need is not from ourselves, so neither are the means of offence or defence. Nor are they means of man's devising. This is a truth which has been overlooked in all ages of the church, to the lamentable injury of the people of God. Instead of relying on the arms which God has provided, men have always been disposed to trust to those which they provide for themselves or which have been prescribed by others. Seclusion from the world (i. e. flight rather than conflict), ascetic and ritual observances, invocation of saints and angels, and especially, celibacy, voluntary poverty, and monastic obedience, constitute the panoply which false religion has substituted for the armour of God. Of this fatal mistake, manifested from the beginning, the apostle treats at length in his Epistle to the Colossians, 2, 18–23. He there exhorts his hearers, not to allow any one, puffed up with carnal wisdom, and neglecting Christ, the only source of life and strength, to despoil them of their reward, through false humility and the worship of angels, commanding not to touch, or taste, or handle this or that, which methods of overcoming evil have indeed the appearance of wisdom, in humility, will-worship, and neglect of the body, but not the reality, and only serve to satisfy the flesh. They increase the evil which they are professedly designed to overcome. A more accurate description could not be given historically, than is here given prophetically, of the means substituted by carnal wisdom for the armour of God. Calling on saints and angels, humility in the sense of self-degradation, or submitting our will to human authority, neglecting the body, or ascetic observances, abstaining from things lawful, uncommanded rites and ordinances, observing months and days—these are the arms with which the church in her apostasy has arrayed her children for this warfare. These are by name enumerated and condemned by the apostle, who directs us to clothe ourselves with the panoply of God, which he proceeds to describe in detail.

Πρὸς τὸ δύνασθαι ὑμᾶς στῆναι πρὸς τὰς μεθοδείας τοῦ διαβόλου. This divine armour is necessary to enable us *to stand against the wiles of the devil.* If our adversary was a man, and possessed nothing beyond human strength, ingenuity, and cunning, we might defend ourselves by human means. But as we have to contend with Satan, we need the armour of God. One part of the Bible of course supposes every other part to be true. If it is not true that there is such a being as Satan, or that he possesses great power and intelligence, or that he has access to the minds of men and exerts his power for their destruction; if all this is obsolete, then there is no real necessity for supernatural power or for supernatural means of defence. If Satan and satanic influence are fables or figures, then all the rest of the representations concerning this spiritual conflict is empty metaphor. But if one part of this representation is literally true, the other has a corresponding depth and reality of meaning. If Satan is really the prince of the powers of darkness, ruler and god of this world; if he is the author of physical and moral evil; the great enemy of God, of Christ and of his people, full of cunning and malice; if he is constantly seeking whom he may destroy, seducing men into sin, blinding their minds and suggesting evil and sceptical thoughts; if all this is true, then to be ignorant of it, or to deny it, or to enter on this conflict as though it were merely a struggle between the good and bad principles in our own hearts, is to rush blindfold to destruction.

V. 12. This is the point on which the apostle most earnestly insists. He would awaken his readers to a due sense of the power of the adversaries with whom they are to contend. He lifts the vail and discloses to them the spiritual world; the hosts of the kingdom of darkness. We have to stand against the wiles of the devil, ὅτι οὐκ ἔστιν ἡμῖν ἡ πάλη πρὸς αἷμα καὶ σάρκα, *because our conflict is not with flesh and blood*, i. e. with men. The word πάλη means *a wrestling*. The apostle either changes the figure immediately, or he uses the word here in a more general sense. The latter is the more probable. " Flesh and blood" does not here or any where else, mean our corrupt nature, as *flesh* by itself so often means; but *men*. So in Gal. 1, 16, " I conferred not with flesh and blood," means, ' I did not consult with man.' The apostle after his conversion sought no instruction or counsel from man; all his knowledge of the Gospel was received by immediate revelation.

Our conflict is not with man, *but against princi-*
palities, against powers, against the rulers of the dark-
ness of this world, against spiritual wickedness in high
places. The signification of the terms here used, the
context, and the analogy of Scripture, render it certain
that the reference is to evil spirits. They are called in
Scripture δαιμόνια, *demons,* who are declared to be
fallen angels, 2 Pet. 2, 4; Jude 6, and are now subject
to Satan their prince. They are called ἀρχαί, *princes,*
those who are first or high in rank; and ἐξουσίαι, *poten-*
tates, those invested with authority. These terms have
probably reference to the relation of the spirits among
themselves. The designation κοσμοκράτορες, *rulers of*
the world, expresses the power or authority which they
exercise over the world. The κόσμος, i. e. mankind,
is subject to them; comp. 2 Cor. 4, 4; John 16, 11.
The word is properly used only of those rulers whose
dominion was universal. And in this sense the Jews
called the angel of death κοσμοκράτωρ. In the following clause τοῦ σκότους τοῦ αἰῶνος τούτου, *of the dark-*
ness of this world; the words τοῦ αἰῶνος, on the
authority of the best manuscripts, are generally omitted. The sense is substantially the same whichever
reading be adopted. These evil spirits are the rulers
of this darkness. The meaning either is, that they
reign over the existing state of ignorance and alienation from God; i. e. the world in its apostasy is subject to their control; or *this darkness* is equivalent to
kingdom of darkness. Rulers of the kingdom of darkness, which includes in it, according to the scriptural

doctrine, the world as distinguished from the true people of God. The word σκότος is used elsewhere, the abstract for the concrete, for those in darkness, i. e. for those who belong to, or constitute the kingdom of darkness, Luke 22, 53; Col. 1, 13. Our conflict, therefore, is with the potentates who are rulers of the kingdom of darkness as it now is.

They are further called τὰ πνευματικὰ τῆς πονηρίας, *spiritual wickedness*, as the phrase is rendered in our version. But this cannot be its meaning; it is not wickedness in the abstract, but wicked spirits, the context and the force of the words themselves show to be intended. Beza and others understand the words as equivalent to πνευματικαὶ πονηρίαι, *spiritual wickednesses*. This would give a good sense. As these spirits are called ἀρχαί and ἐξουσίαι, so they may be called πονηρίαι. But τὰ πνευματικὰ τῆς πονηρίας cannot be resolved into πνευματικαὶ πονηρίαι. Τὰ πνευματικὰ is equivalent to τὰ πνεύματα, as in so many other cases the neuter adjective in the singular or plural is used substantively, as τὸ ἱππικόν, *the cavalry*; τὰ αἰχμά-λωτα, *the captivity*, i. e. captives. *Spirits of wickedness* then means *wicked spirits*. The beings whom the apostle in the preceding clauses describes as principalities, powers, and rulers, he here calls wicked spirits, to express their character and nature.

The principal difficulty in this verse concerns the words ἐν τοῖς ἐπουρανίοις. A very large class of commentators, ancient and modern, connect them with the beginning of the verse, and translate, " our conflict is

for heavenly things;" heaven is the prize for which
we contend. There are two objections to this interpretation, which are generally considered decisive,
although the sense is good and appropriate. The one
is, that ἐν τοῖς ἐπουρανίοις always in this Epistle means
heaven ; and the other is that ἐν does not mean *for.*
The connection is with the preceding clause. These
wicked spirits are said to be in heaven. But what
does that mean? Many say that heaven here means
our atmosphere, which is assumed to be the dwelling-
place of evil spirits; see 2, 2. But τὰ ἐπουράνια is
not elsewhere in this Epistle used for the atmospheric
heavens; neither do the Scriptures give any counte-
nance to the popular opinion of the ancient world,
that the air is the region of spirits; nor does this idea
harmonize with the context. It is no exaltation of the
power of these spirits to refer to them as dwelling in
our atmosphere. The whole context, however, shows
that the design of the apostle is to present the formidable character of our adversaries in the most impressive
point of view. Others suppose that Paul means to
refer to the former, and not to the present residence
of these exalted beings. They are fallen angels, who
once dwelt in heaven. But this is obviously inconsistent with the natural meaning of his words. He
speaks of them as in heaven. It is better to take the
word heaven in a wide sense. It is very often used
antithetically to the word *earth.* ' Heaven and earth,'
include the whole universe. Those who do not belong
to the earth belong to heaven. All intelligent beings

are terrestrial or celestial. Of the latter class some are good and some are bad, as of the angels some are holy and some unholy. These principalities and potentates, these rulers and spirits of wickedness, are not earthly magnates, they belong to the order of celestial intelligences, and therefore are the more to be dreaded, and something more than human strength and earthly armour is required for the conflict to which the apostle refers. This indicates the connection with the following verse.

V. 13. *Wherefore*, i. e. because you have such formidable enemies, and because the conflict is inevitable, ἀναλάβετε τὴν πανοπλίαν τοῦ Θεοῦ, not only arm yourselves, but *take the panoply of God ;* no other is adequate to the emergency. "Ἵνα δυνηθῆτε ἀντιστῆναι ἐν τῇ ἡμέρᾳ τῇ πονηρᾷ, *in order that ye may be able to withstand,* i. e. successfully to resist, *in the evil day.* The evil day is the day of trial. Ps. 41, 2, "The Lord will deliver him in the time of trouble ;" or as it is in the Sept. ἐν ἡμέρᾳ πονηρᾷ ; and Ps. 49, 5, "Wherefore should I fear in the days of evil ;" Sept. ἐν ἡμέρᾳ πονηρᾷ. The day here referred to is the definite day when the enemies previously mentioned shall make their assault. This however is not to be understood with special, much less with exclusive, reference to the last great conflict with the powers of darkness which is to take place before the second advent. The whole exhortation has reference to the present duty of believers. They are at once to assume their armour, and be always prepared for the attacks of their formidable enemies.

Καὶ ἅπαντα κατεργασάμενοι στῆναι, *and having done all to stand.* This is understood by many to refer to the preparation for conflict. Having made every preparation, stand ready for the assault. But that idea is included in the former part of the verse. Others take κατεργάζεσθαι in the sense of *debellare, vincere;* having overcome all opposition, or conquered all, stand. The ordinary sense of the word includes that idea. ' Having done all that pertains to the combat, to stand;' i. e. That you may be able, after the conflict is over, to maintain your ground as victors.

V. 14. With the flowing garments of the East, the first thing to be done in preparing for any active work, was to gird the loins. The apostle therefore says, στῆτε οὖν περιζωσάμενοι τὴν ὀσφὺν ὑμῶν ἐν ἀληθείᾳ, *stand therefore having your loins girt about with truth.* By *truth,* here is not to be understood divine truth as objectively revealed, i. e. the word of God; for that is mentioned in the following verse as the sword. Nor does it mean *sincerity of mind,* for that is a natural virtue, and does not belong to the armour of God; which according to the context consists of supernatural gifts and graces. But it means truth subjectively considered; that is, the knowledge and belief of the truth. This is the first and indispensable qualification for a Christian soldier. To enter on this spiritual conflict ignorant or doubting, would be to enter battle blind and lame. As the girdle gives strength and freedom of action, and therefore confidence, so does the truth when spiritually apprehended and believed. Let not any one imagine that he is prepared to withstand the assaults of the powers of darkness, if his mind is stored with his own theories or with the speculations of other men. Nothing but the truth of God clearly understood and cordially embraced will enable him to keep his feet for a moment, before these celestial potentates. Reason, tradition, speculative conviction, dead orthodoxy, are a girdle of spider-webs. They give way at the first onset. Truth alone, as abiding in the mind in the form of divine knowledge, can give strength or confidence even in the ordinary conflicts of the Christian life, much more in any really " evil day."

Καὶ ἐνδυσάμενοι τὸν θώρακα τῆς δικαιοσύνης, *and having put on the breast-plate of righteousness.* The θώραξ was the " armour covering the body from the neck to the thighs, consisting of two parts, one covering the front and the other the back." A warrior without his θώραξ was naked, exposed to every thrust of his enemy, and even to every casual dart. In such a state flight or death is inevitable. What is that righteousness, which in the spiritual armour answers to the cuirass? Many say it is our own righteousness, integrity, or rectitude of mind. But this is no protection. It cannot resist the accusations of conscience, the whispers of despondency, the power of temptation, much less the severity of the law, or the assaults of Satan. What Paul desired for himself was not to have on his own righteousness, but the righteousness which is of God by faith; Phil. 3, 8. 9. And this, doubtless, is the righteousness which he here urges believers to put on as a breast-plate. It is an infinitely perfect righteousness, consisting in the obedience and sufferings of the Son of God, which satisfies all the demands of the divine law and justice; and which is a sure defence against all assaults whether from within or from without. As in no case in this connection does the apostle refer to any merely moral virtue as constituting the armour of the Christian, so neither does he here. This is the less probable, inasmuch as righteousness in the subjective sense, is included in the idea expressed by the word *truth* in the preceding clause. It is the spirit of the context which determines the meaning to be put on the terms here used. For although *righteousness* is used so frequently by the apostle for the righteousness of God by faith, yet in itself it may of course express personal rectitude or justice. In Is. 59, 17, Jehovah is described as putting "on righteousness as a breast-plate, and a helmet of salvation on his head;" as in Is. 11, 5, it is said of the Messiah, "righteousness shall be the girdle of his loins, and faithfulness the girdle of his reins."

V. 15. In ancient warfare which was in a large measure carried on by hand-to-hand combats, swiftness of foot was one of the most important qualifications for a good soldier. To this the apostle refers when he exhorts his readers to have their feet shod, ἐν ἑτοιμασίᾳ τοῦ εὐαγγελίου τῆς εἰρήνης, *with the preparation of the gospel of peace*. According to one explanation εὐαγγελίου is the genitive of apposition, and the Gospel is the ἑτοιμασία with which the Chris-

tian is to be snod. Then the idea is either that the
Gospel is something firm on which we can rest with
confidence; or it is something that gives alacrity, adding
as it were wings to the feet. Others take εὐαγγελίου as
the genitive of the object, and ἑτοιμασία for readiness
or alacrity. The sense would then be, 'Your feet shod
with alacrity for the Gospel,' i. e. for its defence or
propagation. The simplest interpretation and that best
suited to the context, is that εὐαγγελίου is the genitive
of the source, and the sense is, 'Your feet shod with the
alacrity which the Gospel of peace gives.' As the
Gospel secures our peace with God, and gives the
assurance of his favour, it produces that joyful alacrity
of mind which is essential to success in the spiritual
conflict. All doubt tends to weakness, and despair is
death.

V. 16. 'Επὶ πᾶσιν, *in addition to all;* not above
all as of greatest importance. Besides the portions
of armour already mentioned, they were to take τὸν
θυρεὸν τῆς πιστέως, *the shield of faith.* Θυρεός, literally, a door, and then a large oblong shield, like a door.
Being four feet long by two and a half broad, it completely covered the body, and was essential to the
safety of the combatant. Hence the appropriateness
of the apostle's metaphor. Such a protection, and thus
essential, is faith. The more various the uses of a shield,
the more suitable is the illustration. The faith here
intended is that by which we are justified, and reconciled to God through the blood of Christ. It is that
faith of which Christ is the object; which receives him

as the Son of God and the Saviour of men. It is the
faith which is the substance of things hoped for and
the evidence of things not seen ; which at once appre-
hends or discerns, and receives the things of the Spirit.
It overcomes the world, as is proved by so many examples in the eleventh chapter of the Epistle to the
Hebrews. Faith being in itself so mighty, and having
from the beginning proved itself so efficacious, the
apostle adds, ἐν ᾧ δυνήσεσθε πάντα τὰ βέλη τοῦ πονηροῦ τὰ πεπυρωμένα σβέσαι, whereby ye shall be able to
quench all the fiery darts of the evil one. The obvious
allusion here is to those missiles employed in ancient
warfare, around which combustible materials were
bound, which were ignited and projected against the
enemy. Reference to these fiery darts is made in Ps.
7, 13, " He will make his arrows burning arrows ; "
see Alexander on the Psalms. These darts are said to
be τοῦ πονηροῦ, not of the wicked, as the words are
translated in the English Version, but *of the evil one*,
i. e. of the devil. Comp. Matt. 13, 19. 38. In the
latter passage ὁ πονηρός is explained in ver. 39, ὁ διάβολος. See also 1 John 2, 13 ; 3, 12 ; 5, 18, and other
passages. As burning arrows not only pierced but set
on fire what they pierced, they were doubly dangerous. They serve here therefore as the symbol of the
fierce onsets of Satan. He showers arrows of fire on
the soul of the believer ; who, if unprotected by the
shield of faith, would soon perish. It is a common
experience of the people of God that at times horrible
thoughts, unholy, blasphemous, skeptical, malignant,

crowd upon the mind, which cannot be accounted for
on any ordinary law of mental action, and which cannot be dislodged. They stick like burning arrows;
and fill the soul with agony. They can be quenched
only by faith; by calling on Christ for help. These,
however, are not the only kind of fiery darts; nor are
they the most dangerous. There are others which
enkindle passion, inflame ambition, excite cupidity,
pride, discontent, or vanity; producing a flame which
our deceitful heart is not so prompt to extinguish, and
which is often allowed to burn until it produces great
injury and even destruction. Against these most dangerous weapons of the evil one, the only protection is
faith. It is only by looking to Christ and earnestly
invoking his interposition in our behalf that we can
resist these insidious assaults, which inflame evil without the warning of pain. The reference of the passage,
however, is not to be confined to any particular forms
of temptation. The allusion is general to all those
attacks of Satan, by which the peace and safety of the
believer are specially endangered.

V. 17. The most ornamental part of ancient armour,
and scarcely less important than the breast-plate or the
shield, was the helmet. The Christian, therefore, is
exhorted to take τὴν περικεφαλαίαν τοῦ σωτηρίου, *the
helmet of salvation*. According to the analogy of the
preceding expressions, "the breast-plate of righteousness," and "shield of faith," salvation is itself the
helmet. That which adorns and protects the Christian,
which enables him to hold up his head with confidence

and joy, is the fact that he is saved. He is one of the redeemed, translated from the kingdom of darkness into the kingdom of God's dear Son. If still under condemnation, if still estranged from God, a foreigner and alien, without God and without Christ, he could have no courage to enter into this conflict. It is because he is a fellow-citizen of the saints, a child of God, a partaker of the salvation of the Gospel, that he can face even the most potent enemies with confidence, knowing that he shall be brought off more than conqueror through him that loved him; Rom. 8, 37. When in 1 Thess. 5, 8, the apostle speaks of the hope of salvation as the Christian's helmet, he presents the same idea in a different form. The latter passage does not authorize us to understand, in this place, "helmet of salvation" as a figurative designation of *hope*. The two passages though alike are not identical. In the one salvation is said to be our helmet, in the other, hope ; just as in one place "faith and love" are said to be our breast-plate, and in another, righteousness.

The armour hitherto mentioned is defensive. The only offensive weapon of the Christian is "the sword of the Spirit." Here τοῦ πνεύματος cannot be the genitive of apposition. The Spirit is not the sword; this would be incongruous, as the sword is something which the soldier wields, but the Christian cannot thus control the Spirit. Besides, the explanation immediately follows, *which is the word of God.* "The sword of the Spirit" means the sword which the Spirit gives. By the ῥῆμα Θεοῦ is not to be understood the divine pre-

cepts, nor the threatenings of God against his enemies.
There is nothing to limit the expression. It is that
which God has spoken, his word, the Bible. This is
sharper than any two-edged sword. It is the wisdom
of God and the power of God. It has a self-evidencing
light. It commends itself to the reason and conscience.
It has the power not only of truth, but of divine truth.
Our Lord promised to give to his disciples a word and
wisdom which all their adversaries should not be able
to gainsay or resist. In opposition to all error, to all
false philosophy, to all false principles of morals, to all
the sophistries of vice, to all the suggestions of the
devil, the sole, simple, and sufficient answer is the
word of God. This puts to flight all the powers of
darkness. The Christian finds this to be true in his
individual experience. It dissipates his doubts; it
drives away his fears; it delivers him from the power
of Satan. It is also the experience of the church collective. All her triumphs over sin and error have been
effected by the word of God. So long as she uses this
and relies on it alone, she goes on conquering; but
when any thing else, be it reason, science, tradition, or
the commandments of men, is allowed to take its place
or to share its office, then the church, or the Christian,
is at the mercy of the adversary. Hoc signo vinces—
the apostle may be understood to say to every believer
and to the whole church.

V. 18. It is not armour or weapons which make
the warrior. There must be courage and strength;
and even then he often needs help. As the Christian

has no resources of strength in himself, and can suc
ceed only as aided from above, the apostle urges the
duty of prayer. The believer is—1. To avail himself
of all kinds of prayer. 2. He is to pray on every suitable occasion. 3. He is to pray in the Spirit. 4. He
is to be alert and persevering in the discharge of this
duty. 5. He is to pray for all the saints; and the
Ephesians were urged by the apostle to pray for him.

The connection of this verse is with στῆτε οὖν of
ver. 14. " Stand, therefore, with all prayer and supplication, praying on every occasion, in the Spirit."
Διὰ πάσης προςευχῆς καὶ δεήσεως, may be connected
with the following participle προςευχόμενοι, as has been
done by our translators, who render the passage,
" praying with all prayer and supplication." But this
renders the passage tautological. Others take this
clause by itself, and understand διά as expressing the
condition or circumstances. 'Stand, therefore, with all
prayer, praying at all times,' &c. As to the difference
between προςευχή and δέησις, *prayer and supplication*,
some say that the former has for its object the attaining of good; the latter, the avoidance of evil or deliverance from it. The usage of the words does not sustain
that view. The more common opinion is that the distinction is twofold; first, that προςευχή is addressed
only to God, whereas δέησις may be addressed to men;
and secondly, that the former includes all address to
God, while the latter is limited to petition. The expression *all* prayer, means all kinds of prayer, oral and
mental, ejaculatory and formal. The prayers which

Paul would have the Christian warrior use, are not merely those of the closet and of stated seasons, but also those habitual and occasional aspirations, and outgoings of the heart after God, which a constant sense of his nearness and a constant sense of our necessity must produce.

Not only must all kinds of prayer be used, but believers should pray ἐν παντὶ καιρῷ, *on every occasion;* on every emergency. This constancy in prayer is commanded by our Lord, Luke 18, 1, " Men ought always to pray and not to faint." In 1 Thess. 5, 17, the apostle exhorts believers to " pray without ceasing." It is obvious, therefore, that prayer includes all converse with God, and is the expression of all our feelings and desires which terminate in him. In the scriptural sense of the term, therefore, it is possible that a man should pray almost literally without ceasing.

The third direction is, to pray ἐν πνεύματι. This does not mean *inwardly,* or, *with the heart;* non voce tantum, sed et animo, as Grotius explains it; but it means under the influence of the Spirit, and with his assistance, whose gracious office it is to teach us how to pray, and to make intercessions for us with groanings that cannot be uttered; Rom. 8, 26. The fourth direction has reference to alertness and perseverance in prayer; εἰς αὐτὸ τοῦτο ἀγρυπνοῦντες, *watching unto this very thing.* This very thing is that of which he had been speaking, viz. praying in the Spirit. It was in reference to that duty they were to be wakeful and vigilant, not allowing themselves to become weary or negligent. Ἐν πάσῃ προςκαρτερήσει καὶ δεήσει περὶ πάντων τῶν ἁγίων, *with all perseverance and supplication for all saints.* " Perseverance and supplication " amounts to persevering or importunate supplication. In Rom. 12, 12, the expression is, τῇ προςευχῇ προς-καρτεροῦντες, *continuing instant in prayer.* This persevering supplication is to be offered *for all the saints.* The conflict of which the apostle has been speaking is not merely a single combat between the individual Christian and Satan, but also a war between the people of God and the powers of darkness. No soldier entering battle prays for himself alone, but for all his fellow-soldiers also. They form one army, and the success of one is the success of all. In like manner Christians are united as one army, and therefore have a common cause ; and each must pray for all. Such is the communion of saints, as set forth in this Epistle and in other parts of Scripture, that they can no more fail to take this interest in each other's welfare, than the hand can fail to sympathize with the foot.

V. 19. The importance which the apostle attributed to intercessory prayer and his faith in its efficacy are evident from the frequency with which he enjoins the duty, and from the earnestness with which he solicits such prayers in his own behalf. What the apostle wishes the Ephesians to pray for, was not any temporal blessing, not even his deliverance from bonds, that he might be at liberty more freely to preach the Gospel, but that God would enable him to preach with the freedom and boldness with which he ought to preach : ἵνα μοι δοθῇ λόγος ἐν ἀνοίξει τοῦ στόματός μου ἐν παρρησίᾳ, γνωρίσαι, κτλ. Our translators have paraphrased this clause thus, *that utterance may be given me, that I may open my mouth boldly to make known*, &c. The literal translation is, *that utterance may be given me in opening my mouth, with boldness to make known*, &c. What Paul desired was divine assistance in preaching. He begs his reader to pray ἵνα μοι δοθῇ λόγος, *that the power of speech, or freedom of utterance, might be given to him, when he opened his mouth*. Paul says, 2 Cor. 11, 6, that he was ἰδιώτης τῷ λόγῳ, *rude in speech*. The word λόγος itself has at times the metonymical sense here given to it, and therefore ἐν ἀνοίξει τοῦ στόματος is most naturally taken without emphasis as equivalent to, *when I open my mouth*, i. e. when called upon to speak. Calvin and many others lay the principal stress on those words, and make *with opening of the mouth* equivalent to *with open mouth*, pleno ore et intrepida lingua, as Calvin expresses it. Os opertum cupit, quod erumpet in liquidam et firmam confessionem. Ore enim semiclauso proferuntur ambigua et perplexa responsa. This, however, is to anticipate what is expressed by ἐν παρρησίᾳ γνωρίσαι. Others connect both ἐν ἀνοίξει τοῦ στόματος and ἐν παρρησίᾳ with γνωρίσαι, ' to make known with the opening of the mouth, with boldness the mystery,' &c. This is the construction which our translators seemed to have assumed. But this is very unnatural, from the position of the words and relation of the clauses. Παρρησία (πᾶν ῥῆσις), *the speaking out all, freespokenness.* . Here the dative with ἐν may be taken adverbially, *freely, boldly ;* keeping nothing back, but making an open, undisguised declaration of the Gospel. This includes, however, the idea of frankness and boldness of spirit, of which this unrestrained declaration of the truth is the expression. Μυστήριον τοῦ εὐαγγελίου, *mystery of the Gospel ;* the Gospel itself is the mystery, or divine revelation. It is that system of truth which had been kept secret with God, but which is now revealed unto our glory ; 1 Cor. 2, 7.

V. 20. Ὑπὲρ οὗ, *for the sake of which* Gospel, πρεσβεύων ἐν ἁλύσει εἰμί, *I am an ambassador in bonds.* An ambassador is one through whom a sovereign speaks. "We are ambassadors for Christ, as though God did beseech you by us : we pray you in Christ's stead be ye reconciled with God ;" 2 Cor. 5, 20. The apostles, as sent by Christ with authority to speak in his name, and to negotiate with men, proposing the terms of reconciliation and urging their acceptance, were in an eminent sense his ambassadors. As all ministers are sent by Christ and are commissioned by him to propose the terms of salvation, they too are entitled to the same honourable designation. Paul was an ambassador in bonds, and yet he did not lose his courage but preached with as much boldness as ever.

Ἵνα ἐν αὐτῷ παρρησιάσωμαι, *that therein I may speak boldly.* This may be taken as depending on ἵνα δοθῇ of ver. 19. The sense would then be, ' That utterance may be given to me—that I may speak boldly.' But the preceding ἐν παῤῥησίᾳ γνωρίσαι depends on ἵνα δοθῇ. The two clauses are rather parallel. Paul desired that the Ephesians should pray, 'That utterance should be given him—that is, that he might preach boldly ;' ὡς δεῖ με λαλῆσαι, as I ought to speak. It becomes the man who is an ambassador of God, to speak with boldness, assured of the truth and importance of the message which he has to deliver. That even Paul should solicit the prayers of Christians that he might be able to preach the Gospel aright, shows the sense he had at once of the difficulty and of the importance of the work.

V. 21. In conclusion the apostle informs the Ephesians that he had sent Tychicus to them to relieve their anxiety concerning him ; ἵνα δὲ εἰδῆτε καὶ ὑμεῖς, but that ye also may know, i. e. you as well as other Christian friends who had manifested solicitude about me in my bonds ; τὰ κατ᾽ ἐμέ, the things which concern me, i. e. my circumstances ; τί πράσσω, not what I do, for that they knew already ; but how I do. His health as well as his situation was a matter of anxiety to his friends. Tychicus shall make all known to you ; ὁ ἀγαπητὸς ἀδελφὸς καὶ πιστὸς διάκονος ἐν κυρίῳ ; this admits of a twofold interpretation. It may mean that Tychicus was Paul's διάκονος, servant as well as his brother. This view is commended, though not adopted by Calvin, and is advocated by many of the best commentators, on the ground that it is most natural that the two words ἀδελφὸς and διάκονος should have the same

reference, " my beloved brother and faithful servant ;"
and that in so many other places Paul speaks of those
who attended him and in various forms served him.
The words ἐν κυρίῳ, according to this view, belong
equally to both words. He was a brother as well as a
servant in the Lord, i. e. a Christian brother and servant. It is more common, however, to understand the
apostle as commending Tychicus as a faithful minister
of the Gospel. In Col. 4, 7, he is called a fellow-
servant, which favours the assumption that he was a
fellow-labourer in the ministry. He is mentioned in
Acts 20, 4 ; 2 Tim. 4, 12 ; Tit. 3, 12. None of these
passages, however, throws any light on his relation
to the apostle further than that he was one of his
attendants. As, however, in the next verse Paul says
he had sent him not only that they might know his
affairs, but also, παρακαλέσῃ τὰς καρδίας ὑμῶν, *that he*
might comfort your hearts ; the probability is altogether in favour of his being a minister of Christ, who
could communicate to the Ephesians not only the consolation of favourable intelligence concerning Paul,
but the higher consolations of the Gospel.

V. 23. Εἰρήνη τοῖς ἀδελφοῖς, *peace be to the brethren.*
This is the usual form of salutation or benediction. It
is not concord, but all the fruits of χάρις or favour of
God. Καὶ ἀγάπη μετὰ πίστεως, this does not mean
love together with faith, as though two distinct blessings were intended ; but rather love united with faith.
Faith they had ; Paul's prayer was that love might be
connected with it. The love intended must be bro-

therly love. These blessings are sought ἀπὸ Θεοῦ πατρὸς καὶ Κυρίου Ἰησοῦ Χριστοῦ, *from God the Father and the Lord Jesus Christ.* The Father and Son are united as objects of worship and the source of spiritual and saving blessing. He from whom Paul sought these blessings, is he to whom those who need them must look in order to obtain them.

V. 24. True to the last, as a needle to the pole, the apostle turns to Christ, and implores the divine favour on all who love our Lord Jesus Christ in sincerity. The words ἐν ἀφθαρσίᾳ rendered *in sincerity*, are so understood by Erasmus and Calvin, and by many others. There is however great diversity of opinion as to their true meaning. Ἀφθαρσία signifies *incorruption*, as in 1 Cor. 15, 53. 54, δεῖ γὰρ τὸ φθαρτὸν τοῦτο ἐνδύσασθαι ἀφθαρσίαν, *for this corruptible must put on incorruption.* Hence it means *immortality* as in Rom. 2, 7; 2 Tim. 1, 10. Some connect these words with Ἰησοῦν Χριστόν, *Christ in immortality*, i. e. Christ glorified. Others connect them with χάρις and give ἐν the force of εἰς; ' grace unto immortality, or to eternity; everlasting grace.' Others adopting the same construction, render the passage, ' grace with immortality, i. e. eternal life.' The only natural construction is with ἀγαπώντων; then the meaning is either that expressed in our Version, " Who love our Lord Jesus Christ in sincerity;" or, ' with constancy;' that is, with a deathless or immortal love. In either case, the general idea is the same. The divine favour rests on those to whom the Lord Jesus is the supreme object of love. In 1 Cor. 16, 22, Paul says, "If any man love not our Lord Jesus Christ, let him be Anathema Maranatha." These passages, though so dissimilar, both teach that love to Christ is the indispensable condition of salvation. There must be an adequate reason for this. Want of love for Christ must deserve final perdition, and love to him must include preparation for heaven. This of necessity supposes Christ to be God. Want of love to him must imply enmity to God. It is all a delusion for any one to think he can love the Infinite Spirit as manifested in nature, or in the Scriptures, if he does not recognize and love that same God in the clearest revelation of his character, in his most definite personal manifestation, and in his most intimate relation to us, as partaking our nature, loving us, and giving himself for us. Love to Christ includes adoring admiration of his person, desire for his presence, zeal for his glory, and devotion to his service. It need not be ecstatic, but it must be controlling.

THE END.